MW01427500

THE WORLD OF COMMERCE

BOOK ONE — THIRD EDITION

THE WORLD OF COMMERCE
BOOK ONE THIRD EDITION

E. D. Shade   R. C. Gyles

McGRAW-HILL BOOK COMPANY Sydney
New York San Francisco Auckland Bogotá Caracas
Lisbon London Madrid Mexico City Milan Montreal
New Delhi San Juan Singapore Tokyo Toronto

First published 1980 by Sapphire Books
Reprinted 1981, 1982, 1983
Reprinted 1984 by McGraw-Hill Book Company Australia Pty Limited
Second edition 1986
Reprinted 1987, 1988, 1989, 1990
Third edition 1991

Copyright © 1991 by E. D. Shade and R. C. Gyles

Apart from any fair dealing for the purposes of study, research, criticism or review, as permitted under the *Copyright Act*, no part may be reproduced by any process without written permission. Inquiries should be made to the publisher.

Copying for educational purposes
Where copies of parts of this book are made by an educational institution under the *Copyright Act*, and an agreement exists between the Copyright Agency Limited and the relevant educational authority (Department of Education etc.) to pay the fee for such copying, no further fee is due. In the absence of such an agreement, the law requires that records of such copying be kept. In such cases the copyright owner is entitled to claim payment.

**National Library of Australia
Cataloguing-in-Publication data:**

Shade, E. D. (Elizabeth D.), 1943–
 The world of commerce. Book one.

 3rd ed.
 Includes index.
 ISBN 0 07 452836 X.

 1. Commerce. I. Gyles, R. C. (Robyn C.), 1946–
 II. Title.

380

Produced in Australia by Book Generation Proprietary Limited, Glenroy, Victoria for
 McGraw-Hill Book Company Australia Pty Limited
 4 Barcoo Street, Roseville, NSW 2069
Typeset in Australia by Abb-typesetting Pty Ltd, Collingwood, Victoria
Printed in Singapore by Kyodo Printing Industries (Pte) Limited

Sponsoring Editor: Katherine Jones
Production Editor: Heather Kelly
Designer: Wing Ping Tong
Illustrators: Gerald Carr and Dianne Booth

Contents

Preface — vii

1 The consumer — 1

Wants and needs ▪ Types of wants ▪ Factors affecting consumption patterns ▪ The effect consumption changes have on the community ▪ Types of goods and services available ▪ Choice ▪ Caveat emptor ▪ The assertive consumer ▪ Seller activities which reduce consumers' power ▪ Help for consumers ▪ How much can we buy? ▪ Interdependence in our society ▪ Where can we buy goods and services? ▪ Types of retail stores ▪ Other ways to buy ▪ Unordered goods ▪ Ways to buy services ▪ Documents and records for the consumer ▪ Files and filing

2 Money — 45

The need for money ▪ The circular flow of income ▪ Money ▪ Money in Australia today ▪ Characteristics of money ▪ Functions of money ▪ Motives for wanting money ▪ How do we get money? ▪ Unequal distribution of income and wealth in Australia ▪ Ways of making payments ▪ Budgeting income ▪ The problem of personal debt

3 Business — 91

Three industry groups ▪ Location of industries ▪ Interdependence ▪ Distribution of goods ▪ Types of retail businesses ▪ Common methods of buying goods and services ▪ Documents and records kept by small businesses

4 Labour 130

What is labour? ▪ Specialisation of labour ▪ The results of specialisation ▪ The workforce ▪ Why do people work? ▪ Types of work ▪ Changes in the types of work ▪ The costs and benefits of computers ▪ Apprenticeship ▪ Incomes ▪ Incomes for people who cannot work ▪ Safeguarding against loss of income ▪ Trade unions

5 Law 178

The place of law in history ▪ An introduction to simple rules and laws ▪ Why we need laws ▪ Why we need to change laws ▪ The law in Australia ▪ The parliaments ▪ The courts ▪ Law enforcement ▪ A court case

6 Government 206

The role of government in Australia ▪ Specialisation in government ▪ Local government ▪ State government ▪ The Australian government

Index 243

Preface

The World of Commerce Book One is the first of a series of three volumes which cover all the course content specified in the New South Wales commerce syllabus. We have used a spiral approach to the first two books, covering the same six broad subject areas in each, but treating different aspects of each subject. Book Three contains those topics that are most appropriate for students about to enter the adult world. Clearly, as students gain more background in the subject, and as they mature, their interests, abilities and needs also change. The content of each book has been chosen with these constraints in mind. The subject area 'Records' has been incorporated into other topics, reflecting the way the subject is taught in most schools.

We have provided concrete, practical and up-to-date information, and have tried to make students aware of commerce's relevance and importance in our business-oriented world. We have kept the language as simple as possible and have used commonplace examples to illustrate the concepts and processes. Following each small unit of work is a series of exercises and activities which will give teachers the opportunity to test and reinforce attitudes and values as well as to revise the content.

The topics are presented logically, but each chapter is self-contained so the order of teaching can be varied. As a result, there is sometimes a slight overlap of information in cases where the subject matter is relevant to several chapters.

The third edition of *The World of Commerce* series has been updated in line with revisions in the commerce syllabus, as well as for changes that have occurred in the commercial world since publication of the earlier editions. Other variations have been in response to suggestions by teachers and reflect changes in the methods of teaching commerce. The authors welcome further comments and suggestions.

1 The consumer

All individuals in our society are consumers. Every time we pay for a drink or a video we are being consumers. We may consume *goods* such as books or iceblocks. Goods are physical items we can see and touch. Sometimes we consume *services*, for example when we have a haircut or watch a movie. Services are activities that individuals or firms provide for consumers.

We consume many goods and services each day. Name the goods and services being consumed in these pictures

Wants and needs

We consume two different types of goods and services: essentials and non-essentials. We must have the essentials or 'needs' to survive. Needs are basically the same in any society. They are basic food, water, shelter, clothing (at least in cold climates), simple tools and maybe weapons. As societies become more developed, people look for a wider variety of goods and services. The non-essentials or luxuries are called 'wants'. We could live without movies, fashionable clothes, modern houses and chocolate but they make life more pleasant and interesting.

2 THE WORLD OF COMMERCE

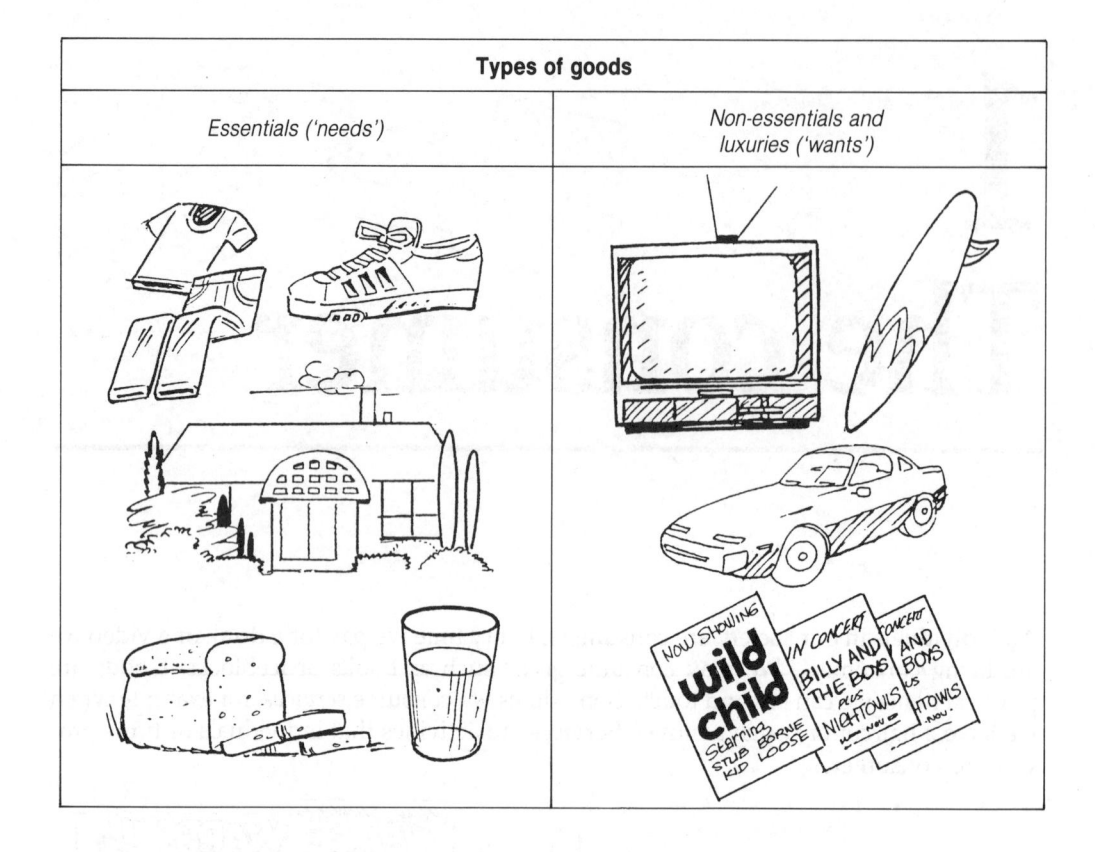

Types of goods	
Essentials ('needs')	Non-essentials and luxuries ('wants')

Types of wants

Even though there is a difference between needs and wants, from now on the term 'wants' will be used to cover all the goods and services we use.

Private wants

Private wants are those we use individually and for which we take personal responsibility. For example we generally buy or make our own food, furniture and entertainment.

Collective wants

Collective wants are generally provided by the government. We rely on the government for roads, hospitals and defence services. Collective wants are used by the community as a whole. It would be too expensive and wasteful for consumers to provide them for themselves. Taxes generally pay for collective wants.

Complementary wants

Complementary wants are used together. Examples are cars and petrol, pies and tomato sauce.

Substitute wants

Substitute wants can be used instead of something else. Examples are tea and coffee, sticky tape and glue.

Exercise 1A

1. Make a list of twenty goods or services you (or your family) have bought in the last two weeks. Divide them into 'wants' and 'needs' as shown in the table.

Goods and services	
Needs	Non-essential wants

2. List five collective wants. Why are collective wants provided by the government?
3. List the following wants in your notebook and beside each write a complementary want for it.
   Wants: writing paper, knitting wool, bread, snow skis, torch, window, camera, video cassette recorder
4. List the following wants and beside each write a substitute want that could replace it.
   Wants: beach mat, ballpoint pen, magazine, hamburger, butter, frozen peas, diamonds

Skills activities

Applying your knowledge

Take a double page in your notebook and write the heading 'Wants' on one page and 'Needs' on the other. Draw (or paste in from magazines) pictures to illustrate at least four examples of each.

Newspaper research

Select a page from the 'classified advertisements' section of your local paper. Colour the advertisements red if they are advertising an essential good or service (a need). Colour them blue if they are advertising a non-essential luxury or want. Outline them in green if they are advertising a service and in black if they are advertising a good.

Factors affecting consumption patterns

Wants (and therefore consumption) vary from one person to another. A survey would show that class members *want* a variety of goods and services. If the survey also included parents, grandparents and friends the range of wants would be vastly increased. Many factors cause wants to vary.

Income

Wants vary with income levels. One girl may expect a personal computer for her birthday while another from a less well-off family may hope for a wristwatch. One couple may plan an overseas honeymoon while another couple is happy with a week on the coast.

Age

Wants vary for the same person at different stages of his or her life. As a child a boy may want a bicycle, as a youth he may want a motorbike, as a married man he may want a car and perhaps eventually he may want a wheelchair in his old age.

Explain why a person's transport wants change with age

Environment

The climate influences consumers' wants. People in cold countries want fur coats, while those in the tropics want swimsuits. Wet weather boosts umbrella sales. People on farms will have some wants that are different from those of people in large cities.

Technology

Technology changes wants. New products replace old ones. Notebooks replaced slates. Personal computers may replace textbooks and notebooks in future. Different countries have different levels of technology, and their consumers' wants vary.

Why is the type of shelter, clothing and transport different in each picture?

Culture

People in the same age group will want different types of clothing, entertainment, housing and food, depending on whether they live in Australia, Papua New Guinea, China or some other country. Even within a country, cultural heritage affects wants. Racial background, religion, gender, family values and peer pressure lead different consumers to buy different goods and services.

Fashion

Fashions affect consumers' choice of cosmetics, car designs, places to go for holidays, jewellery designs, music and especially clothing styles.

Changes in fashion affect the types of clothes we buy. Give examples of changes in music fashions over the years

Status

Some wants depend on people's wish to 'keep up with the Joneses'. Status items can include jewellery, private tennis courts, luxury cars and certain brands of clothing.

Advertising

Advertising has a huge influence on consumers' choice of goods and services. It makes them aware of new products and different brands. Advertising tries to convince consumers that deodorants bring romance, soap brings beauty, soft drinks bring happiness and that certain brands of clothes are trendy.

Habits

Some consumers keep buying the same goods and the same brands of goods because of habit. They may always buy the same brand of electrical goods or go to the same place for their holidays. Some students always have the same lunch order.

Family, friends and peer groups

Other people have a big influence on the goods we buy. Parents may help choose the brand of clothing while friends often influence the type of clothing and music we like.

The effect consumption changes have on the community

Changes in wants and needs have far-reaching effects on the community. They increase demand for complementary goods and reduce the demand for substitute goods. Changes in consumption patterns can change the direction of government spending and affect whole lifestyles. They create some new jobs and destroy others. Some new products add to pollution and other environmental problems while others help to solve these difficulties.

CASE STUDY *The effect the motor car has had on the community*
Cars allow consumers to do and see more than they could before. Cars need better and stronger roads and bridges, leaving fewer government funds for education, medical research and other areas that benefit the community. Before most people had cars, many Sydney families travelled by train to the Blue Mountains for their holidays. Now they can travel much further away, and many motels and caravan parks have been built to cater for them. The Blue Mountains has become less popular as a holiday destination.

The popularity of the motor car has had other effects on the community. Cars have allowed the development of big regional shopping centres and there are now few small general stores in residential areas, except for those attached to late-opening service stations. Before the advent of the car many people lived and worked in the same area, often the area where they were born. Families stayed in close contact. Today it is common for people to live in one area, work in another, play sport and take their entertainment in other areas. They often don't have much time to visit their relatives, who live elsewhere.

The car has created a number of new jobs (such as service station attendant, motor mechanic and workers in car yards and motels) and allowed other workers (such as sales representatives) to do their jobs more efficiently. It has also destroyed jobs, such as those of farriers and workers on some country rail lines. The car has also added to the

The northern approach to the Sydney Harbour Bridge. The motor car has had a major effect on our community   MIRROR AUSTRALIAN TELEGRAPH PUBLICATIONS

community's problems of pollution and traffic accidents. Cars have increased sales of petrol, tyres and other motor accessories and added to our need to import goods from overseas.

Exercise 1B

1. Draw up a table listing each of the factors that influence people's wants. Beside each factor write an example of items that are bought for that reason. One has been done for you.

Factor	Item
1. Age	Toys
2.	
3.	

2. List five goods which were in great demand fifty years ago that are rarely bought today.
3. List four wants you think a space-age child in the year 2100 may demand. Why would there be a change in the types of goods wanted?
4. List five factors that cause wants to change over time.
5. Study the seven 'newspaper headlines'. Each refers to a factor that influences consumers' wants. Copy the numbers 1 to 7 into your notebook and beside each number write the factor influencing wants in each case.

6 SOLUTION TO OIL CRISIS?

2 WARNING: SMOKING IS A HAZARD TO HEALTH

1 NEW CRAZE
A NEW CRAZE for Hula Hoops is

4 TEMPERATURES CLIMB TO 40°

5 One Home in Four now has a Backyard Pool...

3 JAM TO BRING BACK THE MINI SKIRT?

7 NEW RELEASE 'GLAMOUR' MAKEUP NOW ON SALE

6. What effects has the widespread use of television had on the Australian community? In your answer refer to complementary wants, substitute wants, job opportunities created and lost and the effect television has had on our lifestyles.
7. New inventions and changes in technology allow new products to replace old wants. The table below lists some new products and some old products that have been replaced. Copy the table into your notebook and fill in the missing spaces. Add five more products of your own.

Technology changes our wants	
New product	Old product it replaced
1. Refrigerator/freezer	Ice chest
2. Electric light	
3.	Horse and buggy
4.	Smoke signals
5. Electric range	
6.	Straw broom
7.	Copper and scrubbing board
8. Dishwasher	
9.	Hot water bottle
10.	Open fire
11.	
12.	
13.	
14.	
15.	

Skills activities

Newspaper research

Find a newspaper or magazine advertisement that could persuade you to buy a particular article. Paste the advertisement into your notebook and underneath it write
(a) why the advertisement would persuade you to buy the product
(b) which features of the advertisement appeal to you.

Field study and report

Visit the local shopping centre and 'window shop' for ten minutes. Then list the five items you saw that you most want. After returning to class, form into small groups and compare lists. Discuss the reasons for your choices. Write a paragraph explaining why your list differs from the lists of others in your group.

> **Survey and class discussion**
>
> Select ten people: two young children, two your own age, two young adults, two middle-aged adults and two older adults. Ask each one what he or she would do with an unexpected gift of $100. For each person write
> (a) the wants that would be satisfied
> (b) the age group
> (c) their occupation or the occupation of the family breadwinner.
> After completing the survey have a class discussion on the different things that influence wants. Did your survey show any connection between people's wants and their ages and income levels?
>
> **Create an advertisement**
>
> Create a full-page advertisement that would be suitable to place in a magazine. You may draw your own illustrations or construct a collage from other advertisements and photographs. Under your advertisement state
> (a) the product
> (b) the consumers you are targeting (for example age group, gender, income bracket)
> (c) the emotions you are appealing to.

Types of goods and services available

Consumers buy two different types of goods: durables and non-durables. As well, consumers buy a range of services.

Consumer durables and non-durables

Consumer durables are goods which are expected to last a number of years. Furniture, motor vehicles and electrical appliances are consumer durables. They last a long time but they *depreciate* (lose value) over a period of time.

Consumer non-durables are goods which are for single use (such as matches, food and tissues) and those which last for only a short time, such as ballpoint pens. Most items of clothing are classed as consumer non-durables.

The goods which consumers buy are *consumer goods*. They are purchased to satisfy our private or individual wants. When a good is bought to help earn an income and to produce another good or service it is a *capital good*. Some goods can be classed as either consumer goods or capital goods depending on how they are to be used. A lawnmower, bought to mow your own lawn at home, is a consumer good; however, if you buy a lawnmower to use in a lawnmowing business to earn income then the lawnmower is a capital good.

Services

In modern societies consumers want many services, which are things that individuals or firms *do* for consumers. Hairdressers and bus drivers provide services. Services are very

THE CONSUMER

Give three more examples each of consumer durables and consumer non-durables

Goods bought by consumers	
Consumer durables	*Consumer non-durables*

Features

1. Often expensive
2. Usually last a few years at least
3. Often require repairs
4. Not bought often
5. Often bought on credit
6. Often depreciate (lose value) over time as they wear out

Features

1. Inexpensive
2. Used up quickly
3. Bought regularly
4. Bought for cash

important to our standard of living. Life would be less enjoyable without transport, entertainment and other services. Businesses and governments also depend greatly on services. A fruit-canning factory would be less efficient if it had to deliver its own mail, paint its own factory, supply all its own transport and advertise its own products. Government departments also need to have many services provided for them.

Services become more important as a society becomes more highly developed. Tribal Aborigines living in inland Australia have little or no use for travel agents, bank tellers or checkout operators. Australians living in towns and cities find these services essential to keep up their standard of living. Transport is needed at all stages as goods are produced.

In Australia most of the goods and services we buy are produced by private businesses. Business firms produce goods and services so that they can make profits.

Exercise 1C

1. What is meant by the term 'consumer durable'?
2. Some non-durables are called single-use goods. List five single-use consumer goods.
3. List five consumer durables and five consumer non-durables that you would find in the
   (a) classroom
   (b) bathroom
   (c) supermarket.

	Durables	Non-durables
Classroom Bathroom Supermarket		

4. List four services that a family uses regularly.
5. List four services that a manufacturer uses regularly.
6. Why are service industries not important in less-developed societies?

Skills activity

Field survey

List five consumer durables and five consumer non-durables that you have in your kitchen at home. Beside each one, name the firm which produced the good. Write one sentence explaining why firms produce goods and services.

Choice

Most people do not have enough money to buy all the goods and services they want. They must *choose* which wants to satisfy immediately. They may put off other wants and satisfy them in the future, perhaps when they have saved enough money. They may have to completely give up other wants.

Consumers gain the greatest value for their money when they choose carefully. The biggest problem with *impulse buying* (that is, buying goods you hadn't planned to buy) is that consumers may buy goods they do not want as much as something else, and in fact may not really want at all. Shops try to encourage impulse buying. They display goods attractively, and set out their stores so that basic goods are at the back. Shoppers have to pass many other tempting goods to get them. Toys and sweets are at children's eye level. The best way to avoid the trap of impulse buying is to write a shopping list and stick to it.

Which wants to satisfy?

In order to choose between their many wants, consumers work out a list of preferences. A schoolboy wants many things. He may like iceblocks at recess, a movie on Saturday, accessories for his skateboard and playing the pinball machines. He may also want to save money to spend at the Show and he may hope to get a trail bike eventually. He obviously cannot satisfy all these wants every week. He must select which wants to satisfy first. He must also decide which wants, if any, he will give up completely.

List the wants you would like to satisfy

All consumers make choices. They usually satisfy *needs* first. Consumers buy food, shelter and basic clothing before holidays and entertainment. People differ in what they think is essential. Some people spend less on food so that they can afford nice clothes. Others think it is important to eat well even if they cannot often afford to go out. In each case consumers make a choice.

Consumers' choices are influenced by factors such as their age, gender, lifestyle, nationality, religion, occupation and tastes and by the climate, season, fashion and advertising. Consumers can find out *what products are available* to satisfy their wants through discussions with family and friends (that is, by 'word of mouth'), through window shopping and looking through stores, through newspaper and magazine articles and television programs, through advertising and by getting advice from consumer associations.

Which brand or type?

After deciding which wants to satisfy, the consumer must make further choices. For example, a person may decide to buy a sound system. He or she has to choose between the various makes and models and compare the price, quality and appearance of the various brands to see which one best satisfies his or her wants for the amount of money available.

Which seller?

Buyers should compare the prices in different stores. Some stores in small shopping centres are dearer because there is less competition. High rents may raise the price in stores in expensive complexes. Some stores give better customer service. Others provide guarantees and warranties or after-sales service. They may charge more to cover their extra costs. Consumers should consider the services they want and decide if they are willing to pay more for them.

Most goods are bought in ordinary shopping centres. Some families form groups called co-operatives to buy in bulk. They can buy fruit and vegetables from markets and groceries from warehouses. Other consumers go to discount stores or buy from markets such as Sydney's 'Paddy's Market' where goods are less expensive. Many people feel the time and effort involved in shopping in out-of-the-way places is not worth the money saved. They prefer to pay a little more and buy from specialist retailers. Others like to shop at garage sales and through the classified advertisements. They can save a lot of money by buying second-hand items in good condition. The problem is that there is no warranty or after-sales service for most second-hand goods.

When to buy?

An important choice is when to buy. Consumers can often save money by buying goods at sales. Clothes are cheaper halfway through the season when the stores want to make way for the new season's stock. Other shops have sales just before stocktaking. There are often big sales in January to sell the goods not sold before Christmas.

Customers should try to make sure that sale goods are genuine bargains. Some stores buy inferior goods to sell at low sale prices. Another problem is that consumers often have less *choice* during a sale. The size or style they want might not be available.

Buyers can save money at sales. What two problems can arise when buying at sales?

Cash or credit?

Buying on credit involves buying goods with borrowed money. The consumer might buy on bankcard or mastercard or charge the goods to a store account. They are really borrowing money from a bank or finance company. Credit allows the buyers to use and enjoy goods before they have saved enough money to pay for them. Some consumers may have enough money in the bank to buy the goods but they choose to save their cash for emergencies. Others might simply like the convenience and security of paying for most of their purchases in one go each month.

Houses and cars are nearly always bought with borrowed money. Electrical appliances are often bought on credit. Almost anything can be put on a credit card.

There are two main problems associated with credit buying.

1. Some people cannot control their spending when they buy on credit. They spend more than they can afford and the money has to be repaid some time.
2. It usually costs more to buy on credit. Banks and finance companies charge interest on loans. Interest is usually only charged on bankcard and monthly charge accounts if the account is not paid within a certain time.

Exercise 1D

1. Why are consumers not able to satisfy all their wants?
2. What is the problem with impulse buying?
3. How do consumers choose between their many wants? Which wants will they normally satisfy first?

4. Divide about half a page in your notebook into three columns with the headings 'Factor', 'Example 1' and 'Example 2'.
   (a) List the following factors in the first column: age, gender, lifestyle, religion, occupation, taste, weather, season, fashion and advertising.
   (b) Organise the following examples into the second column so that each is on the same line as the factor which influences consumers' choice: ticket to a rock concert or the opera, punk hair cut or pigtails, overcoat or swimsuit, lipstick or shaver, Coke or Pepsi, walking stick or billycart, rosary beads or skull cap, umbrella or sunscreen, overalls or business suit.
   (c) In column 3 write your own example of choices which are influenced by these factors.
5. List the choices that must be made by a young person who has decided to buy his or her first car.
6. Some shopping outlets are cheaper than others. List two places where people can shop to save money and the types of goods they can buy in each place. What problems might the consumer face as a result of buying from these outlets?
7. How can a consumer save money by delaying a purchase until 'sale time'? What are two problems associated with buying at sales?
8. What are the advantages and disadvantages of buying on credit?

Skills activities

Role play

Choose a class member to be a customer and another to be a salesperson. Role play a scene in which the salesperson is trying to persuade the customer to buy an expensive product.

Market research

Buy several brands of potato chips of the same flavour. Put them into plain containers marked simply A, B, C and so on. The teacher should keep a note of which brand is in each container and its price. The class should then 'taste test' the chips and rank them according to taste. After the test is complete, ask the brand name and price of each. What can you conclude about the relationship between price and quality in this case?

Field survey

Do a survey in a large shopping centre to find the range of prices for the following goods:
1. double cassette players
2. 1 kilogram pack of soap powder
3. 1 kilogram of rump steak
4. hair spray
5. 100 gram block of plain chocolate

Try to find the reasons for the range of prices found for each product. Take a page in your notebook for each good and set the work out as shown on the next page.

Product		
Prices	Store/brand	Reasons for differences in price

Newspaper comprehension

Read the newspaper article 'Temptation at the supermarket' and answer the questions that follow.

Temptation at the supermarket

Supermarkets have ways to make you buy, and that applies to children as well as adults. Magazines are placed at checkouts and on the lower shelves, picture books are at toddlers' eye level. There are other traps for the unwary.

- Aroma is a powerful tempter. Some stores install a fan behind the hot bread counter to draw the customers.
- Staple goods such as milk and bread are placed in far corners of the store, drawing customers past attractive displays of goods they were not intending to buy.
- High impact positions at the end of the aisles are kept for displays of goods with high profit margins.
- Impulse lines such as confectionery have high profit margins. They are placed at eye level, which is also 'buy level'—blocks of chocolate at adult eye level and lollipops on the lowest shelves at toddlers' eye level.
- Music helps relax customers and keep them in the store longer so they spend more money.
- Fresh fruit and vegetable stands are attractive so they are placed in sight of the store entrance to entice customers into the store.

Consumer associations advise customers not to shop when they are hungry, to take a shopping list and stick to it, and not to take children with them if they can help it.

1. List two ways supermarkets tempt customers into their stores.
2. List three ways supermarket planners position their goods to tempt consumers to impulse buy.
3. How do stores encourage customers to stay longer?

Caveat emptor

Buyers should examine products very carefully before accepting the goods. The phrase *caveat emptor* is Latin and means 'let the buyer beware'. If customers buy goods and then find they are not what they wanted or that they can buy the goods cheaper somewhere else, they may not be able to get their money back or exchange the goods. In cases where customers were misled and sold damaged goods or goods which do not do what the sellers claim, they are entitled to return the goods. Sellers have a *liability* (responsibility) to consumers to sell goods of 'merchantable quality'. That means the goods must do the job they were sold to do. Signs such as 'No return or exchange' do not take away the consumers' right to goods which do the job for which they are bought. Customers who buy second-hand goods or 'seconds' at a cheaper price cannot claim a refund if the goods are not 'as good as new'.

Examples
1. Belinda bought a tape of her favourite band. When she tried to play it on her cassette player it would not work. She took the tape back to the shop, where it was found to be faulty. She was offered a replacement tape or a refund.
2. Ben also bought a tape, but on his way home he saw the same tape on sale in another store for $5 less. He returned to the first store and asked for his money back. The store owner refused. She was not obliged to refund Ben's money because there was nothing wrong with the tape.

The assertive consumer

Consumers have *rights*. They are entitled to good service and to products which do the task they were bought for. They are entitled to refuse to buy any good which does not do what they want it to. Some consumers put up with poor service and poor quality goods. They may not know their rights or they may be too nervous to insist on their rights. Perhaps the consumers do not speak the language well and are afraid of being confused or feeling embarrassed. Prejudice and social attitudes may make some people unwilling to grant certain consumers their rights.

Consumers need to be *assertive*. Assertive consumers know their rights and feel confident that they are entitled to them. They are not afraid to ask for their rights. Assertive people realise that the people who are prejudiced against them for their gender, race, size or other reason are wrong. *Passive* consumers let sellers (and other customers) decide what they will buy and the standard of service they will get. *Aggressive* consumers try to force their wishes onto sellers and other customers, without considering the other people's rights.

CASE STUDY   *Aggressive, passive and assertive consumers*
Several consumers are waiting to be served at the music counter in a department store. Jim was the last to arrive. He shouts his request to the sales assistant, who ignores him and serves someone else first. Jim makes loud comments about the poor service in the store and storms off.

Joe has been waiting the longest. He is in a hurry because he has a bus to catch. The sales assistant serves several people before him, and has a long chat to one of the customers, but Joe does not say anything. When Joe eventually gets served he finds that the store does not have the disk he wants. He is persuaded to buy a different disk, with the same singer but different songs, even though it is not the one he really wants.

Another customer, Gianna, allows several people to be served before her and then says pleasantly, 'It is my turn now. I have been waiting longer than these other people'. When Gianna finds that the store does not have the tape she wants she asks the assistant to order it for her. She asks for the assistant's name and the department's phone number so she can check whether the tape has arrived.

The aggressive customer (Jim) and the passive customer (Joe) failed to get their wants satisfied. The assertive customer (Gianna) did not get her wants fully satisfied but she has made progress.

Explain why assertive consumers, who know their rights and ask for them firmly, are more likely than aggressive or passive consumers to get what they want

Seller activities which reduce consumers' power

Consumers and sellers have different aims. Well-informed, assertive consumers aim to get the most value for their money. They have a budget, use a shopping list and get expert advice. These all help them spend their money in the way which satisfies the most wants and needs.

Sellers aim to part the consumer from his or her money as easily as possible. The activities they use to reduce consumers' power include advertising, packaging, technical jargon and planned obsolescence.

Advertising

Advertising aims to convince consumers to buy certain goods by stressing things which are important to individuals, such as their appearance and popularity. Advertising also encourages consumers to buy new models of goods they already have, even though the older model still does the job. Advertisements may be targeted at certain groups, making it

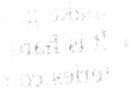

Seller activities which reduce consumers' power
Advertising • Packaging • Technical jargon • Planned obsolescence

Give one example of each technique sellers use to reduce consumers' power

hard for consumers to resist the product. For example, when market research showed that young, poorly educated women were more likely than any other people to take up smoking, cigarette companies pitched their advertising heavily at this group.

Informative advertising *increases* consumers' power. For example, advertisements which let consumers compare prices help them get the best value for their money.

In what ways does excess packaging damage the environment?

Excessive packaging

Excessive packaging reduces consumers' power in several ways.
- It is harder to examine goods before buying them, to make sure they are fresh, well made, in good condition or suitable for the consumers' needs. Bags of apples sometimes contain some bruised fruit. Boxed shirts cannot be tried on before buying. Large cartons make goods appear bigger than they really are.
- It is hard to buy the exact quantity wanted. Some items need three batteries, but batteries come in packs of two or four.

- Packaging can add unnecessarily to the cost of the item. In most cases the wrapping is thrown away when the customer gets the goods home, yet market research shows that packaging helps to sell goods. Consumers will often buy a product in an eye-catching box instead of a similar good in a plain plastic bag.
- Excessive packaging also adds to the problem of rubbish disposal. It is damaging to the environment.

Consumers must decide if it is worth paying more to get goods in attractive packets. They may choose to buy gifts in fancy packs but buy the plainer wraps for their own use. Products such as perfume and cosmetics may give consumers more pleasure when they are in beautiful containers. The extra cost would then be worth while.

Technical jargon

Sellers sometimes use technical jargon to persuade consumers to spend money on goods and services they do not really want or need. An unscrupulous service station owner may convince a non-mechanical customer to pay for unnecessary repairs. A consumer may be talked into buying a music system with more features than he or she needs. Some people are persuaded to have their house treated for termites unnecessarily. People buying motor vehicles, sewing machines, computers and other technical products can be confused by sellers. The best way to avoid this trap is to become as informed as possible about the good you want to buy. Another way is to take a knowledgeable friend to help you shop for technical items.

Planned obsolescence

Planned obsolescence means that goods are designed so that they quickly become *obsolete*, that is, out of date. They need to be replaced in a fairly short time. New models may quickly make the goods seem old fashioned. Perhaps they cannot be repaired because no spare parts are made. The goods may be made in a way that makes it more expensive to repair them than to replace them. Consumers lose the power to buy goods that will last a long time.

Help for consumers

```
                    Help for consumers
                   /        |        |         \
    The Australian     Standards   Business and    Publicity
    Consumers'         Australia   Consumer Affairs  through the
    Association                                       media
```

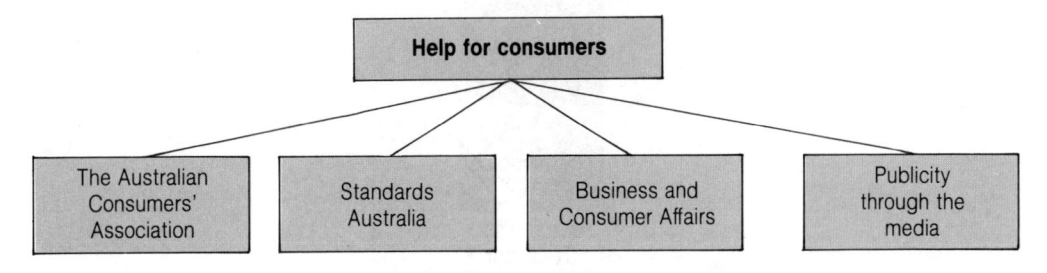

Individual consumers cannot examine every brand of every good on the market. Many buyers do not know how to find information about after-sales service or whether the claims made for a product are true. Help is available from consumer associations, government departments and the media.

The Australian Consumers Association

The Australian Consumers Association (ACA) is an organisation which buys and tests many brands of many products. It has tested products ranging from electrical appliances to slimming preparations and cosmetics. The ASA publishes its findings in *Choice* magazine. *Choice* is sent to members and is also available in most public libraries. Many consumers find the reports very helpful when they are choosing between different brands of a good.

Standards Australia

Standards Australia was formerly known as the Australian Standards Association. It sets national benchmarks which Australian industry must reach (based on safety, acceptable quality levels, parts that are interchangeable and a reduction of unnecessary (or uneconomical) variety) to be able to carry the *Australian Standardsmark*. Any product bearing this mark meets the production standard required by the Australian or international standard. The Standardsmark proves that the goods have met a certain specified quality. Technical experts work out different standards for different products. The standards are worked out on practical industrial and scientific experience. They are constantly revised to keep pace with new technologies.

Standards are set only when an authoritative source (such as a government body, a professional or trade association or private firm or individual) asks for it. Standards Aus-

What does the Australian Standardsmark indicate?

THE NEW AUSTRALIAN STANDARDSMARK

Australian Standard
AS 1270 Lic 999
Standards Australia

An Important Change in the Australian Symbol for Quality, Performance and Safety.

tralia also helps Australian firms exporting to other countries. It gives them information about standards required for goods and services in overseas countries to which they want to export goods.

Business and Consumer Affairs

Business and Consumer Affairs is a New South Wales government body which acts on consumers' behalf. Other states have a similar body called Corporate Affairs. It publishes pamphlets and booklets which give advice on buying a wide range of goods. Consumers can phone or write to Business and Consumer Affairs for advice on action to take if they feel they have been treated badly over the purchase of goods or services. But remember, while consumers have certain rights, it may be hard to enforce them. It is hard to get a refund from a shop which has closed down or to replace an item which is not produced any more. Careful shopping can save problems later.

The media

Newspapers sometimes have columns giving advice to consumers on new products available and ways to get refunds or replacements for faulty products. Some radio stations have consumer advice programs. Consumers can write in or ring the expert on the program for advice on a particular problem. Television programs sometimes demonstrate new products. Programs which follow up consumers' complaints about products which do not work or service which is unsatisfactory are very effective. The bad publicity often causes the firms concerned to fix the problem.

Exercise 1E

1. What is meant by *caveat emptor*?
2. What are a consumer's rights?
3. What is the difference between a seller's aim and a consumer's aim?
4. Explain how sellers use advertising to reduce consumers' power in the market.
5. How does the prepackaging of goods make it harder for consumers to buy wisely?
6. Why do firms sell so many goods in elaborate packages that are simply thrown away?
7. When might it be sensible for the consumer to pay extra to get goods in expensive wrapping? When is it a waste of money?
8. How can the use of technical jargon persuade consumers to buy goods or services they do not really want?
9. Explain how planned obsolescence can cause consumers to buy goods they did not intend to buy.
10. Name two organisations that help consumers. Explain what each organisation does for consumers.

Skills activities

Field survey

Walk through a shop in your local shopping centre and take note of the items that are prepackaged. Time yourself, and see how many you can list in five minutes.

Using the list you drew up in your survey, outline some problems this prepackaging could cause you. For example a recipe calls for 1 cup of flour but the smallest packet of flour contains 1 kilogram.

Role play

A consumer bought a jumper with a tag that said 'Hand washable, dry flat in the shade'. The consumer followed the instructions but the colours ran and the jumper shrank. Role play the scene in the shop when the customer returns the jumper for a refund. One student should play the role of an aggressive consumer, one should play a passive consumer and one should play an assertive consumer. Choose a different student to play the shop assistant in each case.

How much can we buy?

Income

The most important factor determining how much consumers can buy is their income—the amount of money they earn. Incomes depend on the value of the labour and other resources (such as land, buildings and money capital) that they can sell or lend to other people. Doctors generally earn high incomes when they sell their scarce skills and abilities to their patients. Someone who owns many houses can earn a high income by renting them out to other people. Untrained labourers who have only their physical strength to sell to employers earn much less.

A wealthy doctor or landlord can buy far more goods and services than a low-paid labourer. If the labourer or the doctor chose to work longer hours, each could earn more and buy more goods and services. The problem with working longer hours or taking a second job is that the amount of leisure time is reduced. The person may have a higher standard of living but the quality of life may be lower. People who choose to work longer hours and earn more income may find they have more goods and services but they also have less spare time to enjoy their extra possessions.

From our income we must pay taxes to the government. High tax levels leave less income to spend on goods and services. *Gross income* is the total income before any taxes are paid. The amount left after paying taxes is *net income* (or disposable income).

GROSS INCOME − TAX = NET INCOME

Other ways to buy more

Some people can buy more because they win money, for example in Lotto or at the races. Others inherit money. Some people buy goods and services on credit, that is they borrow money to buy them. Borrowing allows them to consume more now but they will need to consume less in future, when they repay the loan. Other people dip into their savings to buy goods they cannot afford from their current income. In this case they consumed less in the past when they were saving and spend more now, when they are drawing on their savings.

Exercise 1F

1. What is the main factor that determines *how much* consumers can buy?
2. List the factors that influence the size of our incomes.
3. What is the difference between gross income and disposable income? Which one is the more important to the consumer? Why?
4. List ways consumers can *buy* more if they do not *earn* more?
5. What choice about current consumption versus future consumption do consumers make in each of the following cases?
   (a) They decide to save money.
   (b) They decide to buy goods on credit.

Skills activities

Newspaper research

Find a newspaper job advertisement that offers a high income and another advertisement that offers a low income. Paste the advertisements in your notebook. Underneath explain in one or two sentences why the person who got the first job would be able to buy more goods and services than the person who got the second job.

Calculation

Collect a *Tax Pack* from a newsagent. Using the tables inside, calculate the net income of a person whose gross income in a year is
(a) $4000
(b) $8000
(c) $16 000
(d) $50 000.

Research

Find and paste in your notebook advertisements for
(a) the Pools
(b) Lotto
(c) borrowing money from a bank, finance company, building society or credit union
(d) bankcard.
Underneath, explain how these *may* be able to help you increase the amount you can buy. Which of them might actually reduce the total amount you can buy?

Interdependence in our society

Australia is a specialised society. Most workers do one main task. This is called *division of labour*. One person sells shoes, another collects and disposes of rubbish. Business firms specialise. They produce one type of good or service. One firm is a furniture factory, others are wheat farms, travel agencies and coal mines. Governments provide services such as transport and defence.

Individuals, businesses and governments depend on each other to produce the goods and services they need. Consumers depend on business firms to satisfy their private wants and on governments to satisfy their collective wants. Workers rely on businesses and government departments for their jobs. Firms need consumers, other firms and governments to buy their finished products so they can make profits. Individuals and firms pay taxes so the government can provide services such as defence and education.

The way in which various parts of a specialised society depend on each other is called *interdependence*. Interdependence causes problems in one area to affect other areas. For example, transport is very important at all stages in the production of goods. Strikes which affect transport can cripple our society. Petrol strikes and bus and train stoppages prevent people from getting to work and goods from being delivered.

Explain why a strike by a small number of workers can affect thousands of people
Source: Sydney Morning Herald

Exercise 1G

1. What is meant by division of labour?
2. What is interdependence?
3. List ten specialists whom wheat farmers rely on to produce the goods and services they require.
4. List ten government services that are important to you and your family.
5. Explain why strikes may disrupt production in a specialised society.

Skills activities

Newspaper research

Find a newspaper article that refers to a recent strike in Australia. Paste it in your notebook. Underneath it list other individuals and business firms that may have been affected by this strike.

Picture interpretation

Look carefully at the illustration below. List the ways in which farmers depend on each of the firms shown.

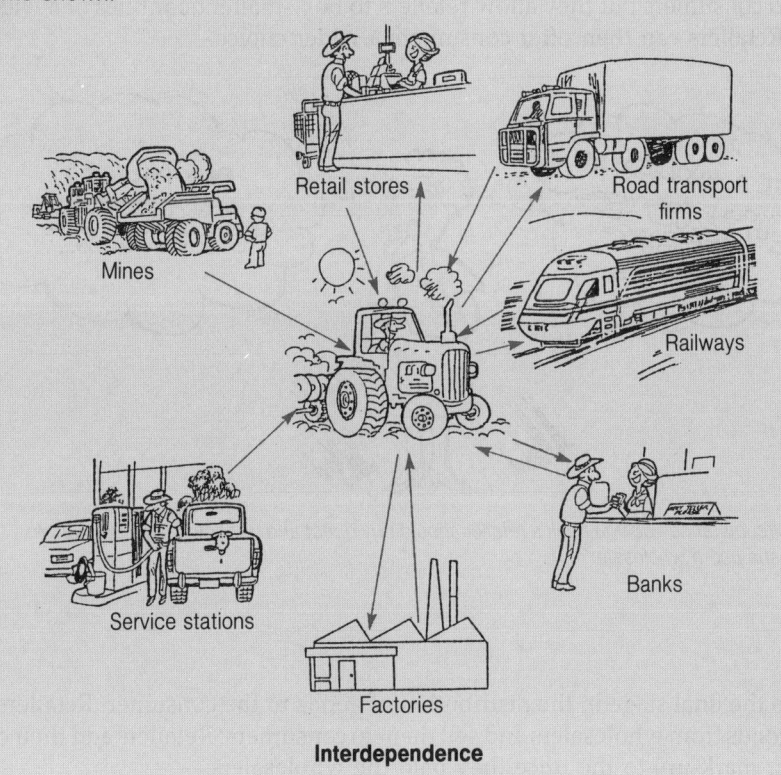

Interdependence

Where can we buy goods and services?

Once goods have been produced in a factory they must find their way to consumers. There are usually two steps in the process—wholesaling and retailing.

Explain the process by which manufactured goods reach the consumer

Wholesaling

Wholesalers buy goods from a wide range of manufacturers and sell them in smaller quantities to retailers. Wholesalers often specialise. For example, there are grocery wholesalers and carpet wholesalers. They allow retailers to select goods from one firm instead of having to deal with different manufacturers. When wholesalers sell goods they add their costs and profit to the price they paid the manufacturers. Wholesalers increase the goods' final cost to consumers but they allow retailers to buy smaller quantities of a wider range of goods. Retailers can then offer consumers a wider choice.

Under what circumstances do you think a retailer should buy direct and under what circumstances should he or she use a wholesaler?

Retailing

Retailing is the final stage in the distribution of goods to the consumer. Retailers usually buy their goods from wholesalers and sell them to consumers. Retailers add their costs and profit (their mark-up) to the price they paid the wholesalers.

Why do consumers usually buy goods from retail stores instead of from a wholesaler?

Types of retail stores

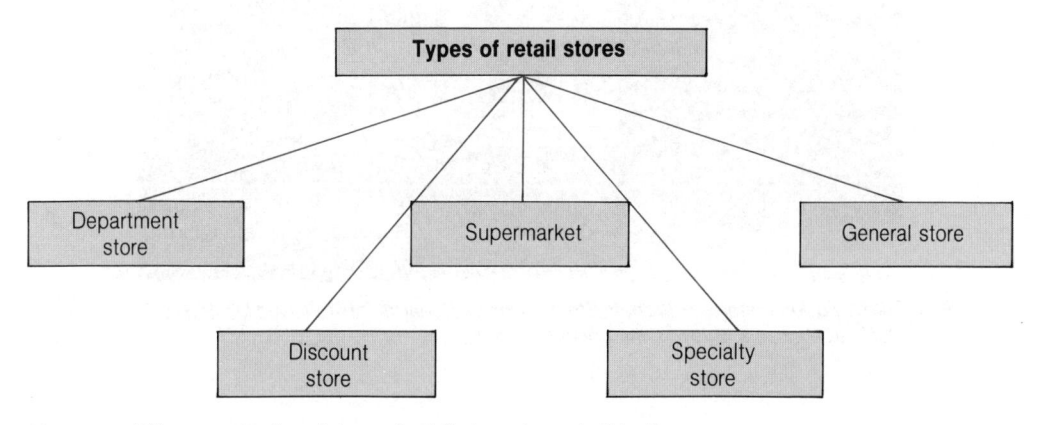

Name a real life example of each type of retail store shown in this diagram

Department stores

Very large shops which sell goods in a wide range of special departments or areas are called department stores. They might have a men's clothing department, a gardening department and a toy department. David Jones and Grace Bros are examples of department stores. Many department stores encourage customers to open charge accounts and buy goods on credit. They usually promote a 'quality' image through their advertising and the atmosphere in the store. Their goods are often in a medium to high price range.

The David Jones store in Elizabeth Street, Sydney. Department stores are located in most large cities and towns throughout Australia DAVID JONES LIMITED

Discount stores

Like department stores, discount stores such as K-Mart, Big W and Venture sell goods in various departments. They sell a smaller range of goods than department stores and have their own brands as well as other brands in a medium to low price range.

Specialty shops

Smaller shops which sell one type of good or provide one type of service are called specialty shops. Examples are dress shops and hairdressers.

General stores

General stores are small shops which sell a variety of goods, mainly food items. They are often located in residential areas away from other shops, especially in older, established suburbs. Some are attached to service stations. Prices in general stores tend to be higher than in supermarkets but they usually stay open for longer hours.

General stores are usually located in areas away from other shops TELECOM AUSTRALIA

Supermarkets

Supremarkets are self-serve shops which sell a wide range of food items and common household goods such as toiletries, cleaning goods and gardening items. They are generally cheaper than specialty shops and general stores. Their high turnover allows them to buy in bulk from suppliers and pass the savings on to their customers.

Regional shopping centres

In recent years 'one-stop regional shopping centres' have been developed. They usually have the following features:
- a car park
- a supermarket
- a department store or discount store (or both)
- a variety of specialty stores, usually including a bank, hairdresser and sometimes a doctor or dentist as well as dress shops, chemist, newsagent, butcher and others.

Exercise 1H

1. What is wholesaling?
2. What is retailing?
3. Name at least one advantage and one disadvantage of shopping in each of the following types of stores:
   (a) department store
   (b) discount store
   (c) specialty store
   (d) general store
   (e) supermarket.
4. List reasons why people sometimes buy goods from general stores when their prices are higher than in larger stores.
5. Name a regional shopping centre you sometimes visit. List its main features.

Skills activities

Survey

Copy the following table into your notebook. List ten stores in your major shopping centre. Beside each store complete the information required. One has been done for you as an example.

Store	Provides good or service?	Type of retailer	Type of good or service
1. Holiday Travel	Service	Specialty store	Travel bookings
2.			
3.			
4.			
5.			
6.			
7.			
8.			
9.			
10.			

Field study

Visit a department store. List ten departments in the store.

Mapping

Draw a simple map of a shopping centre with which you are familiar. Label it clearly. The map should show the following:
(a) the main street
(b) the railway station and bus stops
(c) the main shops in the area
(d) any regional shopping centre, arcade or mall.

Report

Write a short report (one paragraph) to explain how the *availability of transport* has influenced the location of the main shopping centre in your area.

Survey

Divide into groups of three or four and construct a survey to find out the things that influence consumers to shop at particular retail outlets. Below is an example of a survey but you may prefer to make up your own.

Example
For each person to be surveyed have a page divided into three columns. The columns are headed 'Item', 'Where bought (Card A)', and 'Reason (Card B)'.
In the 'Item' column list the following goods: groceries, meat, fruit and vegetables, stationery items, clothing, gifts, cosmetics, magazines, electrical items.

Each interviewer will also need two cards. On Card A write 'general store, specialty shop, supermarket, department store, discount store, other (specify).' On Card B write 'closeness, quality, price, convenience, variety, credit facilities, other (specify)'.

Each group should survey at least five people. As each person is questioned he or she should choose the answer from the appropriate card and the interviewer should write the answer in the space on the survey sheet.

Other ways to buy

Goods can be distributed to consumers by methods other than through retail stores.

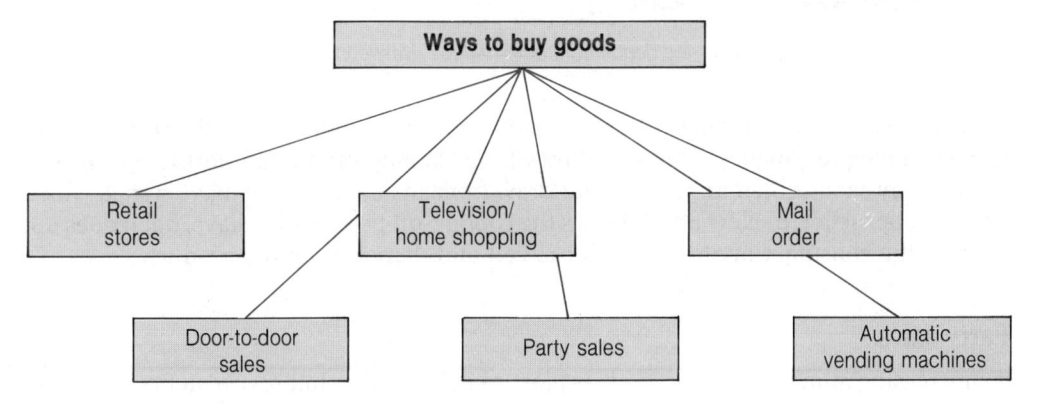

Give one example of a good commonly sold in each of these ways

Door-to-door sales

To make door-to-door sales a seller calls at the consumer's home and demonstrates the product. Cleaning materials and cosmetics are often sold door-to-door and this method is also used by some religious groups. It can be a convenient way to buy goods, especially for people who cannot easily get to shops because they have young children, have no transport or are handicapped through old age, ill health or physical disability.

There are disadvantages to buying from home.
- It is hard to compare prices with those charged by other sellers.
- Consumers do not see the full range of goods available, so they cannot choose the one that best suits their needs.
- Door-to-door selling is sometimes used by unscrupulous business people to take the customers' money (for example as a 'deposit') and then not deliver the goods as promised.
- Some people find it hard to refuse to buy goods they do not want or cannot afford. They may be especially vulnerable in their own homes where they are used to treating guests politely. Sometimes consumers agree to buy goods just to make the salesperson leave.

What are the disadvantages of buying goods from door-to-door salespeople?

The *Door-to-Door Sales Act* gives consumers some protection from high pressure door-to-door selling techniques. This Act allows for a 'cooling off' period during which consumers may change their minds and withdraw from any contract they have signed with a door-to-door seller. In New South Wales the cooling-off period is ten days, but it does not apply if the consumer invites the seller to call and demonstrate the product.

Party sales

An increasing number of goods, such as plastic kitchenware, clothes, cosmetics, wine and books are sold through parties. 'Hosts' invite some 'guests' to their home where the product is demonstrated and orders are taken. Consumers often enjoy the social contact as well as the chance to buy goods, but they do not have the opportunity to compare prices with those of other sellers. As well, there is often a lot of pressure on consumers to buy unwanted goods or pressure to host the next party. This pressure comes because the host is usually given a present by the demonstrator, and the value of the present depends on the value of the sales from the party and the number of future parties booked.

Mail order sales and direct marketing

Some firms sell their goods by advertising in magazines and newspapers. Consumers fill in a coupon and send it, with the money, to the address given. Mail order firms may get lists of customers in certain categories such as families with school-age children, owners of luxury cars or people nearing retirement age. The firms then send these people advertisements for goods likely to appeal to them. Some large department stores send catalogues to country customers who can then order goods by mail.

Mail order shopping can be convenient, especially for people who cannot easily get to shopping centres because of distance, lack of transport or other handicaps. Shoppers who regularly shop by mail are less able to compare prices and shop for value than people who regularly visit a variety of shops. Mail order shoppers also risk losing money to fly-by-night operators who take the money but do not send the goods, and disappear without trace from the address. Others send goods which are not as good as they sounded in the advertisement. The risk is much greater when customers are asked to send the order and money to a post office box number. One way to reduce the risk is to shop only with well-established firms or to order the goods 'cash on delivery' (COD), which means you pay once the goods arrive.

What are fly-by-night operators? Explain why mail order customers are vulnerable to these people

Automatic vending machines

A number of goods can be bought from machines in which the customer places certain coins, presses a button and receives the good. Some machines give change. These machines are commonly found on railway stations and in rest rooms. Among the many goods they are used to sell are cigarettes, snack foods, drinks and toothbrushes.

Television/home shopping

Some firms advertise goods on television and invite consumers to order them by telephone. The goods are then delivered to the consumer's home by courier. To avoid hoax calls sellers usually insist the customer pays for the goods and delivery charge by credit card when placing the order. One problem with buying goods this way is that it may be impossible to get a refund if the goods are not satisfactory. A 'money-back' guarantee is no use if you cannot trace the seller. It is also risky to give your credit card number over the phone, except to a well-known, reputable firm. Dishonest sellers can charge goods to your account on other occasions and it is hard to prove that you did not order them.

Unordered goods

Some unscrupulous sellers send goods to people who have not ordered them, hoping that the consumer will be too busy or too lazy to send back the goods. If the consumer uses the goods, he or she is obliged to pay for them. Consumers who do not want these goods should either return them to the seller (at the seller's expense) or contact the seller to pick them up. If the seller tries to get payment by threatening to contact a debt collector or endanger the consumer's credit rating, the consumer should report it to Business and Consumer Affairs.

Ways to buy services

Many services such as bus rides and visits to the movies are 'used up' at the place of purchase. Other services continue for a longer period of time. An insurance policy to cover a house in case of fire or burglary normally lasts for one year and is then renewable. Rates paid to the council ensure that garbage will be collected for the next twelve months.

Services are provided by private firms, governments and local community organisations. Private firms which provide services include travel agents, dentists and painting contractors. Governments provide services such as education and public transport. Local community organisations such as Apex, Lions and Rotary sometimes provide services to aged people, children's homes and needy individuals in their area. Other local community services (such as drug referral centres, women's and teenagers' refuges and community health centres) are often financed jointly by churches or charities and governments and run by volunteers.

Exercise 1I

1. Name at least one product sold by each of the following methods:
   (a) door-to-door sales
   (b) party sales
   (c) mail order
   (d) automatic vending machine
   (e) television/home shopping.
2. Which people benefit from being able to buy goods from door-to-door sales people?
3. List three possible disadvantages of buying from a sales person who calls door-to-door.

4. How does the *Door-to-Door Sales Act* give consumers some protection against high pressure door-to-door sales people?
5. What problems is a consumer likely to encounter at a 'party' to sell products?
6. Which people are most likely to benefit from mail order sales?
7. List three possible disadvantages of buying goods by mail order.
8. What two actions can consumers take to protect themselves against losing their money when they order goods by mail order?
9. What problems may be faced by a consumer who orders goods from a 'telephone order' firm and pays for them by giving a credit card number over the telephone?

Skills activities

Research

Find a magazine advertisement or a leaflet which invites consumers to buy goods by mail, maybe by filling in a coupon and sending it in with some money. Paste the advertisement into your notebook.

Analyse information

PUMP IT FOR FREE

Entry Form must be completed in full.

☐ Mr
☑ Mrs
☐ Ms
☐ Miss

SURNAME: GREENE
FIRST NAME: TERESA
PARTNER'S SURNAME: GREENE
FIRST NAME: JACK

Tick (✓) ☑ Married ☐ Single ☐ Other

Age Group A ☑ 18–24 B ☐ 25–40 C ☐ 41–60 D ☐ Over 60

Address: FOREST WAY
Suburb: TIMBERTOP   P/code: 2159
Current Occupation: RANGER
Partner's Occupation: GREEN KEEPER
Telephone (Home): 653 1100   (Work): 630 2222

MINI HOUSEHOLDER SURVEY

Homeowner Tick (✓) ☑ Yes ☐ No

Value of Home

A ☐ Under $85,000   B ☑ $85,000–$150,000   C ☐ Over $150,000

Place of Entry: TIMBERTOP   Date of Entry: 30-3-97

Consumers who filled in the coupon on page 37 were entered into a competition in which they could win free petrol for a year.

1. In about half a page, describe the household of the person who filled out this form.
2. What kinds of goods and services would this household be in the market for?
3. What kinds of advertisements would it be worth while for a direct marketing firm to send this household?
4. Copy the coupon into your book and fill in the details as though one of your parents was doing it.
5. What kinds of advertisements would it be worth sending to your place?

Research project—junk mail

Collect all the 'junk mail' that is put in your letterbox for one week. In your notebook list the following for each leaflet:
(a) the good or service being advertised
(b) whether the seller is from your area or from out of the area
(c) whether your family is likely to buy the good or service as a result of this advertising.
Paste any suitable leaflets into your notebook.

Short report—shopping from home

Assume that in about twenty years' time consumers will do most of their shopping from home, using their personal computer, a catalogue and a home delivery service. Put the heading 'The Consumer of the Future' in your book and write a paragraph outlining the advantages and disadvantages of this form of shopping.

Documents and records for the consumer

Cash dockets and cash register slips

Cash dockets and cash register slips both give proof that the customer bought the goods from a particular store and has already paid for them. This proof will be important if the customer is suspected of shoplifting or if the goods need to be returned for some reason. Wise shoppers keep cash dockets and cash register slips until they are sure they will not want to return the goods or until the warranty has expired.

Receipts

A receipt proves that an amount of money was paid. Receipts used to always be given when customers paid bills such as for electricity or household repairs. They were a record as well as proof of payment.

These days receipts are less necessary as most accounts are paid by cheque. The cheque butt has the same details as the receipt and is the customer's record. However,

THE CONSUMER 39

receipts are still given when the customer asks for them. Doctors and dentists always give receipts so patients can claim a refund from their health fund.

What is the main reason for giving cash dockets, cash register slips and receipts to customers?

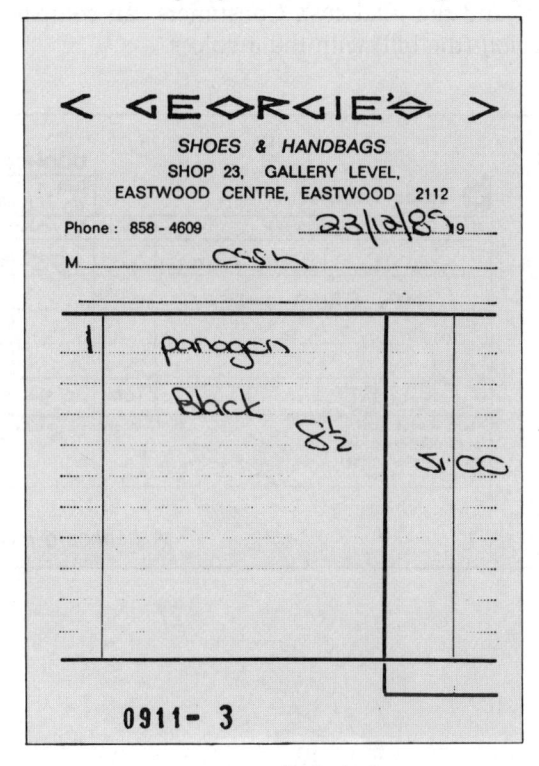

Cash docket

Cash register slip

Receipt

Invoices

Firms give invoices to customers who buy on credit. Customers need a record of the goods they do not pay for immediately. When they get the bill they need to be able to refer back to the invoice to see what the charge is for. The invoice has details of the goods, the quantity, their price, any discount and the total cost. Consumers can compare all the amounts on their *statement of account* (the bill) with the invoices.

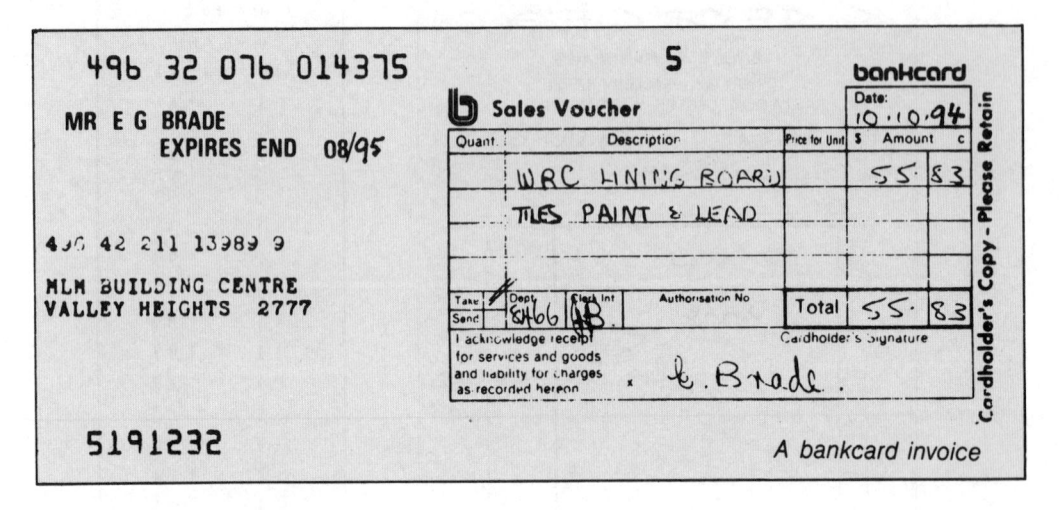

A bankcard invoice

What is the main purpose of an invoice?

Files and filing

Documents and records prove that an event has occurred. People must be able to *find* the documents when they need that proof. Households and firms need a good filing system.

Some individuals and families keep their important documents in a box or special drawer. The documents need to be organised or filed in some way. All guarantees and warranties might be kept together in a large envelope, along with instructions on how to use household items. Marriage and birth certificates and passports might be in another envelope. Health care receipts and the health fund book might be in another, bills to be paid in another and so on. The envelopes might all be kept in a box or drawer, in alphabetical order. Any document could be found quickly and easily. Some families use concertina folders to file their documents and records. Concertina folders are divided into a number of compartments and expand as more documents are filed.

Business firms have a lot more paperwork than most families. They may need a special filing cabinet to organise their records. Filing cabinets are sets of deep drawers with strong paper folders hanging inside them. Letters, documents, price lists and so on can be put safely in their own special files.

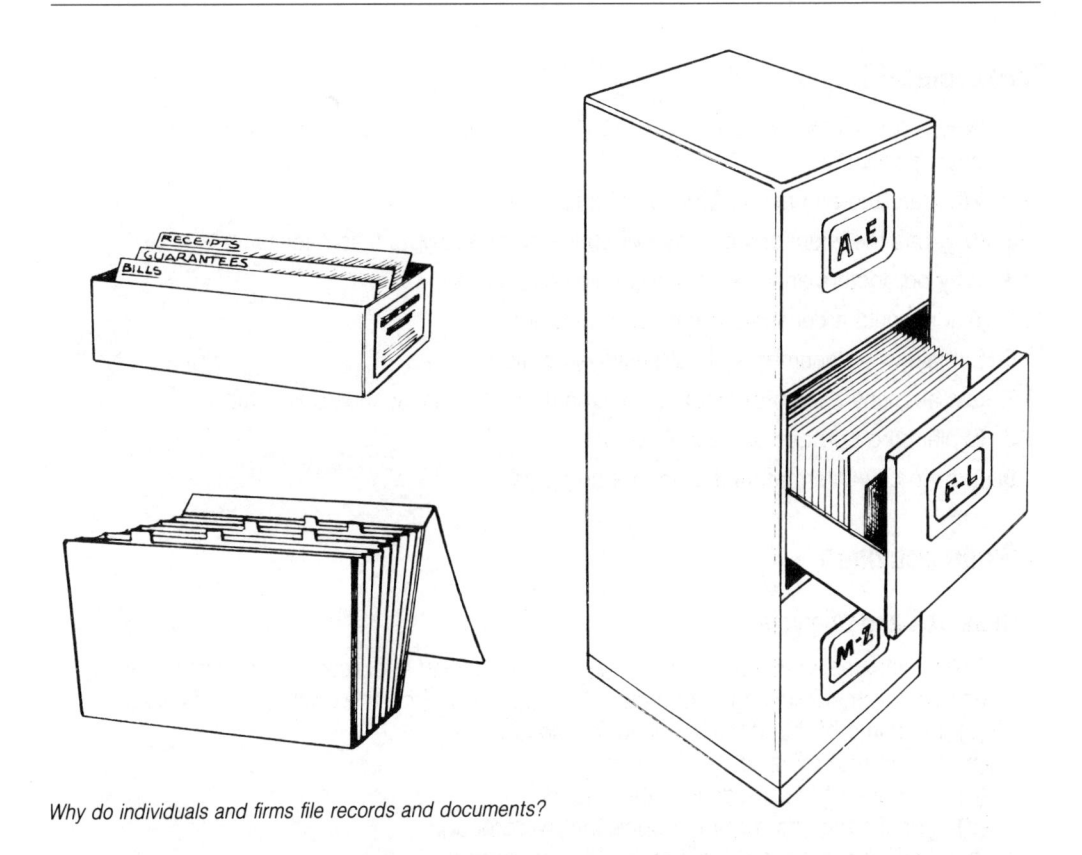

Why do individuals and firms file records and documents?

Most items are filed in alphabetical order. Sometimes the file is first divided into broad categories. There might be sections labelled 'Correspondence', 'Creditors', 'Debtors', 'Staff members' and so on. Within each of these categories the items will be filed alphabetically. Filing systems vary from firm to firm and from household to household, depending on their own particular needs. A book publisher may have a whole drawer in the filing cabinet for authors. Each author would then be filed alphabetically (surname first) with details about the person in an individual folder. Another drawer might be for books in production, while another might be for the customers, the bookshops. A retail store, a car repair firm and a doctor's surgery would also have different filing systems.

Filing by computer

Computers are machines that follow instructions in a set way. They can also record and store information for later use. Computers store information on a magnetic storage device, usually a disk or a tape like those used in cassette recorders. When the computer is being used the disks (or tapes) rotate at high speed and allow the information to be typed in, via the keyboard, read back from the monitor or printed out. The data stored on the magnetic tape or the disk are stored in files of data called *datasets*. The files are accessed in various ways, depending on the system being used. One way is by typing the name of the document required.

Exercise 1J

1. Why is it wise to keep cash sale dockets and cash register slips for some time after buying goods?
2. What are the two main purposes of a receipt?
3. Why has the widespread use of cheques made receipts less necessary?
4. Why do doctors and dentists always give receipts?
5. When would a consumer be given an invoice?
6. Explain why documents should always be filed.
7. List as many as you can of the documents that a family should file safely.
8. Explain the purpose of a filing cabinet.
9. Explain how information is filed in a computer.

Skills activities

Research and analysis

1. Collect and paste into your notebook a cash sale docket and a cash register slip. Beside each, write the following information that you will find on the dockets themselves:
   (a) the name of the store that sold the goods
   (b) the date of the sale
   (c) the price of the goods and the total cost
   (d) a brief description of the goods that were bought.
   (This information is not available on all cash register dockets.)
2. Obtain an invoice and paste it into your notebook. Using the information provided on the invoice write:
   (a) the name of the firm from which the goods or services were bought
   (b) the date on which the purchase was made
   (c) a brief description of the goods or services that were bought on credit
   (d) the amount of money owing on this purchase.
   (If you cannot obtain an invoice yourself, copy the bankcard invoice in the previous section and take the information from it.)

Practise filling in forms

Collect a variety of forms and documents and fill them in, using information about yourself. Paste the completed forms into your notebook.

Revision activities

New terms

In your notebook put the heading 'Important new terms and their meanings'. Copy the first term from List A into your notebook and select its correct meaning from the definitions in List B. Continue until you have listed each term and its meaning.

List A

Capital good, caveat emptor, collective want, complementary want, consumer, consumer good, credit, durable good, filing system, gross income, interdependence, invoice, need, net income, non-durable good, private want, receipt, retailer, specialisation, substitute want, technology, want, wholesaler.

List B

1. A person who buys or uses goods and services
2. A good used by individuals and families, e.g. toothpaste, clothing
3. A good or service we like to have but which is not necessary for our survival
4. A good or service we need in order to survive, e.g. food, water
5. Method of producing goods and services
6. A good that is expected to last a number of years, e.g. furniture
7. A good that is only used once (e.g. matches) or which will last only a short time, e.g. exercise book
8. A good used by business firms to help produce other goods or services, e.g. factory building, cement truck, typewriter
9. Total income earned before taking out tax
10. Income left to spend after taking out tax
11. A way of buying goods or services now but paying for them later
12. The need to rely on other firms, other people or other countries to provide some of the goods required to satisfy wants
13. Concentrating on doing one particular task or producing one particular product
14. Firms which buy goods from manufacturers, store them and resell them in smaller quantities to retailers
15. Firms which sell goods to consumers
16. A warning to buyers that once they have bought something they may not be able to return it for a refund if they find it is not what they wanted
17. Wants that people in the community use together: they are usually provided by the government, e.g. street lights, roads
18. Wants that arise when consumers satisfy another want, because the use of one good makes another good necessary, e.g. cars and petrol
19. Wants that are used in place of something else, e.g. coffee instead of tea
20. Wants that are satisfied by the individual consumer from his or her own net income
21. The document given when customers buy goods on credit
22. The document given as proof that money has been paid
23. A method of organising information so that it can be found again easily

44 THE WORLD OF COMMERCE

Vocabulary exercise—crossword puzzle

Complete the following crossword puzzle in your notebook.

Clues

1. The person who buys or uses goods and services
2. Something necessary for survival
3. Firms which sell to consumers
4. An example of a want
5. Goods or services that make life more pleasant but which are not necessary for survival
6. The income left after income tax has been taken out
7. An example of a need
8. Short for 'each'
9. This influences wants and needs at any time
10. An example of a need
11. Another name for a cash register
12. Fashion influences our wants for these
13. This was used as money in Ancient Rome
14. The same person will have different wants at a different _ _ _
15. Lawful
16. Some expensive goods may be bought as _ _ _ _ _ _ symbols
17. This is taken out of most wages before they are paid to the wage earner
18. A form of money in the early days in Australia
19. Australian Consumers Association (initials)
20. This is very important in determining both what we buy and how much we buy

2 Money

The need for money

The subsistence society

Subsistence societies such as nomadic Aboriginal tribes in Australia had little need for money. To satisfy their needs the group members gathered the goods from the local area. They hunted and fished, and grew or gathered food. They found building materials for their homes. They made their own tools, weapons and cooking utensils.

Barter

People in subsistence societies produce only the bare necessities. They usually produce goods for their own use only. When they do trade, they simply swap what they have for something else they want. Exchanging goods for other goods is called barter. Barter can cause problems. It needs a *double coincidence of wants*. People must find others who have what they want and who will exchange it for what they have.

Example
One villager has a spare pig and he needs a clay pot.
- He must find someone who has a spare clay pot *and* wants some pork.
- They must agree on how many clay pots this pig is worth. The value of the pig will have to be measured in clay pots, not in dollars.
- If they agree that the pig is worth five clay pots, the pig owner cannot exchange one-fifth of his pig for one clay pot.

Barter is a very clumsy and inconvenient way of doing business. It only works in societies with very little trade. These societies have very low living standards because they produce few goods.

What problems are caused by barter?

The specialised society

Australia is a specialised society. People usually produce one type of good or service. Doctors treat the sick, graziers raise sheep or cattle and jewellers make or sell jewellery. People rely on others to produce the goods and services they need for their daily lives.

Barter is not practical in a specialised society. The mechanic who wanted his appendix removed would have to find a doctor with car trouble. The dentist who wanted her children educated would have to find a teacher with toothache. It would be hard to value the services. How many lessons would the dentist's children receive in exchange for the teacher having his teeth filled?

These problems are overcome when goods and services are exchanged for money. The patient pays the doctor a sum of money for an operation. The doctor then pays the gardener for mowing the lawn and pays the coach for tennis lessons. Each of these people can then pay for other goods and services they want.

Money is used to buy goods and services. People get money by selling something to another person or firm. The gardener sells his or her skill and effort to the doctor. An item's *price* shows its value. Money allows people to exchange goods and services without the problems connected with barter.

The circular flow of income

Money flows between the main groups in the community. These money flows show how *interdependent* the groups are.

Individuals combine into household groups, usually families. Some household members sell their labour (that is their time, effort, skills and training) and other resources to

MONEY 47

Explain how the use of money simplifies transactions between the doctor, patient, gardener and tennis coach

business firms. They are paid money wages or other forms of income such as rent, interest and dividends. The firms use the labour and other resources to produce goods and services. Household members spend their money incomes to buy goods and services from business firms. When wages rise, wage earners have more money to spend, but firms' costs rise. When firms put up their prices to cover their higher costs, wages do not buy as much as they did before the price rise.

Households and firms save part of their income, allowing others to borrow the money saved. When interest rates rise, savers receive more income and they can buy more. At the same time, borrowers' costs go up. They have less money to spend on other goods. Households and firms pay taxes to the government. The taxpayers have less money to spend the way they choose, but the government uses the funds to pay pensions, nurses' wages, road builders and on other forms of government spending. The money flows back to the community.

The flow of money between various groups in the community is called the circular flow of income.

48 THE WORLD OF COMMERCE

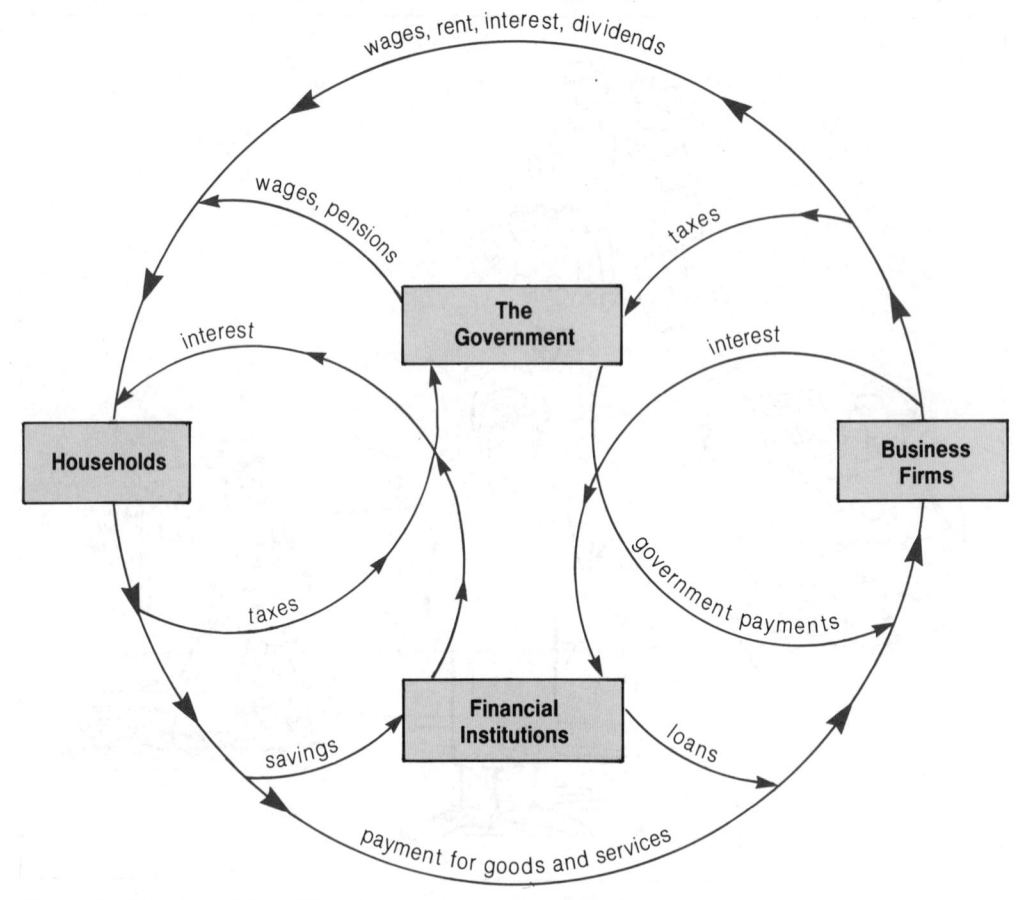

Money circulates to and from different groups in the community

Exercise 2A

1. Explain what is meant by the term 'barter'.
2. Why is a 'double coincidence of wants' necessary for barter?
3. Why is barter possible in a primitive society?
4. Would you have as wide a choice of goods in a primitive society as you have at present? Explain your answer.
5. What is a 'specialised society'?
6. Outline the problems you would have if you wanted a skateboard but all you had to give in exchange was a record.
7. Use an example to show how money allows us to exchange our skills and abilities for goods and services.
8. Explain how specialisation and the use of money increases people's *interdependence* in modern communities.

Skills activities

Apply your knowledge
1. List ten ways in which people in your local area earn an income.
2. Think of an area totally different from the area where you live. For example, if you live in a city, think of a farming or mining community. List five ways the people in that area could earn a living. Use different examples to those in Activity 1.

Barter
Barter your pencil case's contents with other class members. You will need to work out an exchange rate for each swap. For example, one ruler for two pencils. Then draw up a list of the advantages and disadvantages of barter as a method of exchanging goods and services.

Money

Most primitive societies gradually grew into larger communities. They began to specialise and produced more than their basic needs of food, clothing and shelter. They began to weave cloth and make pottery and jewellery. They could trade some of the items they made for other goods they wanted. Barter was awkward when trading a variety of goods. A new system was needed to make trade easier.

Trading communities needed to invent something which would be generally acceptable to everyone wanting to exchange goods or services. This item, whatever it was, would be money. Money overcomes the problems linked with barter. It allows people to exchange goods and services and to compare their values. Money also allows people to save for the future and to record the value of *debts* (amounts owed).

Earliest forms of money

For thousands of years people all over the world have used objects as money. Some Pacific islanders used sharks' teeth. People in Papua New Guinea used cowrie shells. Small pieces of leather were used in Ancient Egypt. The early Romans used salt to pay wages—our word *salary* comes from the Latin word for salt. Rum was used to pay soldiers' wages in early Australia. Cigarettes are sometimes used as currency in gaols. Any item is 'money' if people accept it in exchange for goods or services or to pay debts.

Money around the world

The coins and banknotes used to buy goods and services are called a country's *currency*. There are more than one hundred and fifty different currencies in the world. Most are only

50 THE WORLD OF COMMERCE

Items used as money

Where has each of these items been used as money?

accepted within the country that issued them. Travellers must change money into the currency of the different countries they visit. The table shows some of the world's currencies.

Currencies from various countries			
Country	*Basic unit*	*Subdivision*	*Abbreviation*
Australia	Dollar	100 cents	$A
Brazil	Cruzeiro	100 centavos	Cr
China	Yuan	10 jias or 100 fen	Y
Finland	Markka	100 pennia	F Mk
Hungary	Forint	100 filler	Ft
India	Rupee	100 paise	I R
Uganda	Shilling	100 cents	U Sh

Source: Reader's Digest Great Illustrated Dictionary, p.422

Exercise 2B

1. Why was it necessary for our ancestors to invent 'money'?
2. Define money.
3. List some of the earliest forms of money.
4. What condition is necessary before objects such as cowrie shells can be used as money?
5. What is one word used to describe the official banknotes and coins used to buy goods and services in any country?

Skills activities

Library research

Find out the units of currency used in the following countries: Canada, Denmark, Fiji, Greece, Indonesia, Japan, Lebanon, Mexico, New Zealand, Papua New Guinea, Turkey, United Kingdom. United States of America, Union of Soviet Socialist Republics, Vietnam.

Vocabulary exercise—crossword puzzle

Complete the following crossword puzzle in your notebook.

Clues
1. An amount owed to someone
2. Exchange goods directly for other goods without using money
3. Produce one type of good or service
4. A type of shell once used as money in Papua New Guinea
5. To sell some goods and buy goods from someone else
6. A precious metal sometimes used as money
7. Anything generally accepted in exchange for goods and services
8. What something is worth
9. Keep for future use
10. This indicates a good's value
11. Swap

Money in Australia today

Modern Australian money consists of coins, notes, bank deposits which can be transferred by cheque or electronically, and 'plastic money' or credit cards.

Australian $1 coins being packaged for delivery to banks
MIRROR AUSTRALIAN TELEGRAPH PUBLICATIONS

Coins

The first coins with fixed values were issued in Lydia (now western Turkey) in about 1000 BC. These coins were stamped with the face of the emperor. Now most countries issue coins for the smallest units of their currency. In Australia coins are minted at the Commonwealth Mint in Canberra, Perth and Melbourne. They are distributed through banks. We have 5c, 10c, 20c, 50c, $1 and $2 coins. They are made from metal, a durable (hard-wearing) material. Coins are used so often they would wear out quickly if made from a less durable material.

Notes

Goldsmiths in England used to issue notes as receipts for gold and silver which had been left with them for safekeeping. The notes gave the owners (depositors) proof that they were entitled to claim back (withdraw) their gold and silver when they wanted to buy something. After the sellers were paid they could deposit the precious metal with a goldsmith and they, in turn, would be given their own note. Some sellers agreed to accept the note itself in payment for goods, saving two trips to the goldsmith. Once the receipts began to be used in this way they became money, the first 'banknotes' or paper money.

One problem with using the receipts as money was that they were often for odd amounts such as two pounds ten shillings and four pence. This problem was overcome when the goldsmiths began to issue their receipts in standard amounts such as one pound and five pounds. Many of the early goldsmiths developed into banks. At that time all banks in England had the right to issue banknotes. The system gradually changed so that by 1921 the only bank allowed to issue notes in England was the Bank of England. In Australia the Reserve Bank of Australia is the only bank to issue notes.

A problem with paper money is that it wears out with continued use and needs to be replaced frequently. This problem is being overcome in Australia by replacing paper notes with ones made from plastic. The plastic material is cleaner, lasts longer and is harder to forge than paper. Australian banknotes are printed in Melbourne. They are distributed by the Reserve Bank to other banks which pay them to their customers. Notes are used for the larger currency values: $5, $10, $20, $50 and $100. Banknotes are much lighter than metal coins so it is easy to carry around large sums of money in note form. Of course, it is not very safe to do so, as they can be lost or stolen.

Why is it not wise to carry large sums of money in note form?

Deposits in financial institutions

In today's society many payments are made without using notes and coins. People can transfer funds in some accounts in banks and other financial institutions (such as building societies or credit unions) directly to another person or firm's account. They can write a cheque or use a plastic card in an electronic terminal to transfer the funds to pay for goods and services. Cheques and electronic transfers are explained later in this chapter.

Credit cards

Many people shop by credit card. Mastercard, bankcard, Visa card and store charge cards let them buy goods and services on credit. They receive a monthly statement which shows how much they owe. The customers may pay the account using notes and coins but many do not use currency at all. They simply transfer funds from their account by writing a cheque or by using an automatic teller machine or even a telephone to transfer the funds electronically.

Legal tender

Many sellers are willing to accept credit cards, cheques and electronic transfers in payment but they are not legally obliged to do so. In fact, when you are buying something, sellers can ask to be paid in any way they choose. They can insist on being paid in cabbages if they wish! If you do not want to pay the way they say you do not buy the goods. But when you are paying a debt that already exists, the *creditor* (the person to whom the money is owed) must accept the country's legal tender. When notes and certain values of coins are offered (or 'tendered') to pay a debt they must be accepted or the debt is cancelled. By law, people to whom money is owing must accept the following values of coins and notes:
- 1c and 2c coins to the value of 20c;
- 5c, 10c, 20c and 50c coins to the value of $5;
- $1 coins to the value of $10;
- $2 coins to the value of $20;
- notes to any amount.

This means that a person can refuse to accept $10 paid in 5c coins as payment for a debt. The *debtor* would still owe the money. You could pay a $4 debt in 5c coins, however. But the Roads and Traffic Authority can refuse to accept 5c coins in bridge tolls and bus drivers can refuse to accept them in bus fares because the consumer is paying for *new* purchases.

Exercise 2C

1. In what Australian cities are coins minted?
2. What values in our currency have a single coin to represent them?
3. Why are coins made from a durable material such as metal?
4. Describe how paper notes came to be used as money.
5. Which bank is able to issue banknotes in Australia?
6. In what city are Australian banknotes printed?
7. What values in our currency are represented by single notes?
8. What is the advantage of using notes for the larger units of money?

9. What is one problem of making banknotes from paper? How is this problem being overcome?
10. Describe how deposits in financial institutions can be used as money.
11. Why are plastic credit cards a form of money?
12. What is legal tender?
13. If the train fare was $1, could the ticket seller refuse to accept twenty 5c coins? Why or why not?
14. Mary did not have any money with her but the paper seller, who knew her well, said she could pay for her papers tomorrow. The next day she offered the paper seller twenty 10c coins. Could the paper seller have refused to accept these coins in payment of Mary's debt? Give a reason for your answer.

Skills activity

Vocabulary exercise—crossword puzzle

Complete the following crossword puzzle in your notebook.

Clues

1 (across). Notes and coins
1 (down). This can be used to transfer money from one person's account in a financial institution to another person's account
2. Metal objects that form part of the currency
3 (with 5). Notes and coins that must be accepted in payment of a debt
4. The place where coins are produced in Australia
5 (with 3). Notes and coins that must be accepted in payment of a debt
6. The smallest money unit in Australia
7. Coins are made of this
8. Two-dollar coins to this number of dollars are legal tender in Australia
9. A precious metal that often used to be used as money
10. Amounts owed to other people
11. This was sometimes used to pay wages in Ancient Rome
12. A place where many people keep their savings
13. It is legal tender to offer _ _ _ _ dollars worth of 'silver' coins in payment of a debt
14. One hundred cents equals one _ _ _ _ _ _
15. A unit of paper or plastic money
16. Up to this number of one-dollar coins is legal tender

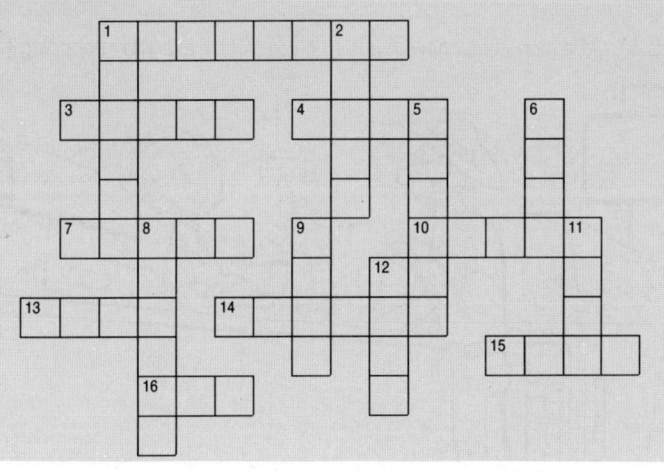

Characteristics of money

Money was invented to overcome the problems of barter. The items used as money had to have certain features to make them easy to use. The characteristics are still the same today. Money must be able to be divided into large and small units. It must be easy to recognise. It must keep well if it is not going to be spent straight away. It must be scarce, easy to recognise and hard to forge. Above all it must be acceptable to other people.

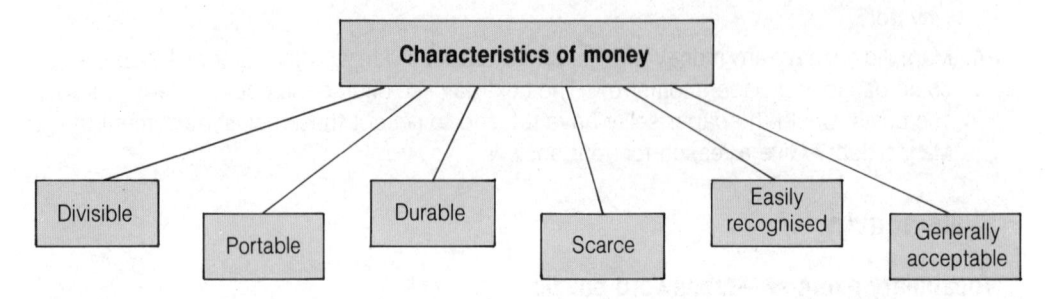

```
                    Characteristics of money
    ┌──────────┬──────────┬──────────┬──────────┐
 Divisible  Portable  Durable   Scarce    Easily      Generally
                                         recognised  acceptable
```

Divisible

Money must be able to buy inexpensive items such as sweets and magazines as well as very valuable items such as houses and cars. Diamonds could not be used to pay for a bus ride. Dollars and cents are so divisible that buyers can compare the value of goods worth say 49 cents and 50 cents. Buyers can also use dollars and cents to buy a 5-cent sweet or a million-dollar mansion.

Portable

Buyers need to be able to carry their money with them. Thousands of dollars in banknotes can easily fit into a wallet. Grain, on the other hand, is so bulky compared to its value that it would not make a good unit of money. A $100 note is far more portable and convenient than two thousand 5-cent pieces.

What characteristics should a money unit have if it is to be useful for everyday shopping?

Durable

It is very important that money will keep well, when it is being saved and also when it is being used. It must not spoil if it is kept for a time or if it is handled often. Metal coins are very durable so coins are used for the small units of currency which are used more often. Paper notes are gradually being replaced by plastic notes because they are more durable. Coins and notes do not decay if they are stored for a long time.

Scarce

No one would be willing to work or to sell valuable goods if they were paid in pebbles or leaves that people could pick up easily for themselves. The Reserve Bank controls the amount of notes and coins available and keeps them scarce compared to the amount people would like to have. It is also important that the items used as money be hard to copy or *forge*. If ice cubes were used as money we could all make our own in the freezer and they would have no real value.

Easily recognised

A problem with using a valuable commodity (like diamonds) as money is that it often takes an expert to recognise its real value. Most people cannot tell the difference between a good quality diamond and one that is inferior. But it is easy to tell the difference between a $10 note and a $50 note. It is not so easy to tell the difference between a $10 note and a good forgery.

Generally acceptable

Acceptability is the most important characteristic of money. An item may be portable, divisible, durable, scarce and easily recognised, but unless people are willing to accept it in exchange for goods and services it cannot be used as money. In Australia people accept paper or plastic notes (which have very little *real* value) in exchange for food, clothes and hard work, because they know that they can exchange the notes for other valuable goods and services they want. We all accept money because we know other people will accept it from us. Non-smokers in prisoner-of-war camps would accept cigarettes as payment for goods because they knew they could exchange the cigarettes for other things they wanted. The cigarettes were a form of money.

Why will people accept paper or plastic notes, which have little real value, in exchange for valuable goods and services?

58 THE WORLD OF COMMERCE

Explain why prisoners of war would accept cigarettes as a form of money even if they did not smoke

Exercise 2D

1. List the important characteristics of money. Write one sentence to explain why each of the characteristics is necessary.
2. Draw the following table in your notebook. For each item listed as a form of money, write the words 'good', 'fair' or 'poor' in each column to show the extent to which it has the necessary characteristics.

Form of money	Divisible	Portable	Durable	Scarce	Easily recognised	Generally accepted
Cow						
Grain						
Ice cubes						
Rum						
Diamonds						
Notes						
Coins						

3. Which of the characteristics listed in question 2 finally determines whether or not an object is really money?
4. Why do people accept paper or plastic notes in exchange for their labour or in exchange for goods that have real value, such as food and building materials?

Skills activities

Applying your knowledge—barter

Select something valuable you own (for example, a watch, a bicycle or a radio). Ask each of five friends what items of their own they would give you for it. In your notebook, draw up the following table. Explain why you would or would not accept that item in exchange for your own.

My good	Goods offered	Why accept/Why reject

Vocabulary exercise—crossword puzzle

Complete the following crossword puzzle in your notebook.

Clues

1. **(across).** Anything which is generally accepted in exchange for goods and services
1. **(down).** Units of money made from this are very durable
2. A unit of currency made from paper or plastic material
3. **(across).** Animals used as money by some tribes in Papua New Guinea
3. **(down).** Australian banknotes will be made of this material in future
4. A characteristic of money which means it is easy to carry about
5. A characteristic of money which means it is in short supply
6. Banknotes were made of this for many years because it made them very portable
7. A characteristic of money which means it will keep well
8. The parts or divisions of something like the currency
9. To copy the currency illegally
10. **(with 13).** A characteristic of money which means people have no trouble telling what it is worth
11. A characteristic of money which means it can be broken down into smaller measures
12. Money was invented to overcome the problems caused when goods and services were traded this way
13. See 10
14. The most important characteristic of money is that it must be _ _ _ _ _ _ _ _ _ accepted

Functions of money

Money was invented to do a number of tasks. These are its *functions*. Money makes it easier to exchange (trade) goods. It helps people save part of their income. It makes it easier to measure and compare the value of different goods. Money also makes it easier for people to record and pay debts.

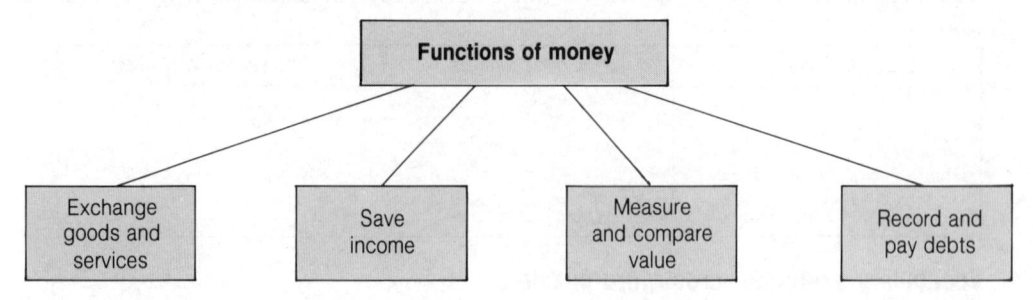

```
                    Functions of money
            ┌───────────┬──────────┬───────────┐
    Exchange         Save       Measure      Record and
    goods and       income    and compare    pay debts
    services                     value
```

Exchange for goods and services

In a specialised society people may do work or produce goods they never use themselves. A man who does not dance might spend his working life making ballet shoes. He is paid a money *wage* which he spends buying the goods and services he wants. Other people lend money for *interest*, let others use their buildings in exchange for *rent* or operate their own business and earn *profit*. They exchange the money they earn for goods and services they wish to buy. Money is the go-between that lets them trade their labour or goods and services they produce for other goods and services they want.

What function is money performing here?

A means of saving for the future

Many people do not spend all their income when they earn it. They save some to buy more expensive goods in future or simply to have security in an emergency. People who do not use money can store grain or dried meat to use when they cannot grow or hunt food. But many goods cannot be saved. Some rot easily. Others are bulky and take a lot of storage room. The problems are overcome if goods are sold for *money* and the surplus money is saved. Money in the form of notes, coins and bank deposits does not perish and a lot of value can be stored in a small area.

Money is not always a good store of value. When prices rise rapidly (that is, when we have inflation) money savings will not buy as much as before. The money itself does not deteriorate but it loses some of its value.

What function is money performing here?

A measure of value

Money makes it easy to place a definite value on a good or service. People are paid a definite amount of money—their wages—for the work they do. Goods have a definite value—their price. We do not measure the value of a compact disk by saying it is worth two books. Instead we say the disk is worth $20 and the books are worth $10 each. Money is a measure, like a ruler, which lets us compare the value of different goods. For example, it shows that a pencil is worth about half as much as a chocolate bar and a movie ticket is worth about five times as much as a chocolate bar.

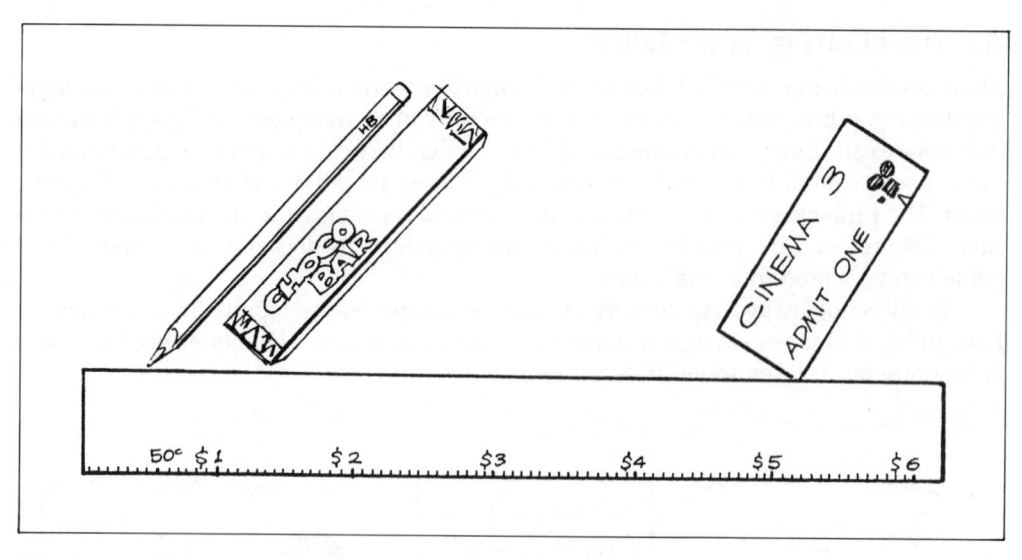

What function is money performing here?

A means of recording and repaying debts

Credit makes it possible for most people to buy expensive items such as a car or electrical goods. Items such as clothing, haircuts and restaurant meals are often put on bankcard. Buyers may pay for the goods next month or they may pay them off over many months or even years. The only satisfactory way to buy on credit and pay back the debts is to measure the future repayments in money. Those repaying the debt then know exactly how much they must pay, including any credit charges and interest. Those being repaid know exactly how much they will receive. If debts were recorded in goods, say kilograms of tomatoes, their value would change with changes in the price of the goods.

Exercise 2E

1. List four 'functions of money'.
2. How does money help people exchange goods and services?
3. Why is it usually better to save spare income in the form of money rather than as goods?
4. When would it be better to keep savings as certain types of goods instead of saving money?
5. How do we use money to compare the value of different goods and services? Give examples.
6. Why is it important to be able to use money to record and repay debts?

Skills activities

Apply your knowledge

1. Paste (or draw) in your notebook a picture of someone buying an item. Underneath it write the function of that money.
2. Collect (or draw) a newspaper advertisement from a bank or other financial institution which offers interest on savings. What function is money fulfilling when it is being saved?
3. Find an advertisement which shows the *price* of the good. What is money's function in this case?
4. Collect an advertisement asking customers to put down a deposit and pay off the good. What is the function of money here?

Motives for wanting money

Money itself has no *real* value. You cannot eat it, drink it or wear it. Money's value comes from what it will buy. People want money to satisfy their present and future wants. People have material wants, for example for clothes, cars and entertainment. They want other people to recognise their success. They also want security. Money helps satisfy all these wants.

To satisfy material wants

People need certain goods and services in order to survive—food, clothing and shelter. They want other things to make life more comfortable—television, holidays and electric blankets. They may want to save for the deposit on a car. Money makes it much easier to get all these things. People with a lot of money can have a much higher standard of living than people without it because they can buy more goods and services.

To gain status

In our society people's position or 'status' often depends on the job they have and the amount of money they earn. Money also lets people buy status symbols such as jewellery, luxury cars, speedboats and expensive holidays. Sometimes people keep accumulating more money than they will ever want to spend, because it gives them a feeling of power over others.

To gain security

Most people like to have a certain amount of money put aside to give them some security for 'rainy days'. If they fall ill, have an accident or lose their jobs they need money to see them through. They must buy food, pay bills, meet their credit repayments and pay their other expenses until they can earn an income again. Many people also try to save some money for their old age so they have a little more to live on than the pension.

64 THE WORLD OF COMMERCE

Vocabulary exercise—crossword puzzle

Complete the following crossword puzzle in your notebook.

Clues

1 **(with 8 and 10).** This is higher for people with a lot of money than for poorer people
2. Some people like to accumulate a lot of money because it gives them a feeling of _ _ _ _ _
3 **across (with 4).** The name given to a good which is bought to impress other people
3 **(down).** People need to have a certain level of savings for this
4. See 3 across
5. A person's reason for wanting something
6. People like to have a certain amount of savings in case they become _ _ _ and cannot earn a living
7 **(with 12).** A term given to an unfortunate event that might occur in the future
8. See 1
9. People need some savings in case they lose this and cannot earn income
10. See 1
11. The only real value of money is the goods and services it can _ _ _
12. See 7

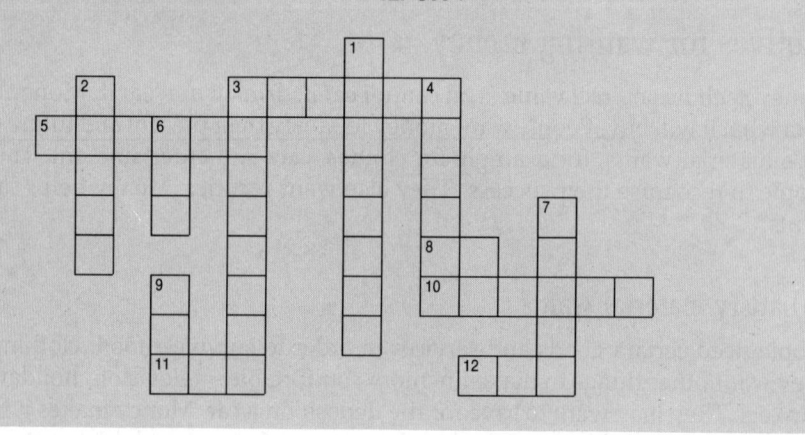

How do we get money?

About nine out of ten income earners in Australia work for business firms, the government or other people. They use their *labour* (that is, their skills and effort) to earn their income. Other income earners receive income by letting property to others, by lending money to others, by investing in companies and by operating their own businesses.

Income from labour

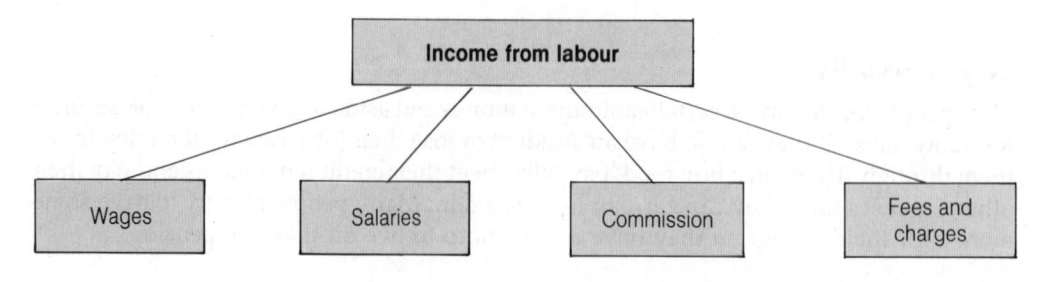

Income from labour
- Wages
- Salaries
- Commission
- Fees and charges

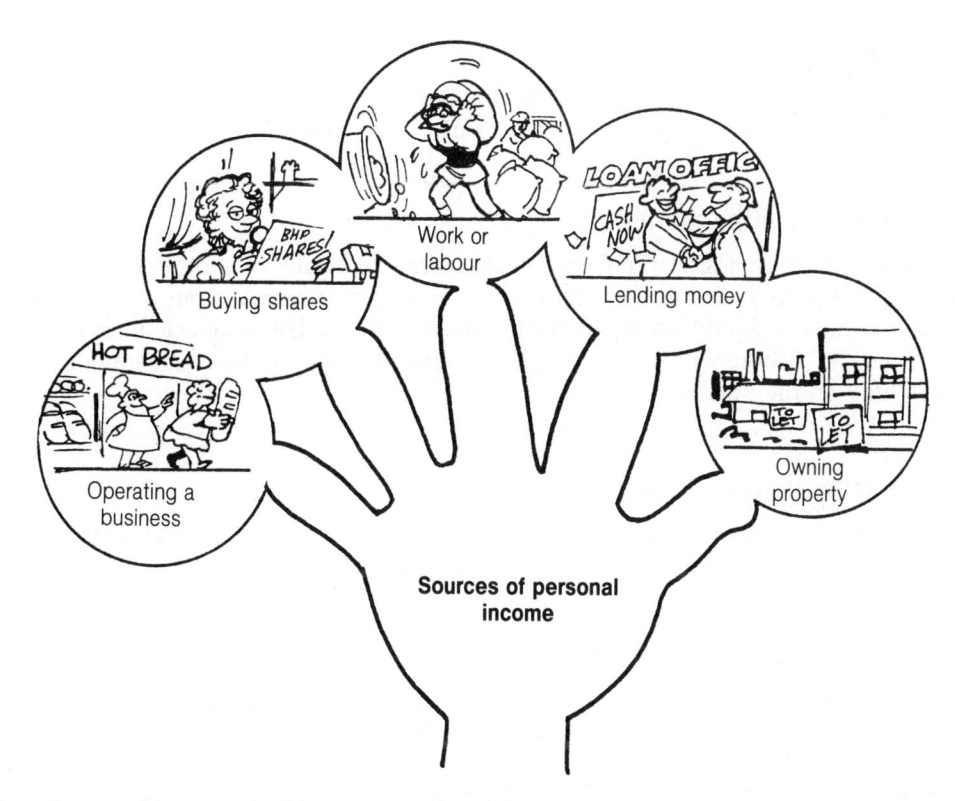

Name the type of income earned from each of these sources

People earn various kinds of money incomes. The name given to their income depends on the type of work they do.
- Sales assistants, clerical workers, labourers and many other employees receive *wages*. People on wages are paid extra money called *overtime* if they work longer than the hours stated in their award. The *award* sets out the hours employees should work and the lowest wages they can be paid. Awards help to make sure employees are paid a fair amount for their labour.
- Many people in management positions and professional people (such as teachers and accountants) receive *salaries*. Salaries are usually higher than award wages but the people who are paid salaries do not get overtime if they work longer hours.
- Self-employed professional people such as doctors, dentists and solicitors are paid *fees*, while self-employed tradespeople such as plumbers and electricians are paid their *charges*.
- Business people who act on behalf of another person are generally paid *commissions*. These people include real estate agents, employment agencies, agents for actors and singers, and some sales representatives. Commissions are a certain percentage of the value of the contract or sale. For example, singers might pay their agents 10 per cent of the fee the agents negotiate for them to appear in a concert.

Income from land

In Australia people who own land or buildings may earn money from them by letting them to other people. The property owner's income is called *rent*.

Income from lending money

People who have savings can put their spare money in a bank or another financial institution such as a credit union. They may lend it to the government by buying government bonds, or lend it to a public company by buying *debentures*. The income lenders receive is called *interest*. People with large enough amounts of money to lend can support themselves fully on the interest.

Income from shares

Some people buy shares in public companies. In this way they become part owners of the companies and share in their profits. The payments they receive are called *dividends*.

Income from owning a business

Some people have their own businesses from which they hope to make a *profit*. Profit is the amount left over after all the business expenses have been paid. Business owners usually expect to make more money from their own business than they could make working for someone else. Owning your own business usually involves risk, worry and long hours of work, however, and not all businesses make big profits.

Inherited wealth

Some people inherit money or property. The inheritance can be used to earn an income. The *heir* (person who inherits) can invest the money or let the property and earn income that way.

Winnings

A few lucky people win large amounts of money in lotteries, through other forms of gambling or as prize money for professional sport. Some of them spend their winnings on goods and services while others invest the money to earn future income in the form of interest, rent, dividends or profit.

Income for people who cannot earn money

Some people in our society are unable to earn their own living. They may be physically or mentally handicapped, too old, too young, unable to find a job or needing to care for young children. These people need to be provided with income so they can buy the basic necessities. In Australia the federal government provides *social security benefits*. Money for these benefits comes from taxes.

Unequal distribution of income and wealth in Australia

Australia is one of the world's wealthy countries. Most Australians are well fed, well clothed and live in nice homes. Most families have a car, colour television and the telephone. Workers are generally reasonably well paid.

However, there is a darker side. Incomes are not spread evenly among all Australians. In 1989 Australia was thought to have 30 000 millionaires and also 40 000 homeless people. The poorest 40 per cent of people receive only 15 per cent of the total income earned in a year, while the richest 20 per cent of people get 47 per cent of the total.* Between two and three million Australians live in poverty. The poorest people in Australia are found among

- the unemployed, particularly those with young families and those over fifty years of age
- single-parent families, particularly those headed by a woman
- old people dependent on the age pension
- Aborigines and newly arrived, unskilled migrants
- unskilled workers with large families.

Reasons for unequal income distribution

There are many reasons why some people earn more or less money than others.

- Some people inherit wealth or win large sums of money which they can invest. Their high income is the result of good luck.
- Some people have skills for which employers are willing to pay high wages. Unskilled people (or people with skills that employers do not want) cannot earn as much. In some cases they may not be able to get a job at all.
- Some people work long hours in hard jobs and earn more money because of the extra effort they put in. Others prefer to have an easier life and more leisure time. They earn less.
- Some people belong to strong trade unions which have been able to win high wages for them. Others belong to weaker unions and their award wages are lower.
- Some people save some of their income and put it to work to earn more money for them. They take out insurance to help them if they suffer financial losses. Others spend all their income and do not take out insurance. They have nothing to fall back on in an emergency like ill health, unemployment, accidents or other misfortune. Perhaps they have different values or maybe they do not earn enough to be able to save money or pay insurance premiums.
- Some people train for a long time to get a better-paid job. Others do not have the ability or the motivation or they cannot afford to get the higher education that would lead to a better-paid job.
- Some people cannot get better-paid jobs because of *discrimination*. Some women, Aboriginal people, migrants, handicapped people and others may be refused certain jobs because employers believe they would not do the job well.
- Some people cannot get a job because they are too old, in poor health or needing to look after young children. They depend on social security payments for their income.

* UNICEF, *The State of the World's Children*, 1989.

68 THE WORLD OF COMMERCE

Skills

Inheritance and luck

High award wages

Many dependants

Investments

Reasons for unequal distribution of income

Poor English language skills

Education and training

Long hours and hard work

Unable to work

Discrimination

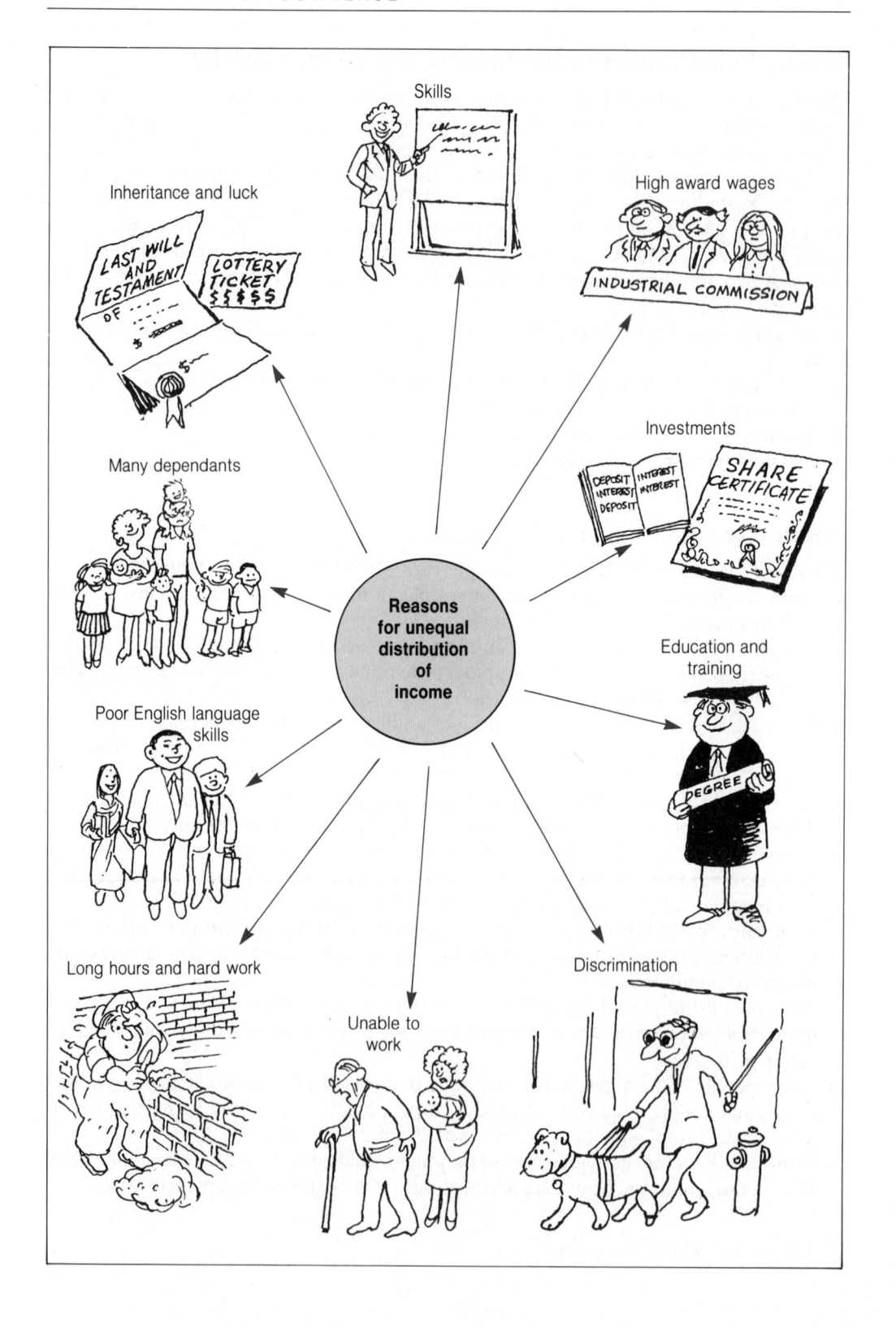

- People who do not speak English well often have trouble getting a well-paid job, even if they have all the other qualifications needed.
- Some people support many dependants. When the income has to be shared among a large family there is less for everyone.

Effects of unequal income distribution

Standard of living
In specialised countries like Australia a household's *standard of living* depends mainly on the amount of money it has to spend. The area in which we live, our housing, and the quality of our food, clothes, entertainment and holidays all depend, to a very large extent, on the household's income. Unequal distribution of income means that the very rich can afford to live in luxury while the very poor are struggling to survive.

Vicious circles
Richer people can afford to give their children a better education, allowing them to get better-paid jobs in future. They can also leave money and property to their children in their will, giving the children the chance to earn even more income. When people are well off their children are likely to be well off too, but people with a poor background are likely to remain poor. A child who cannot afford to stay on at school or go to university has less chance of getting a well-paid job than one who gets a good education. The children of poor parents will also have to depend on their own earnings because they are not likely to inherit many possessions from their parents.

Social effects
Unequal income distribution may lead to despair and resentment among those on very low incomes. Their anger may lead them into vandalism and violence to others in society or towards their own families. Their despair may cause them to turn to drugs or alcohol. Their health may suffer through poor housing and a shortage of good food. Low self-esteem may make it even harder for poorer people to get a better-paid job.

Social security payments
An unequal distribution of income increases the need for programs to help needy people. About one in four families in Australia depend on government welfare payments as their main form of income. Social security payments are worth about 10 per cent of the total value of goods and services produced in Australia in a year.

70 THE WORLD OF COMMERCE

People on low incomes generally have poorer housing and a lower standard of living than people on high incomes. Compare the two houses shown in these two pictures
MIRROR AUSTRALIAN TELEGRAPH PUBLICATIONS

Exercise 2F

1. How do most people in Australia earn their income?
2. Name the type of income earned by
   (a) factory workers and bus drivers
   (b) a solicitor who is employed by a legal firm
   (c) self-employed architects
   (d) travel agents.
3. How, in Australia, do we make sure that wage earners are paid a fair amount?
4. What is the income received by property owners who allow other people to use their land or buildings?
5. Name three institutions which accept loans from the public. What form of income can be earned by lending money?
6. What is the income received by shareholders? Why are they entitled to this income?
7. Explain the term 'profit'.
8. How can an inheritance or a gambling win be used to earn an income?
9. Why does the federal government pay money to people who are unable to earn an income? What name is given to these payments? How does the government get the money to make these payments?
10. Give two examples to illustrate the unequal distribution of income in Australia.
11. List the groups of people most likely to be found at the poorest end of the income scale in Australia.
12. List ten reasons for the unequal distribution of income in Australia.
13. What effects does the unequal distribution of income have on living standards in Australia?
14. Give two reasons why people are more likely to become wealthy if they have a wealthy background. Why is it harder for the children of poor people to become rich?

Skills activities

Class discussion topics

1. If all the wealth in Australia were divided evenly among the population we would soon have the same distribution of income as we have at present.
2. Social security payments only encourage people not to look for jobs.

Vocabulary exercise—crossword puzzle

Complete the following crossword puzzle in your notebook.

Clues

1 **(with 2).** The lowest amount employers can pay to workers doing particular jobs
3. Income to people who allow others to use their land or buildings
4. Charges made by self-employed professional people such as doctors and dentists
5. Payment to a shareholder from a comapny's profit

72 THE WORLD OF COMMERCE

6. People lending money to public companies buy these
7. Income received from lending money
8. **(across).** People buy these when they become part-owners of a company
8. **(down).** The earnings of a professional person. The person receiving this does not usually get paid for overtime
9. This sometimes prevents certain people from getting jobs
10. A form of income received by business people who act on behalf of another person
11. Incomes may be unequally distributed because the relatives of wealthy people sometimes _ _ _ _ _ _ _ large amounts of money
12. The income received by a person who owns his or her own business
13. Most families in Australia _ _ _ _ their living
14. **(with 24).** Wage earners are paid at a higher rate for this
15. Cash social service benefits (initials)
16. These people often find it hard to get a job, especially if they do not speak English very well
17. People who gamble hope to make money from these
18. Mental and physical effort used to produce goods and services
19. The name given to the money, property and other assets people own
20. Sometimes a person's income and wealth depends on this
21. Single-parent households headed by these people make up a large proportion of the poorest group in Australia
22. People with this are usually able to get better-paid jobs
23. Money from this helps to pay social security benefits
24. See 14
25. Between two and three million Australians are believed to live in this

Ways of making payments

Currency

Currency means the notes and coins issued by the government. Consumers usually use currency to pay for inexpensive items and everyday purchases such as a bus ride or a milkshake. Firms usually use notes and coins from the *petty cash box* to pay for low cost, unplanned purchases such as stationery that is needed before the main order is due. Consumers are unlikely to use currency for expensive purchases such as a house or a car because it is not safe to carry around such large amounts of cash. Firms prefer to pay for most goods by cheque because it is safer and they have a record of the payment. Currency should never be sent through the post because of the risk that it could get lost or stolen.

Explain why notes and coins should not be sent through the post

Cheques

A cheque is a written order to a bank from one of its customers. It tells the bank to pay a certain amount of money to someone else.

Cheques allow one person to withdraw funds from a bank account and deposit the funds in another account, without having to handle the money or change the funds into notes or coins.

Cheques are widely used as a means of payment in our society, but a cheque is not legal tender. It does not have to be accepted by anyone to whom it is offered in payment of a debt. Cheques do have many advantages over cash as a means of payment, however, and they are widely accepted.

Advantages of cheques

- Cheques are *convenient*. It is easier to carry a cheque book, which allows you to spend the money in your bank account, than to carry large amounts of currency. As well, you can write a cheque for the exact amount of the bill you are paying, removing the need to get change. A cheque may be written for any amount as long as the person or firm

writing the cheque has enough money in the account to cover it. Sometimes the bank will allow a customer to write cheques for more money than they have in the bank. In this case the bank gives the customer an *overdraft*. The banks charge interest on overdrawn accounts.
- Cheques are *safer* than currency. They can be crossed 'not negotiable' so that the wrong person cannot get the money. The ways to cross a cheque are explained in more detail below. The customer can also ask the bank to *stop payment* on a cheque if the goods turn out to be unsatisfactory.
- Cheques provide a *record* of each payment. The person who wrote the cheque (the *drawer*) has the cheque butt as his or her record. After it pays the money, the bank keeps the cheque plus details of the account to which the money was paid. They can be used to prove that certain payments were made.

The cheque butt

Most cheque forms are attached to a cheque butt. The butt stays in the cheque book after the cheque itself is torn out. The person writing the cheque should always fill in the details on the butt when he or she writes out the cheque. The butt has space for the date, the person or firm named on the cheque to be paid the money (the *payee*) and the reason for paying the money. There may also be spaces for the drawer to keep a record of funds deposited in the bank and the amount still in the account.

In the following example Lisa Clucas has written a cheque for Ben Jones to pay him for some books. She had $40 in the bank until yesterday, when she deposited another $25.

How much does Lisa have in her cheque account after writing this cheque?

The parties to a cheque
- The person or firm who has the cheque account is the *drawer* of the cheque.
- The bank where the account is kept is the *drawee* of the cheque.
- The person named on the cheque to be paid the money is the *payee*.

Crossed cheques

To make a cheque safer it may be crossed by drawing two parallel lines across its face. The cheque must then be paid into a bank account. When a cheque is not crossed the money can be paid in cash to the person presenting the cheque to the bank.

MONEY 75

Name the drawer, the drawee and the payee

Not negotiable

To make the cheque even more safe, the words 'not negotiable' should be written between the two parallel lines. These words mean that the person receiving the cheque has no more right to the cheque than the person who gives it. In other words, if you accept a cheque from a person who found or stole someone else's cheque, you are not entitled to keep the money, even if you accepted the cheque in payment for something. You may have to pay the money back to the rightful owner. However, if the rightful owner gives you a 'not negotiable' cheque, you become the rightful owner yourself and you are quite entitled to keep the money.

When people write the words 'not negotiable' on a cheque they make it safer for themselves and the rightful owner. But anyone who accepts a 'not negotiable' cheque should be quite sure that the person who gives it to them is honest. Otherwise they could end up losing their money.

Computers and cheques

At the bottom of each cheque form is a series of numbers printed in a special magnetic ink which can be 'read' by a computer. An operator at the bank records the amount of the cheques in the same magnetic ink and all the information is relayed to the bank's central computer which automatically adjusts the records of the drawer's cheque account.

The computer automatically deducts federal and state taxes that must be paid on withdrawals from or deposits to the account as well. After a certain time the computer prints out the details of each account. This *bank statement* is then posted to the account holder.

Bank statement

People who have a cheque account receive a bank statement at regular intervals, usually every month. The bank statement is a record of all money that has been deposited in the account in the period since the last statement was sent. It also records all money that has been withdrawn from the account, by the drawer writing cheques or withdrawing cash or by the bank to automatically make certain regular payments or to pay bank fees and government charges. As well, the bank statement shows how much is left in the bank at the time the statement was prepared. Deposits *add* to the balance in the account while withdrawals *reduce* the balance.

The bank statement illustrated shows that at the beginning of July the account had $1032.82 in it. On 4 July $1500.00 was deposited into the account in the Handybank at Taree. On 14 July a further $60.00 was deposited into the account. These deposits are listed in the *credit* column of the bank statement. During the month of July the bank charged the Bensons $16.60 as a fee for having this account. The federal government charged them $3.55 as tax on their debits (withdrawals) and the state government charged them tax of $1.50 on deposits. As well, fifteen cheques were presented to the bank for payment during July and they got a new cheque book. Stamp duty on the cheque book was $3. These withdrawals are all listed in the *debit* column on the statement. The numbers in the *particulars* column refer to the numbers on the cheque forms. According to the bank, they had $289.17 left in the account.

Bank reconciliation statement
On the cheque butt the drawer should write all deposits and details of all cheques written, and keep a record of the balance left in the account. If these records are accurate and up to date, people should know at any time how much they have left in the bank. However, quite often when they receive the bank statement they find that the final balance on the statement does not match the balance on the cheque butt.

A difference in the balance shown on the cheque butt and the final balance on the bank statement does not mean that either the bank or the account holder (the drawer) is wrong. What it does mean is that the bank might not have all the information the drawer has. Or perhaps the bank had information that the drawer did not have.

1. The drawer may have deposited some money in the bank just before it closed on 29 July —too late for it to have been recorded on the bank statement. The drawer knew about the deposit but the bank did not know about it when the statement was prepared.
2. The drawer may have written some cheques and posted them on 28 July, but unless they had been taken to the bank and the money drawn out of the account by 29 July, they will not appear on the statement.
3. On the other hand, the drawer would not know exactly how much was going to be charged in bank fees and taxes so they would not be listed on the cheque butt.

When the drawer receives the bank statement he or she should take the following steps.
1. Check through the statement for charges such as fees, taxes and interest (if the account has been overdrawn).
2. Take the charges away from the balance shown on the cheque book.
3. Do a bank reconciliation statement, which
    (a) starts with the balance shown on the bank statement
    (b) adds any deposits that have not appeared on the statement and
    (c) takes away any cheques that are not shown.

The result should *reconcile* the balance with that on the cheque butt, that is, bring them back into agreement.

Statement of account

Westpac Banking Corporation

Arcadia   NSW

                                           5204

Mr M C Benson & Mrs B W Benson
39 Glen St
Arcadia   2159

Account No. 830801

Sheet No. 131

Name of account

Mark Charles Benson & Beth Wendy Benson

Date	Particulars	Debit	Credit	Balance
1994	BROUGHT FORWARD			1032.82 CR
1JUL	FEE	16.60		
	FEDERAL TAX ON DEBITS	3.55		
	STATE DUTY ON DEPOSITS	1.50		
	772200	35.00		
	772201	72.80		903.37 CR
4JUL	HANDYBANK TAREE 02/07/94		1500.00	
	772182	240.00		
	772199	12.00		2151.37 CR
5JUL	772202	50.00		2101.37 CR
6JUL	772198	60.00		2041.37 CR
7JUL	772204	472.00		1569.37 CR
8JUL	772203	1000.00		
	772205	54.60		514.77 CR
13JUL	772209	30.80		483.97 CR
14JUL	DEP		60.00	543.97 CR
15JUL	772206	15.00		
	772207	20.00		508.97 CR
19JUL	772208	10.00		498.97 CR
22JUL	597674	3.00		
	772210	14.80		481.17 CR
28JUL	597671	192.00		289.17 CR

Last statement to	This statement to	Total debits	Total credits		
30 JUN 94	29 JUL 94	2303.65	1560.00	CR credit	OD overdrawn

Proceeds of cheques etc. accepted for collection will not be available till cleared.
All entries for the last few business days are subject to verification and authorisation. Any items not paid, or withdrawn, will be adjusted by reversal entry on a later statement.
Please see reverse for additional information.

AB60
62901

Example

Mr and Mrs Benson received their bank statement and deducted the fee, taxes and stamp duty from the balance on their cheque butt. The cheque butt then showed they had $338.65 in the account on 29 July 1994. However, their bank statement showed a final balance of $289.17. When Mrs Benson compared the bank statement with her own records she found several differences.

1. The $400 deposit she made on 29 July had not been listed.
2. Cheque 597672 for $150.52 and cheque 597673 for $200 had not been paid.

She did the following bank reconciliation statement and found that her records and the bank's records were both correct.

Bank Reconciliation Statement of M C & B W Benson as at 29 July 1994

			$
Balance as per bank statement			289.17
Add deposit 29 July 1994			400.00
			689.17
Less cheques	597672	150.52	
	597673	200.00	350.52
Balance as per cheque butt			338.65

Credit cards

An increasing number of goods and services are bought on credit, using credit cards such as bankcard, mastercard, Visa and American Express. There are a number of reasons why credit cards have become popular.

- Some people use credit cards because they cannot afford to pay cash for the goods they want. Credit cards allow them to have the goods now and pay for them later.
- Other people use credit cards because they want to buy goods without taking the risk of carrying large sums of cash around with them.
- Credit cards are very convenient. More and more people now get paid by having their wages paid straight into bank accounts. Credit cards give them another alternative to either visiting the bank to withdraw cash to spend or paying by cheque.
- Credit card statements provide a record of goods bought and their prices. These records can help people work out their budgets.
- Some credit cards (such as bankcard) do not charge interest if the account is paid within a set time. Customers using these cards can save money by paying for all their purchases once a month, using just the one cheque.
- Most sellers prefer to accept a credit card than take the risk of a cheque which might 'bounce'. Credit cards also help to increase sales by encouraging customers to 'impulse buy' when they do not have the ready cash.
- Banks have encouraged the use of credit cards. They save the time and paperwork involved in processing large numbers of cheques. By reducing the amount of cash handled by banks they have also increased staff safety and reduced the risk of loss through armed hold-ups.

Electronic Funds Transfer at Point of Sale (EFTPOS)

Electronic funds transfer is a process that transfers messages about financial transactions from one computer to another through the telecommunications network. Funds are transferred electronically when bank customers use automatic teller machines and when they do their banking by telephone or home computer. *Electronic funds transfer at point of sale* involves customers paying for goods by using a plastic card to transfer money directly from their own bank account to the seller's bank account. The seller passes the card through a card reader on the terminal. This sends a message to the bank. The customer uses his or her *personal identification number* (PIN) on the hand-held key pad. (The PIN is a secret number that account holders use to identify themselves when they use electronic banking services. It is like an electronic signature.) The bank sends back a message electronically, approving the payment if there are enough funds in the account. The docket is printed out by the seller's terminal and given to the customer as a record.

EFTPOS machines provide a convenient alternative for payment at many retail outlets   NORMAN NICHOLLS

EFTPOS is like paying by cheque except that the process is much quicker. It allows customers to spend the money in their accounts without withdrawing it in cash first. Cards which allow money to be transferred in this way are called *debit* cards. They debit the customer's own account. They are different to *credit* cards in that customers do not use them to buy on credit. Some cards can be used as either debit or credit cards. Customers can choose whether to spend money in their own bank accounts or buy goods on credit.

EFTPOS is used mainly by supermarkets and variety stores which have many customers who each spend relatively small amounts. It is not suitable for buying expensive goods because most banks set limits on the amount that can be withdrawn in a day.

Advantages

- Banks and retailers save money as electronic payments cost less to process than cash, cheques or credit cards which involve paper records.
- Banks and retailers get paid instantly. They do not risk bad debts and they have more money to invest as it is not tied up in cash registers.
- As long as customers do not record their PIN number there is little chance of their money being lost or stolen.
- Customers can withdraw cash from retail outlets using EFTPOS as well as pay for their purchases. This is convenient as banks are open for much shorter hours than shops and service stations.
- Banks and service stations do not need to keep as much cash on the premises, reducing the risk of robbery and increasing staff safety.
- Consumers do not need to carry as much cash, reducing the risk of loss or theft.

Disadvantages

- Many consumers find it hard to manage their money when they can withdraw funds so easily from their accounts.
- EFTPOS is harder to use (than cash) for consumers who are old or mentally handicapped. For example they may have trouble remembering their PIN but it is risky for them to write it down.
- It can be hard to prove any errors in operating the account.
- EFTPOS can store information about individual consumers' purchases and buying patterns. Marketing firms can use this information to design advertising aimed at particular groups or even particular consumers. In extreme cases the government could even use it for surveillance.

Exercise 2G

1. What do we mean by the word 'currency'?
2. List ten items that are usually paid for with notes and coins.
3. Why is it not wise to use currency when making payment through the post?
4. What is a cheque? Give four benefits of using cheques.
5. Cheques are not legal tender. What does this mean?
6. List three advantages of using cheques to pay for goods and services.
7. What information should be recorded on the cheque butt?

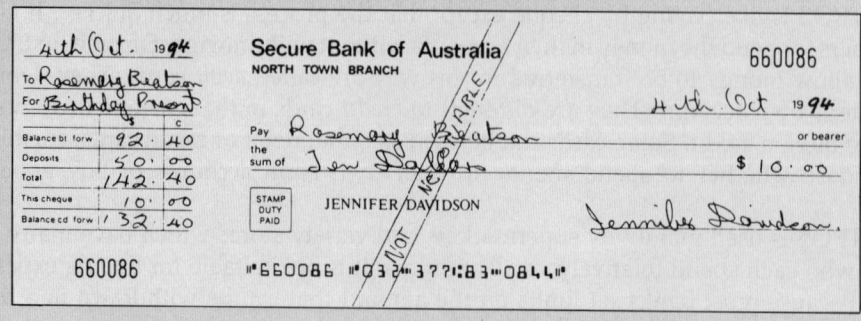

MONEY 81

8. Refer to the above cheque. Answer the following questions.
   (a) Who is the drawer?
   (b) Who is the drawee?
   (c) Who is the payee?
   (d) On what date was the cheque written?
   (e) How much does Jennifer Davidson think she will have left in her account after this cheque is presented to the bank?

9. Draw a cheque form in your notebook. Pretend that you bank with the Secure Bank of Australia at the North Town branch. Write a cheque for $1000 to Benjamin Brothers Pty Ltd for the deposit on a car. You had $1200 in the bank before you wrote the cheque. Don't forget to fill in the cheque butt.

10. On the cheque you wrote in question 9 who was the drawer? Who was the drawee? Who was the payee?

11. What does it mean when a cheque is 'crossed' by two parallel lines?

12. Explain what 'not negotiable' means when it is written on a cheque.

13. Rachel bought a basketball from Judith and paid for it with a 'not negotiable' cheque. Judith lost the cheque and it was found by Irene who took it to the local shop. The storekeeper recognised Rachel's signature on the cheque and, knowing Rachel was honest, accepted the cheque in payment for the goods Irene bought. When Judith realised she had lost the cheque she telephoned Rachel who contacted her bank. When the storekeeper banked the cheque he was told he would not be paid the money from Rachel's account.
   (a) Explain why the storekeeper was not entitled to the cheque, even though it had been given to him in exchange for goods from his store.
   (b) How would the situation have been different if Judith had given the cheque to the storekeeper?

14. What is a bank statement?

15. Give two reasons why the balance the bank statement says you have in your account is rarely the same as the balance shown on your cheque butt.

16. Your bank statement says you have $75 in the bank on 30 June. Your cheque butt says you have $50. When you compare your bank statement with your cheque butts you find that a deposit of $10 on 30 June is not recorded on the bank statement and that three cheques have not been presented to the bank. The cheques are number 220149 for $12, number 220151 for $10 and number 220152 for $13. Prepare the bank reconciliation statement to show that neither you nor the bank is wrong.

17. List seven reasons why credit cards are a popular method of paying for goods.

18. What is EFTPOS?

19. Read through the list of advantages of EFTOPS. Which reason do you think would be most likely to encourage people to use it?

20. Read through the list of disadvantages of EFTPOS. Which reason do you think would be most likely to make people reluctant to use it.

Skills activity

Vocabulary exercise—crossword puzzle

Complete the following crossword puzzle in your notebook.

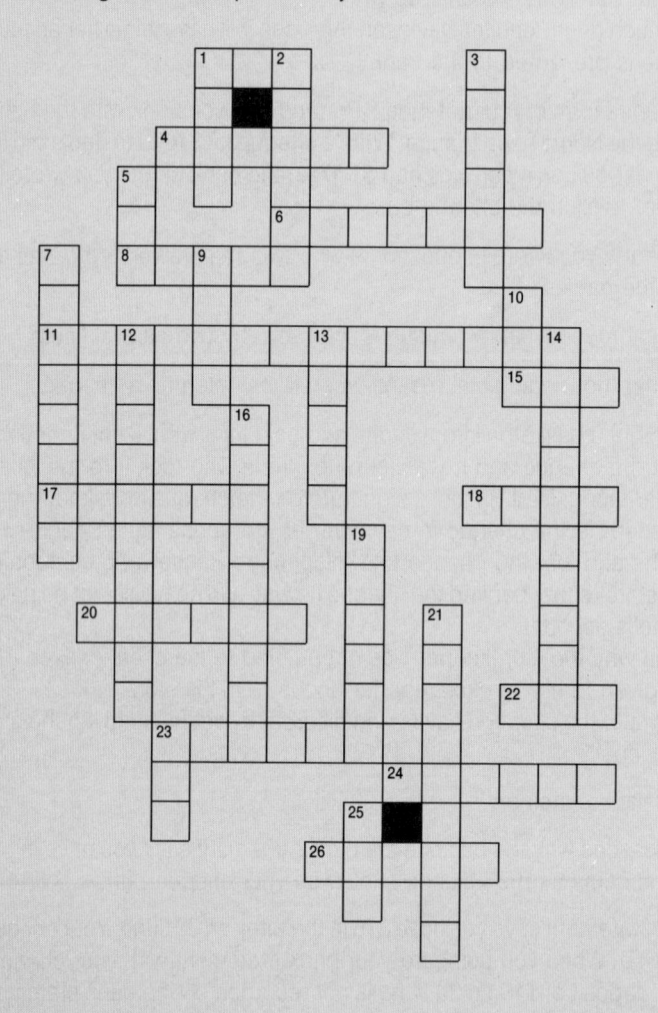

Clues

1 (across). These letters, which sometimes appear on bank statements, stand for 'financial institutions duty'. They show that a tax has been charged on withdrawals from the bank account

1 (down). A cheque is written on a _ _ _ _ from a cheque book.

2. When you do a bank reconciliation statement you must _ _ _ _ _ _ any unpresented cheques from the balance shown on the bank statement

3. The person or firm who writes a cheque

4. Deposits to the account are listed in the _ _ _ _ _ _ column in the bank statement

5. When you do a bank reconciliation statement you _ _ _ any deposits which have not been credited to the account

6. This type of cheque must be deposited in a bank account. It cannot be cashed over the counter by the bank

7. The term given to notes and coins which have been issued by a country to be used as its official money units

MONEY 83

8. Cheques which have been drawn on the account are listed in this column in the bank statement
9. **(with 11 and 21).** People with cheque accounts should do this when they receive their bank statement, to bring their cheque butt and bank statement into agreement
10. **(with 14).** When this is written across the face of a cheque it warns that the holder of the cheque has no more right to it than the person who gave it to them
11. See 9
12. This word describes cheques and credit cards. It means 'handy'
13. **(with 24).** Cheques are not this, but many sellers are willing to accept them in payment of a debt
14. See 10
15. This number of $1 coins is legal tender
16. People who have this are allowed to write cheques for more money than they have in their account
17. A written instruction to a bank to pay a certain amount of money to a certain person or firm
18. The part of a cheque that the drawer keeps as his or her own record
19. The bank where the cheque account is kept
20. Many people prefer to pay by cheque than by cash because the cheque butt provides this
21. See 9
22. Banks charge this for keeping accounts
23. **(across).** This is charged when people overdraw their cheque account
23. **(down).** Computers can read markings on a cheque written in magnetic _ _ _
24. See 13
25. A charge that must be paid to the government. It is charged on deposits and withdrawals from bank accounts
26. The person named on the cheque to receive the money

Budgeting income

Budgeting simply means planning income and spending. People must make *choices* about what goods and services to buy now, which to put off buying for the time being and which ones to give up altogether. Budgeting helps them to plan these choices. Without a plan people may spend their money on less important items and not have enough left for the things they really want.

What can a budget do?

- Budgets help people see where their money goes. They are often surprised to find out how much they spend on certain items.
- Budgets help people plan their spending so they can buy the goods and services they really want.
- Budgets help prevent people from getting too deeply into debt and help them to bring their debts under control.
- Budgets help people save towards particular goals.
- Budgets help people see if they have spare funds which they can invest to earn more income.

Preparing a budget

1. Work out your normal income

For a school student normal income consists of regular pocket money plus income from a regular part-time job. Wage earners should count their normal wage. Do not count unreliable income such as gifts, overtime (which varies from week to week and could cut out unexpectedly), winnings or inheritances. If your old aunt leaves you a fortune in her will, enjoy it—but don't count on it.

2. List your expenses
Expenses can be divided into several categories.

(a) Fixed and essential expenses: Wage earners may have to pay fares and board or rent. Families must pay electricity bills, rent or mortgage payments and rates and instalment payments on items bought on credit. People trying to save for a long-term goal should include a certain amount of savings in this category.

(b) Essential but not fixed expenses: You may have to pay for your own school lunches and sports fees. Families must pay for food, clothes, toiletries and haircuts. In each case the individual and family can choose more or less expensive items.

(c) Non-essential expenses: Entertainment, gifts and holidays are non-essential because no one is forced to spend money on them and they can be given up, at least temporarily, if necessary. This is not the same as saying spending on these items is not important. It is only when a person or family spends more than they can afford on them that they become a problem.

(d) Regular expenses: These expenses have to be paid each payment period. You might pay for lunches, fares and entertainment from your pocket money each week. Your family might pay for rent or the mortgage, food, petrol, pocket money and loan repayments on the car from each pay cheque.

(e) Periodic expenses: You probably have to pay for expenses such as gifts and special outings which come up from time to time. Families have to allow for electricity and telephone bills, car maintenance costs, medical bills, clothes and other periodical expenses. The best way to make sure there is enough money to pay these expenses is to try to work out the total amount spent on them the previous year, add about 10 per cent to allow for price rises and divide the total amount by the number of pay periods. This is the amount the budgeter needs to set aside each pay.

3. Is your income greater than your expenses?
When you have worked out your income and expenses you can see if your income is greater than your expenses. If so, you have money to save and invest or you may choose to spend more. The budget lets you see how you would most like to use the extra money. If your expenses are greater than your income, you are living beyond your means. There are two ways to solve this problem:
- try to earn more
- spend less.

The budget helps show where you could reduce your spending. For example, you may decide to cut your own lunch—and still go to the pictures on Saturdays. A family might decide to take it in turns to cook Friday night's tea instead of getting take-away food, and put the saving towards a yearly holiday.

4. Stick to your budget
The important thing about a budget is that once you have worked it out you should stick to it or you have wasted your time. This is one reason why the budget should not be too strict.

MONEY 85

If you cut out all the things you enjoy so that you can save an unrealistic amount you may become so miserable that you give up altogether. It is easier to save if you have a definite goal in mind. It also helps if you bank your savings immediately so that you are not tempted to spend the money after all.

Why should you put savings aside when you first get your income instead of saving whatever is left over at the end of the week?

This could be the weekly budget of a young person who has recently started work and who is living at home:

Income		*Expenses*	
Wages (after tax)	$300	Board	$ 70
		Savings for car	$ 80
		Fares	$ 30
		Medical insurance	$ 5
		Clothes	$ 60
		Entertainment	$ 40
		Lunches	$ 15
	$300		$300

The problem of personal debt

One result of bad budgeting is *overcommitment*. This means that the individual or family has more bills than they can afford to pay. Overcommitment may be the result of people spending their income on non-essential items and not having enough money to pay the rent and other bills. Overcommitment can also result from people using credit to buy goods they simply cannot afford.

Sometimes a budget can show overcommitted people how to spend less and save the money to gradually pay off their debts. There are several ways they can do this.

- Creditors (firms to whom people owe money) might extend their agreements, allowing the debtors to pay back smaller amounts over a longer time.
- A bank or finance company might lend them the money to pay off all their debts, and help them work out a plan to repay this one loan at a rate they can manage.

Sometimes an individual or family has barely enough money to pay for essentials. There is none left to pay off debts. There can be a number of unfortunate consequences for the debtor in this case.

- Services such as electricity and the telephone may be cut off if the bills are not paid. It costs extra money to get them reconnected once the bills do get paid.
- In some cases the goods bought with a loan may be repossessed (taken back) by the creditor.
- A creditor can take the debtor to court and get a *garnishee order* on his or her wages. This means that the employer will take a certain amount out of the person's wages each week to pay off the debt.
- The court may give a creditor power to sell some of the debtor's property or goods to get the money to pay the debt.
- Sometimes debtors try to avoid being forced to pay the money or lose the goods by moving house. This can add to the stress faced by the individual and his or her family.

Exercise 2H

1. What is a budget? Why do people need to budget?
2. List five different things a budget can do.
3. Explain why you should only count regular income when working out your budget.
4. Give an example of a fixed essential expense your family must pay.
5. Give an example of an essential but not fixed expense in your family. How could you reduce the cost of this item in your family budget?
6. Which non-essential expense in your family would be easiest to give up if you needed to save money? Would all members of the family agree with your answer? Explain why or why not.
7. Name five regular expenses your family faces.
8. Name five periodic expenses your family faces.
9. What are the two ways of overcoming the problem of living beyond your means?

MONEY 87

10. What problem might you have if you make your budget too strict?
11. Look at the budget on page 85. What problems would the budgeter face if there was an unexpected expense such as a birthday present? Change the budget to allow for unexpected expenses.
12. Imagine that you have just started work and take home $300 per week. You live at home. Make up a budget. In one paragraph, explain why your budget differs from the one shown on page 85?
13. What is meant by overcommitment?
14. Suggest two ways overcommitted people could change their affairs to make it easier for them to repay their debts.
15. List five unfortunate things that could happen to people who cannot repay their debts.

Skills activities

Research

1. Find out the types of bills or expenses that a house owner must pay and approximately how much they are for a full year. List them in your notebook.
2. Find out the expenses that a car owner has to pay and approximately how much they are for a full year. Write them in your notebook.

Calculation

Using the information in activities 1 and 2, calculate how much you would need to put aside each week to make sure you could pay the bills on your house and car.

Vocabulary exercise—crossword puzzle

Complete the following crossword puzzle in your notebook.

Clues

1. People who do not budget carefully may not be able to pay these
2. Having this helps give a person the incentive to save regularly
3. People who are living beyong their means must either earn more or spend _ _ _ _
4. This is the part of a budget that shows the maximum amount you can afford to spend
5. The category of expenses that *must* be paid
6. A person who owes money
7. If a person does not keep up payments for goods which have been bought on credit, the creditor can sometimes do this to the goods
8. A budget is a _ _ _ _ of income and expenses
9. This is the only type of income that should be counted when a person is drawing up a budget
10. This word means the costs or payments listed in a budget
11. This is an essential but not fixed expense in a family budget
12. This word describes expenses which cannot be changed
13. This word describes expenses that do not have to be paid in every pay period
14. Money which is owed to someone else
15. A plan of income and expenses

88 THE WORLD OF COMMERCE

16 (with 20). This allows an employer to take some money from an employee's wage to help pay off a debt
17 (with 25). These are essential, periodic expenses. They are more expensive for parents with children at private schools
18. People who cannot pay their bills may be taken here by their creditors
19. The person or firm to whom money is owed
20. See 16
21. People on low incomes and those who have not budgeted carefully may not be able to afford to do this. As a result they are in an even worse situation if their goods are stolen or damaged
22. This is a fixed, essential expense for people who do not own their own homes
23. A regular repayment to reduce a debt
24. Overcommitted people need to spend less or earn _ _ _ _
25. See 17
26. This is a fixed, essential expense for people who are paying off their home
27. These are periodic, non-essential expenses

Revision activity

New terms

In your notebook put the heading 'Important new terms and their meanings'. Copy the first term from List A into your notebook and select its meaning from the definitions in List B. Continue until you have listed each term and its meaning.

MONEY 89

List A
Bank statement, barter, budget, cheque, circular flow of income, credit card, creditor, currency, debt, debtor, discrimination, drawee, drawer, electronic funds transfer at point of sale (EFTPOS), garnishee order, inflation, interest, labour, legal tender, money, overdraft, payee, personal identification number (PIN), profit, rent, social security benefit.

List B
1. Exhange goods directly for other goods
2. Money owed to another person or firm
3. Anything people are generally willing to accept in exchange for goods and services
4. Money flows back and forth between different groups in the community
5. Coins and banknotes
6. A plastic card which people can use to buy goods and services and pay for them at a later date
7. Certain values in notes and coins that must be accepted by creditors in payment of a debt
8. A time when prices are rising rapidly
9. Human skill and effort used to produce goods or services
10. Income received by people who allow others to use their land or buildings
11. Income received by people who lend money to others
12. Income received by people who own their own business
13. Money or other benefit the government gives to the needy, e.g. pension
14. Less favourable treatment in the job market because of some personal characteristic which has nothing to do with the job
15. A written instruction to a bank to pay an amount of money to a person or firm
16. The amount that a bank's customer borrows by writing cheques for more money than is in the account
17. The person who writes a cheque or who owns the account on which a cheque is drawn
18. A term meaning that the holder of a cheque has no more right to the cheque than the person who gave the cheque to him or her
19. A record, sent regularly to account holders, of all money deposited and withdrawn from cheque accounts (and some other accounts) during a certain time, e.g. one month
20. A process which allows customers to use funds still in a bank account to pay for goods and services. Funds are withdrawn electronically from the customer's account and deposited in the seller's account
21. The bank where a cheque account is kept
22. The person named on a cheque to be paid the money

23. A secret number that account holders use to identify themselves when they use electronic banking services
24. A plan for income and expenses to help people buy the things they really want, increase their savings or avoid getting into debt
25. People and firms to whom money is owed
26. People and firms who owe money
27. A court order which instructs employers to take money from a person's wage and pay the money to that person's creditors

3 Business

Three industry groups

Production means making goods and services to satisfy the wants and needs of the community. Production of a good includes all the activities from obtaining the raw materials through to the sale and delivery of the good to the buyer. A good has not been fully 'produced' until it has been sold to the final buyer. There are three industry groups concerned with producing goods and services.

Primary industries

Primary industries obtain or produce materials largely supplied by nature. There are five different branches of primary industry—grazing, farming, mining, lumbering and fishing. The goods made by primary industry are called *primary products*.

Secondary industries

Secondary industries manufacture goods. Manufacturers use the raw materials they get from primary producers to make semi-finished and finished goods. Flour mills turn wheat into flour. The bakery uses the flour to make bread. Both the flour mill and the bakery are secondary industries.

Tertiary industries

Tertiary industries distribute goods and provide services. After crops have been grown and other raw materials have been turned into finished products, services are needed to deliver them to consumers. Cattle are killed at the abattoir but people cannot buy 1 kilogram of steak there. Many services are needed before the steak can be cooked at home. Transport workers take the carcass to the butcher's shop. Butchers cut up, weigh and sell the meat. The transport workers and butchers do not produce a 'good', but they do provide an essential 'service' in helping to distribute the meat.

What industry groups are concerned with producing goods and services?

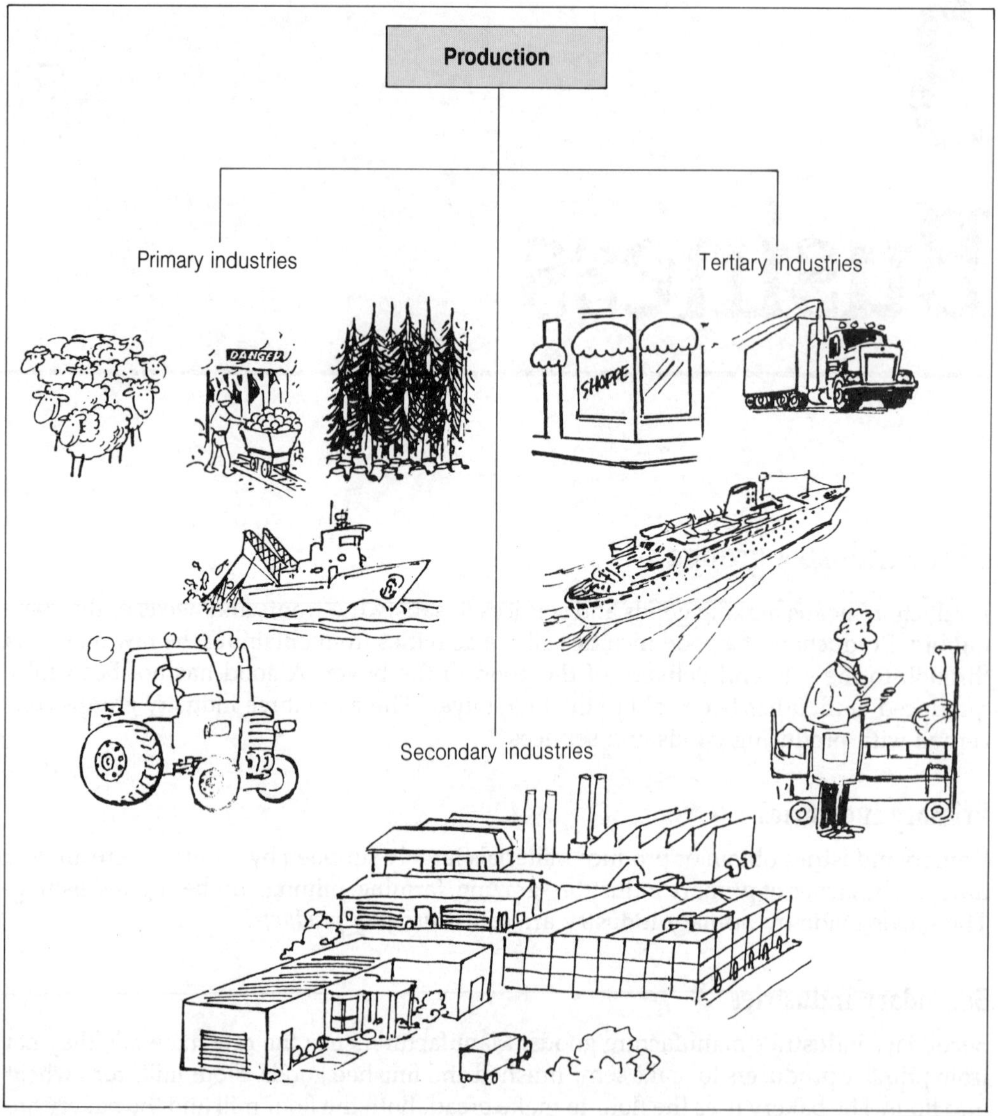

There is a great demand for other services in our society. These services are not to do with distributing goods, they are the services provided by people such as teachers, models, doctors, garbage collectors, bank tellers, television repair people, painters and police officers.

Specialisation

Each industry group specialises in a certain stage of production. Within each group there is even more specialisation. Primary industries specialise in producing foodstuffs and raw

BUSINESS 93

What are the five branches of primary industry?

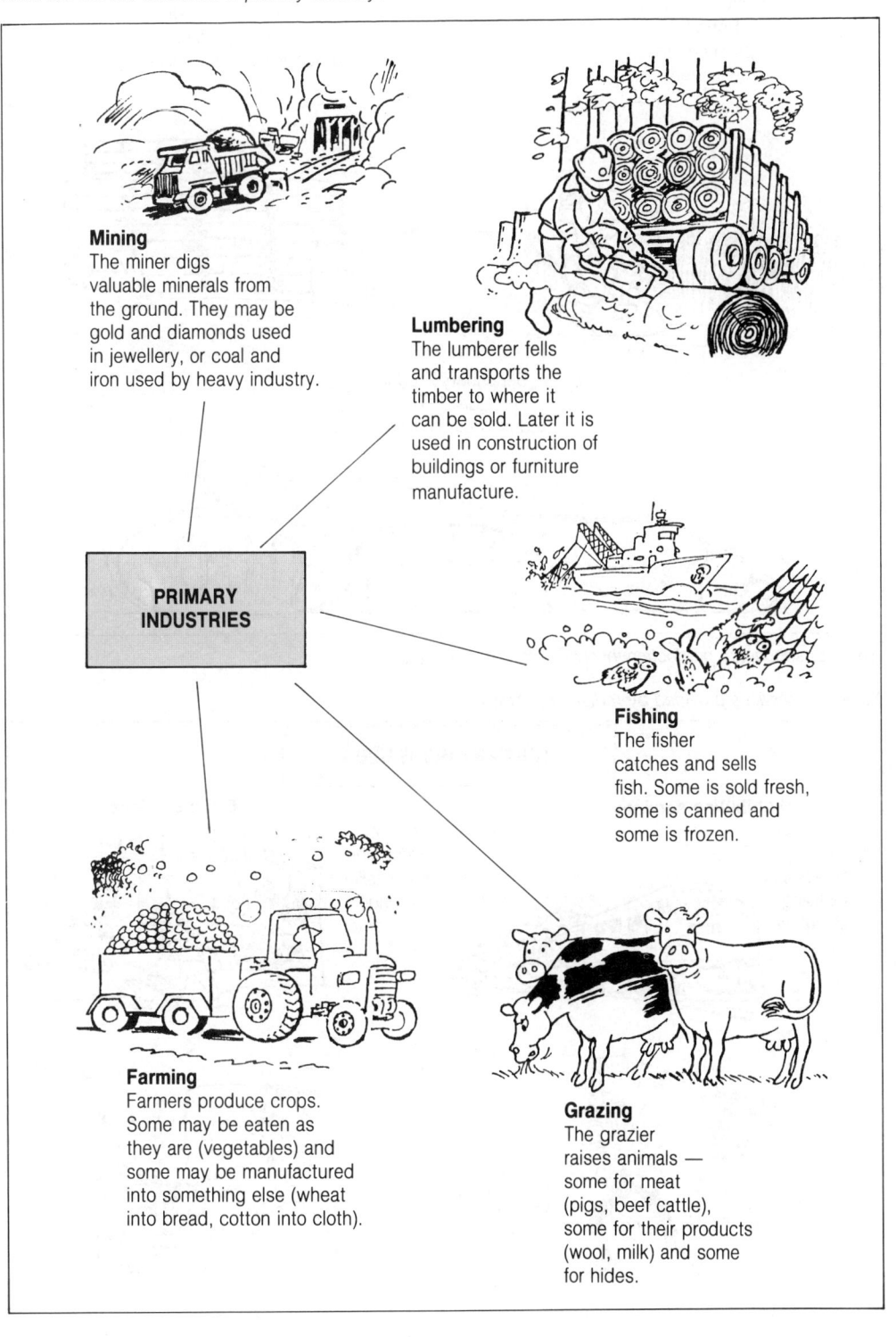

Mining
The miner digs valuable minerals from the ground. They may be gold and diamonds used in jewellery, or coal and iron used by heavy industry.

Lumbering
The lumberer fells and transports the timber to where it can be sold. Later it is used in construction of buildings or furniture manufacture.

PRIMARY INDUSTRIES

Fishing
The fisher catches and sells fish. Some is sold fresh, some is canned and some is frozen.

Farming
Farmers produce crops. Some may be eaten as they are (vegetables) and some may be manufactured into something else (wheat into bread, cotton into cloth).

Grazing
The grazier raises animals — some for meat (pigs, beef cattle), some for their products (wool, milk) and some for hides.

94 THE WORLD OF COMMERCE

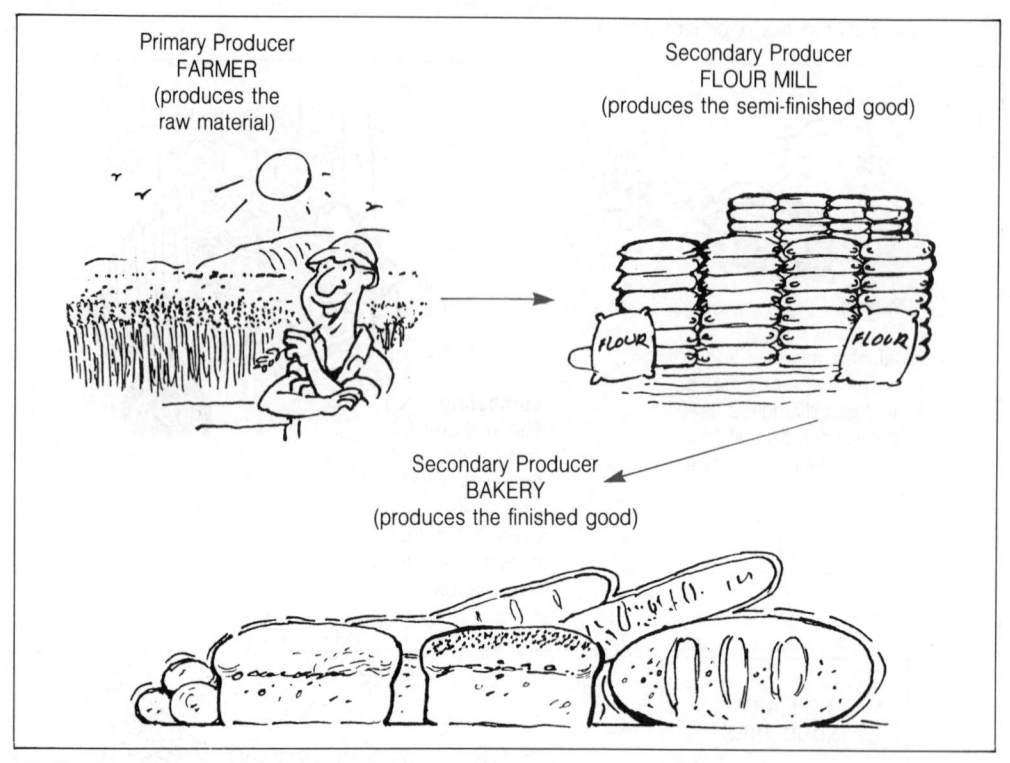

Primary Producer
FARMER
(produces the raw material)

Secondary Producer
FLOUR MILL
(produces the semi-finished good)

Secondary Producer
BAKERY
(produces the finished good)

Why may secondary production involve more than one stage?

Name five services provided by tertiary industries

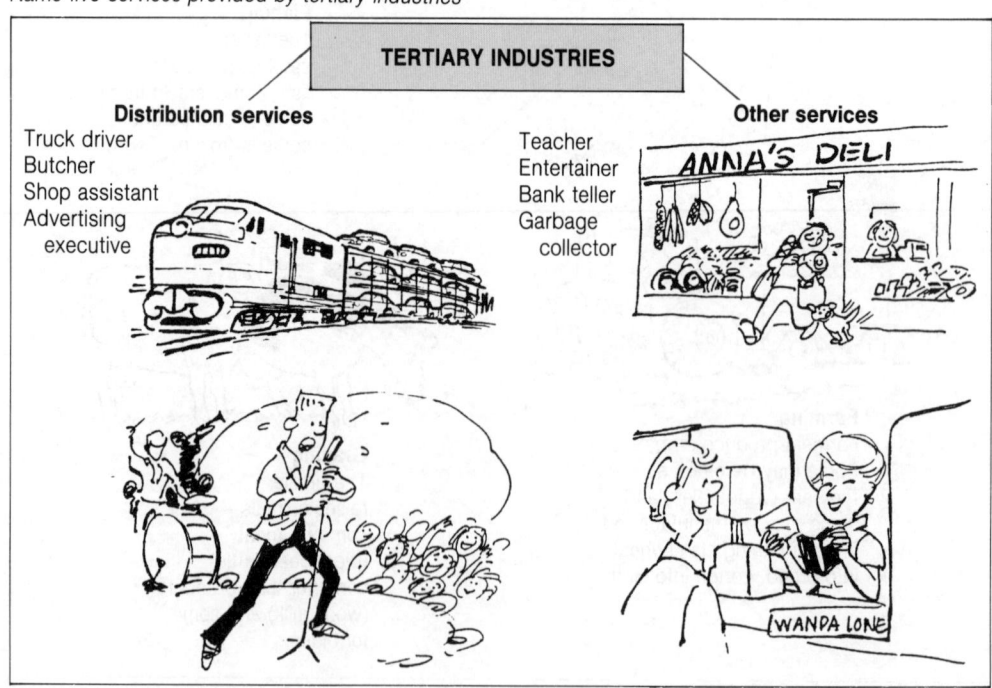

TERTIARY INDUSTRIES

Distribution services
Truck driver
Butcher
Shop assistant
Advertising executive

Other services
Teacher
Entertainer
Bank teller
Garbage collector

materials. Farmers can specialise even further by growing only one crop, such as wheat. A grazier might only produce fine merino wool. Secondary and tertiary industries also specialise. One furniture manufacturer might only make kitchen cupboards; another might only make lounge suites. One transport company might provide delivery only in the local area; another might provide interstate or even international delivery services.

In India, where farming methods are very simple, most people have to work in primary industries to grow enough food to feed the population. In Australia few people are needed to work on farms. Most of the work is done by large machines such as tractors and harvesters. Yet these farms produce enough food and raw materials to satisfy Australia's needs and some to trade.

Exercise 3A

1. What is production?
2. When is the production of goods and services completed?
3. What are primary industries?
4. List the five branches of primary industry.
5. What are secondary industries?
6. What are tertiary industries?
7. List all the jobs in tertiary industry that would be important in the production of
   (a) a magazine
   (b) a pie, bought at a pie shop.
8. Name ten important services that are *not* concerned with the distribution of a good.
9. Select three different activities in primary industry and explain the type of good that each specialises in.
10. Why are so few people needed in farming and mining in Australia? Why are so many people needed to produce food in India?

Skills activities

Apply your knowledge

1. (a) Divide your page into three columns. Head them 'Factory', 'Raw materials used' and 'Goods produced'.
   (b) In the first column list five factories you know. If possible choose factories from your local area.
   (c) In the second column list the raw materials these factories use.
   (d) In the third column list the finished or partly finished goods these factories produce.

2. From newspapers and magazines obtain pictures of activities carried on in each of the three industry groups. Name the activities and arrange them under the headings 'Primary', 'Secondary' and 'Tertiary'. Write a short description of each activity.
3. Find or draw pictures to illustrate the whole process involved in the production of a good such as a magazine or a pie. Arrange the pictures in order of the three industries involved—from primary, to secondary, to tertiary. Name the activity and industry involved. Indicate with a capital T where transport would be needed.

Draw and interpret graphs

Examine the two pie charts and do the exercise and answer the questions below.

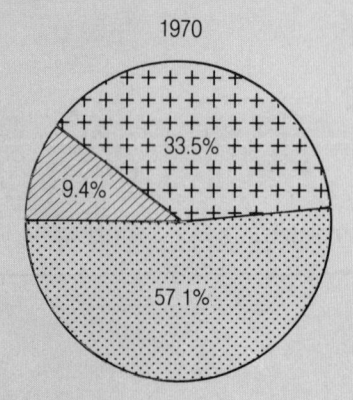

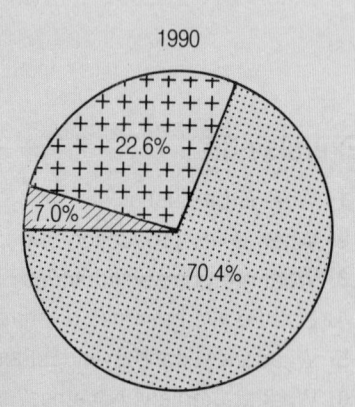

1970
- 33.5%
- 9.4%
- 57.1%

1990
- 22.6%
- 7.0%
- 70.4%

Percentage of workforce employed by industry groups

Key

- Primary industry
- Secondary industry
- Tertiary industry

Source: Compiled from figures supplied by the Australian Bureau of Statistics

1. Draw bar graphs to show the percentage of people employed by each industry in 1970 and 1990. Use a scale of 1 centimetre to 10 per cent.
2. Which industry employed the most people in 1970 and in 1990? Name ten occupations included in this industry.
3. Which industry employed the least people in 1970 and in 1990? Name ten occupations included in this industry.
4. Which industry increased the percentage of the workforce it employed between 1970 and 1990? Suggest two reasons why this would have happened.
5. Which industry employed a smaller part of the workforce in 1990 than it did in 1970? Suggest two reasons why this would have happened.

Mix 'n match

In your notebook draw up this table.

Industry occupations		
Primary	Secondary	Tertiary

Read the list of occupations below. Match each occupation with the industry group to which it belongs by writing it under the correct industry heading.

Doctor, coal miner, electrician, butcher, abattoir worker, cabinet maker, plumber, fisherperson, tailor, boot maker, bank teller, waiter, welder, panel beater, pastry cook at Sara Lee.

Scrambled words

Rearrange the letters of the four scrambled words below to form four words associated with production. Write the answers in your notebook.

YRBUE

RVSCEISE

IDBIRTSIOUTN

MFUCAUNTEARR

Print the numbered letters in your notebook.

Unscramble the letters to find an important industry group.

Location of industries

It is very important for every business to be set up in the area where it will have most chance of being successful. Different locations are chosen for different businesses or industries. Different factors influence them.

Primary industries

A farmer will need to consider features about the land itself and the climate. A wheat farmer needs flat land because of the machinery used. Banana farmers can grow crops on hillsides but they need a warm, wet climate. Graziers need to consider the amount of water and feed available for their stock. Mines can be located only where there is a valuable mineral deposit that can be reached. Coal situated under Sydney would not be mined because of the difficulty and expense.

The Ulan open cut mine at Dubbo. Mines must be located where there are mineral deposits NSW DEPARTMENT OF MINERALS AND ENERGY; PHOTOGRAPH BY DAVID BARNES

Secondary industries

Manufacturers are interested in transport—its costs, reliability and efficiency. They need a power supply and people to work in factories. They must also take into account government regulations about zoning, and public relations with the community. Environmental concerns are starting to have a much greater influence on the location of businesses.

The manufacturers will choose the locations which give them the greatest chance for success. If they are producing goods such as house bricks or soft drinks, which are heavy and expensive to transport, they will probably set up the factories close to their customers. However, if their raw materials are heavy, bulky or perishable they will probably choose sites near their source of raw materials. Sugar mills are located close to sugar-cane farms and timber mills close to forests. Many factories are built near railway stations or wharves or on major highways.

Factories that use a lot of water must be near a good water supply. High-pollutant industries are best located away from towns and cities; for example, alumina refineries in northern Tasmania.

List the factors that determine the location of secondary industry

The Victoria Sugar Mill in Queensland. Sugar mills are usually located close to sugar cane fields to save transport costs   CSR LIMITED

Tertiary industries

Firms in tertiary industry such as restaurants, solicitors and banks provide services. These businesses need to be set up in towns and cities where there are plenty of customers. In a large city such as Sydney there is a wide variety and a large number of competing firms to choose from. In a small country town, where their are few customers, the number and quality of services offered may be limited. Some small farming and mining areas have a shopping centre with only a hotel, a general store which may also be an agent for the post office and bank, and perhaps a service station.

The environment and industry

Businesses are not free to set up wherever they choose. Councils have long zoned areas for certain use—residential, commercial or industrial. Recently, however, environmental issues have begun to influence where industry can be located. Political parties and associations such as the Australian Democrats and the Environment Independents have been set up to help to protect the environment. Protestors try to stop logging in national forests. Conservation groups such as the Australian Conservation Foundation try to influence governments and industries to stop logging and mining activities in disputed areas.

New laws are being made. Factories which dump waste materials into rivers and the sea face heavy fines. Logging is limited in national forests. The Australian government stopped sand mining on Fraser Island and prevented the Franklin River dam from being built in Tasmania.

The Commonwealth Bank building, Martin Place, Sydney. Banks need to be located in areas where customers have easy access to them
MIRROR AUSTRALIA TELEGRAPH PUBLICATIONS

The decision to build a third runway at Sydney airport was delayed for environmental reasons. Residents living in flightpath areas formed an action group called Residents Opposed to Runway Three to fight the building of the runway. The Australian government first gave permission for the runway to be built in March 1989, subject to the findings of an Environmental Impact Statement (EIS), which had to carry out research into noise pollution. Between 4000 and 6000 submissions were made by members of the public.

The development of a $20 million tourist complex by the Western Australian government was stopped in November 1989 by the Supreme Court in Western Australia. The stoppage was supported by two unions which banned their members from working on the site. The unions were in sympathy with Aboriginal protestors who claimed that the old Swan Brewery site in Perth is a sacred resting place of the Dreamtime rainbow serpent Wagyl.

Why are political parties and associations that aim to protect the environment becoming more important?

Exercise 3B

1. List some factors that determine where primary industries can be located.
2. List some factors that determine the location of secondary industries.
3. When will manufacturers choose to locate their factory near the source of raw materials rather than near their customers?
4. Why do tertiary industries locate in towns and cities?
5. State the way in which local councils control the location of industry.

6. Name three groups that were set up to influence governments to protect the environment.
7. State two activities stopped by the Australian government in order to protect the environment.
8. State three other activities that have either been stopped or delayed for environmental reasons.

Skills activities

Apply your knowledge

1. Name a factory which is located close to your home. State what it produces. List the reasons why you think it was set up in your area.
2. List ten manufactured food items in your kitchen pantry at home. Opposite the name of each item, write the name of the place where it was made. (You will usually find this information on the label.) Place a tick (√) beside the items that were made within 40 kilometres of a large city such as Sydney or Newcastle. An example has been done for you.

Food item	Where produced	Within 40 km of a large city
1. Cottees Apricot Conserve	Liverpool	√ Sydney

Strict laws needed for toxic factories

The NSW Government is to introduce new laws covering the location of dangerous and offensive industries. This follows a chemical fire which released toxic clouds in the residential suburb of Seven Hills. The Premier has promised that the Government will act to protect residents and the environment close to such factories. He said such incidents were too common.

The Minister for Local Government and Planning, Mr Hay, has said that NSW needs these industries for its economic development. Mr Hay also said that it is important not to allow factories to adversely affect the health of the residents or the environment in which they lived. Mr Hay gave out a draft policy which would control the location of industries, including panel-beating shops.

The regulations also control noise pollution and odour. Mr Hay stated that if industries do not stick to the regulations they can be closed down. He stated that local councils would have to consider public comment before approving applications.

Newspaper comprehension

1. Read the newspaper article entitled 'Strict laws needed for toxic factories' and answer the following questions in your notebook.
   (a) Why does the New South Wales government plan to introduce new pollution laws?
   (b) What is meant by 'toxic clouds'?

104 THE WORLD OF COMMERCE

(c) What do you think Mr Hay would mean by 'economic development'?
(d) List three ways by which the new laws could help prevent this type of incident from happening again.

GAS BLAST

Residents in terror as explosions rock city

Hundreds pour in to help

Greiner waits for reports

Fireballs in gas blast

Gas highly flammable LIQUID

1000m fireballs

Firemen tame vast inferno

FIREMEN today tamed the raging inferno that shook Sydney and destroyed a gas storage depot in a spectacular blaze that reached white-hot 1000 degrees.

Terrified shrieks as night turns into day

Map showing: Peters, Botany Rd, Gardeners Rd, Mascot, Sydney Airport, Rockdale, Botany Bay.

2. Read the newspaper article entitled 'Gas explosion rocks Sydney' and answer the following questions in your notebook.
   (a) Why do you think the LPG storage tanks are located in a highly populated area?
   (b) Give two reasons why the New South Wales government could decide to force the plant to be relocated.

Gas explosion rocks Sydney

Thousands of residents from four Sydney suburbs were evacuated last night while 16 fire brigades tried desperately to fight explosions in a gas plant which were shooting fireballs 1000 metres into the air. The gas plant is part of an industrial estate surrounded by residential areas.

A large number of ambulances were rushed to the area but no one was injured. The first of 15 explosions occurred at about 8.45pm at the plant in Canal Rd, St Peters. There was a second explosion at about 10pm.

Windows were shattered in houses and a huge fireball leapt into the sky. Police described the evacuation of residents as the biggest emergency operation in Sydney in 20 years.

The NSW Government has launched an enquiry into the explosion of the liquefied petroleum gas (LPG) storage tanks. Sydney airport was closed during the explosions as the flightpath was directly overhead. The Premier, Mr Greiner, refused to say whether the Sydney plant would be allowed to be maintained. A decision would be made after a full investigation.

The storage of dangerous substances in densely populated areas can present a danger to the community. This photograph shows fire fighters controlling explosions in an LPG gas plant in St Peters, Sydney MIRROR AUSTRALIAN TELEGRAPH PUBLICATIONS

Class discussion

'A clean environment is a luxury Australia cannot afford. The development of industry and increased employment are important.'

Interdependence

Individuals, firms, areas and nations specialise in producing certain goods and services. As a result we depend on others to satisfy our many wants and needs.

Individuals

A farmer may specialise in growing rice or wheat. Factory workers may be skilled in various trades. The welder, fitter and boilermaker are all specialists. Tertiary workers provide many services, ranging from garbage collection to transplant surgery. We all depend on many others in our society.

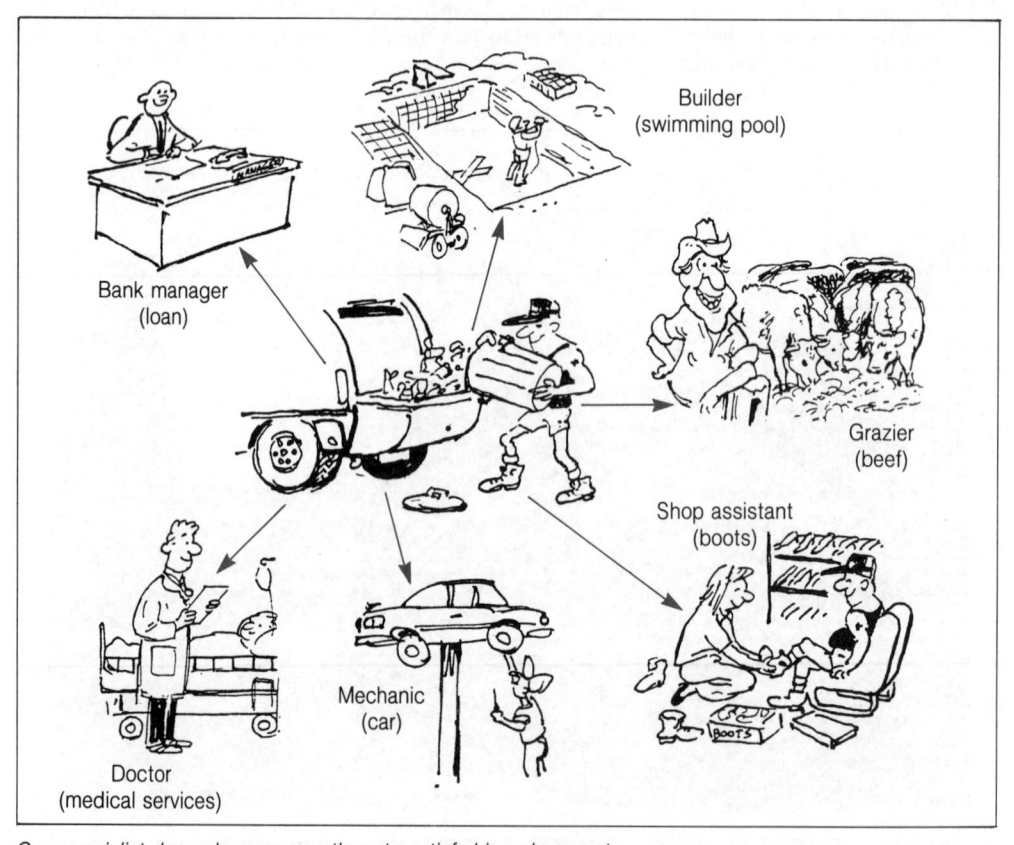

One specialist depends on many others to satisfy his or her wants

Areas

Areas also tend to specialise. As a result they too are interdependent. No city or farming area can produce everything it needs. Sydney relies on the Hunter Valley for wine, on Queensland for tropical fruits and on nearby regions for dairy products. Each of these areas in turn relies on Sydney to produce and supply it with many manufactured goods.

Nations

Countries depend on each other. Japan provides Australia with manufactured goods. The Middle East supplies oil. Malaysia supplies rubber. Australia supplies wool, wheat and minerals to many countries.

People are both consumers and producers. When working in a factory or bank we are producers. Firms depend on us for our labour and pay us an income. We rely on those firms for our employment and income. Consumers depend on firms to produce the goods and services they want to buy. Governments rely on individuals and firms for the taxes needed by them to provide services. Primary industry relies on secondary industry to buy its products and on tertiary industry to distribute them. Secondary industry depends on primary industry to supply it with raw materials and so on.

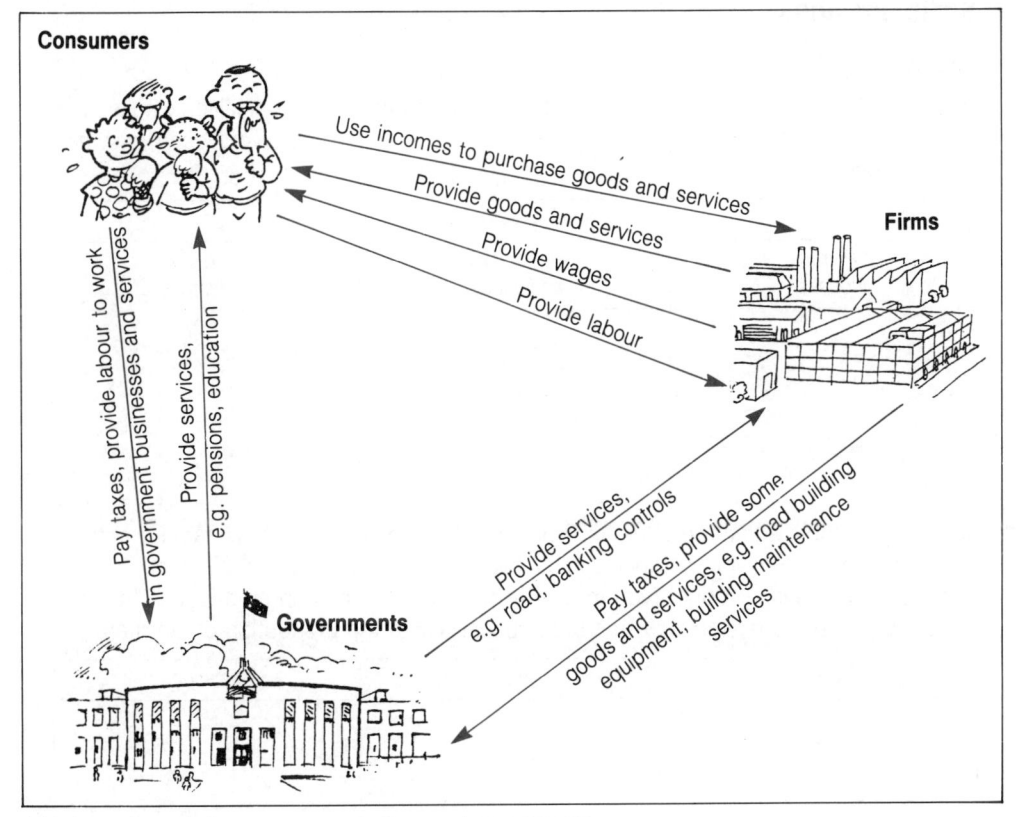

Interdependence between consumers, firms and governments

At all stages in producing a good—from obtaining the raw material to the manufacture and final sale—certain services are extremely important. The farmer who grows and harvests the wheat, and the miller who produces the flour, need to be insured against loss. The wheat has to be transported to the silo, to the flour mill, to the baker and to the shop on roads provided by councils. The farmer, the flour miller, the baker, the shopkeeper and the council all need banking services. In modern societies all producers depend on many others.

Exercise 3C

1. State one way in which each of the following takes place:
   (a) a dressmaker is both a producer and consumer
   (b) governments rely on individuals
   (c) consumers rely on firms
   (d) firms rely on governments
   (e) governments rely on consumers
   (f) Australia relies on an overseas country for goods.

2. Transport, banking and insurance services are important at all stages of production. Briefly explain how they are important in the production of milk.

Skills activities

Tables

1. Draw up a table (as shown below) and write the names of five specialists who work in primary, secondary and tertiary industries. Choose examples from your local area wherever possible.

Specialists who work in:		
Primary industries	Secondary industries	Tertiary industries
1.	1.	1.
2.	2.	2.
3.	3.	3.
4.	4.	4.
5.	5.	5.

2. Draw up a table with three columns. From the following table copy the headings and the list of products into your notebook. In the middle column write one area that specialises in producing each product (you may refer to a land-use map in an atlas). In the next column write the reason why that area specialises in the production of that item.

Product	Area	Reason
1. Wine		
2. Coal		
3. Iron ore		
4. Motor vehicles		
5. Iron and steel		
6. Bananas		
7. Wheat		
8. Gold		
9. Beef		
10. Clothes		

3. Draw up a table with three columns in your notebook. In the first column list five consumer durables (such as motor vehicles, furniture) and five food items that were produced in another state or country. In the second column state where the good was produced. In the third column state the reason why you think the good was produced outside New South Wales.

Crossword puzzle

Complete the following crossword in your notebook.

Clues
1. The industry group which turns raw materials into semi-finished and finished goods
2. The industry group which obtains or produces materials largely supplied by nature
3. The industry group which distributes goods and supplies services
4. These can only be located where there is a valuable mineral deposit that is accessible
5. Tertiary industries must do this to goods before production can be complete
6. People employed in this tertiary industry include football players and boxers
7. These are only one example of tertiary producers
8. Nearly all producers _ _ _ _ _ _ against loss
9. Factories tend to set up near a good source of _ _ _ _ _ _
10. _ _ _ _ _ _ _ _ _ is important to all industries
11. _ _ _ materials are produced by primary industries
12. Manufacturing takes place in a _ _ _ _ _ _ _
13. Most businesses _ _ _ money to their suppliers
14. A very important part of tertiary industries is involved in supplying _ _ _ _ _ _ _ _ to their customers

Distribution of goods

It is essential that goods are distributed efficiently, especially in a country as specialised as Australia. Once the good has been manufactured it must reach the consumer. From the manufacturer the good is often sold to a wholesaler, then to a retailer and finally to the consumer. Sometimes the manufacturer sells directly to the retailer or the consumer. Sometimes the wholesaler sells directly to the consumer. The more steps involved in the distribution process, the higher the price the consumer must pay. This is because each businessperson adds costs and profit to the price.

Wholesalers

A wholesaler buys in large quantities from the manufacturer and sells in smaller bulk quantities to the retailer. Wholesalers use warehouses to store their goods, which they buy from a large number of manufacturers. They can then give retailers a wide choice of goods from one location. The main disadvantage of the wholesaler is that he or she adds a cost to the price of goods. Nowadays there are some 'wholesaler–retailers' who sell in bulk to consumers; for example, bulk purchase butcher shops. Consumers buy meat in bulk at lower prices than in an ordinary butcher shop.

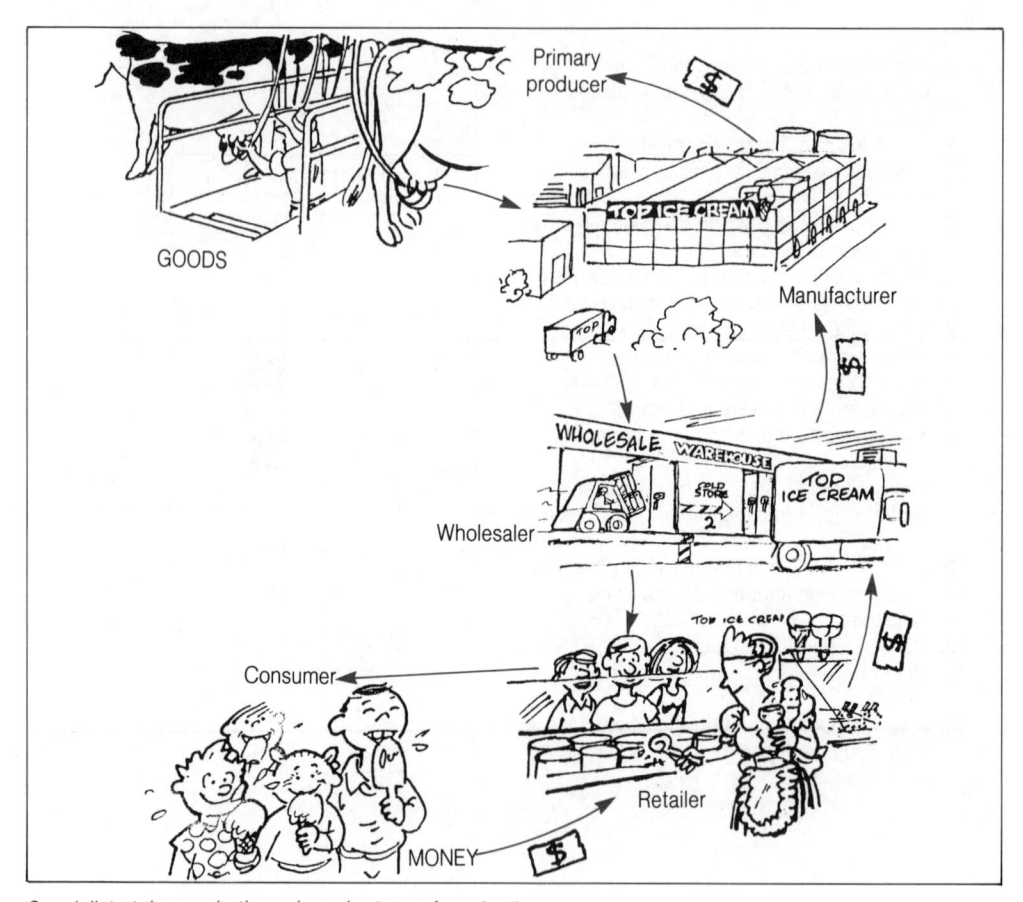

Specialists take goods through each stage of production

Bonded stores

Bonded stores play a small but important role in the distribution of goods. Many goods which we buy have a sales tax and an import duty placed on them by the Australian government. The government lets these goods be placed in a 'bonded store' by the wholesaler or retailer. They do not pay the tax until they need the goods. The taxes must be paid before the goods are removed from bonded stores.

Retailers

Retailing is the sale of goods and services directly to the consumer. Generally retailers obtain their goods in bulk from wholesalers and sell in single units to consumers. It is the final stage in the production process. In recent years there have been very big changes in retailing. There has been a big drop in the number of small shops such as grocers and mixed businesses. There has been a drop in the number of department stores in the cities. There are now many more department stores in suburban shopping centres.

Some of the oldest retailing firms in Australia still in existence include David Jones, Angus and Coote, and Lowes.

Exercise 3D

1. In a brief paragraph describe the work of a wholesaler. State one advantage and one disadvantage of the wholesaler to the consumer.
2. What is a bonded store?
3. What is retailing?
4. State two changes that have taken place in retailing in recent years in Australia.
5. Name three of the oldest retailing firms in Australia.
6. Name four small retailers in your local shopping centre.

Skills activities

Flow diagram

Draw a flow diagram in your notebook to show the steps involved in the production of one good from the raw materials to the final stage where it is bought by consumers. Choose any good you are familiar with such as jeans, a surfboard or a chair.

Apply your knowledge

Assume that you bought a packet of corn chips yesterday. In ten lines describe the work involved by different business firms to get these corn chips from the farmer to you.

Types of retail businesses

A 'simple' organisation—the corner shop

Corner shops used to be common in residential areas. Some still exist, particularly in older suburbs. They are small and mainly provide basic food and grocery needs. They rarely sell meat, although they often sell 'staple' vegetables and fruit.

Advantages
- It is convenient and close to home. This can be important when you only need to buy one or two items.
- It provides personal service. The owner of the store often knows the customers.
- It is open for longer hours than large stores.
- Credit is sometimes given to established customers.
- Sometimes goods are delivered free of charge.

Disadvantages
- It charges higher prices for goods. The owner cannot obtain big discounts by buying in bulk.
- It has limited choice in the variety and range of goods it can offer for sale.
- It has a smaller turnover, so the stock is sometimes older than at large supermarkets.

A more 'complex' organisation—the supermarket

The growth of supermarkets has helped kill off the small corner or general store. Supermarkets have large and varied stocks at lower prices. Weekly 'specials' are offered on groceries, meat and vegetables. Consumers can select their own food without help from shop assistants. This reduces the supermarkets' costs. Often facilities such as packing the groceries, home delivery and parking areas are provided. Supermarkets are usually found in shopping centres. They are usually owned by large companies.

Department stores

Department stores cater for a wide range of shoppers' needs. Generally they are owned by companies and are located in shopping centres. The stores are divided into a number of departments or areas. Each department provides a different good or service. The departments include men's clothing, children's shoes, women's nightwear, cosmetics, furniture and hardware. Some of the largest department stores in New South Wales include David Jones and Grace Bros. At first they were found only in Sydney. Now they are in many towns and cities throughout New South Wales.

Specialty shops

Specialty shops are often small and provide a wide range of one type of good. Darrell Lea's stores sell only sweets. Other stores might sell a selection of closely related goods—gift stores are an example. Often the owner is also the manager and works in the business. In specialty stores, such as interior decorating businesses, the customer is provided with help and advice that may not be available in a larger store.

Chain stores

Chain stores operate under the same name in many different towns and suburbs. Some chain stores have been in existence for many years, for example Coles and Woolworths. There are now many chains of specialty stores. Some sell only pharmaceutical goods, others sell footwear or casual clothes, and some operate restaurants.

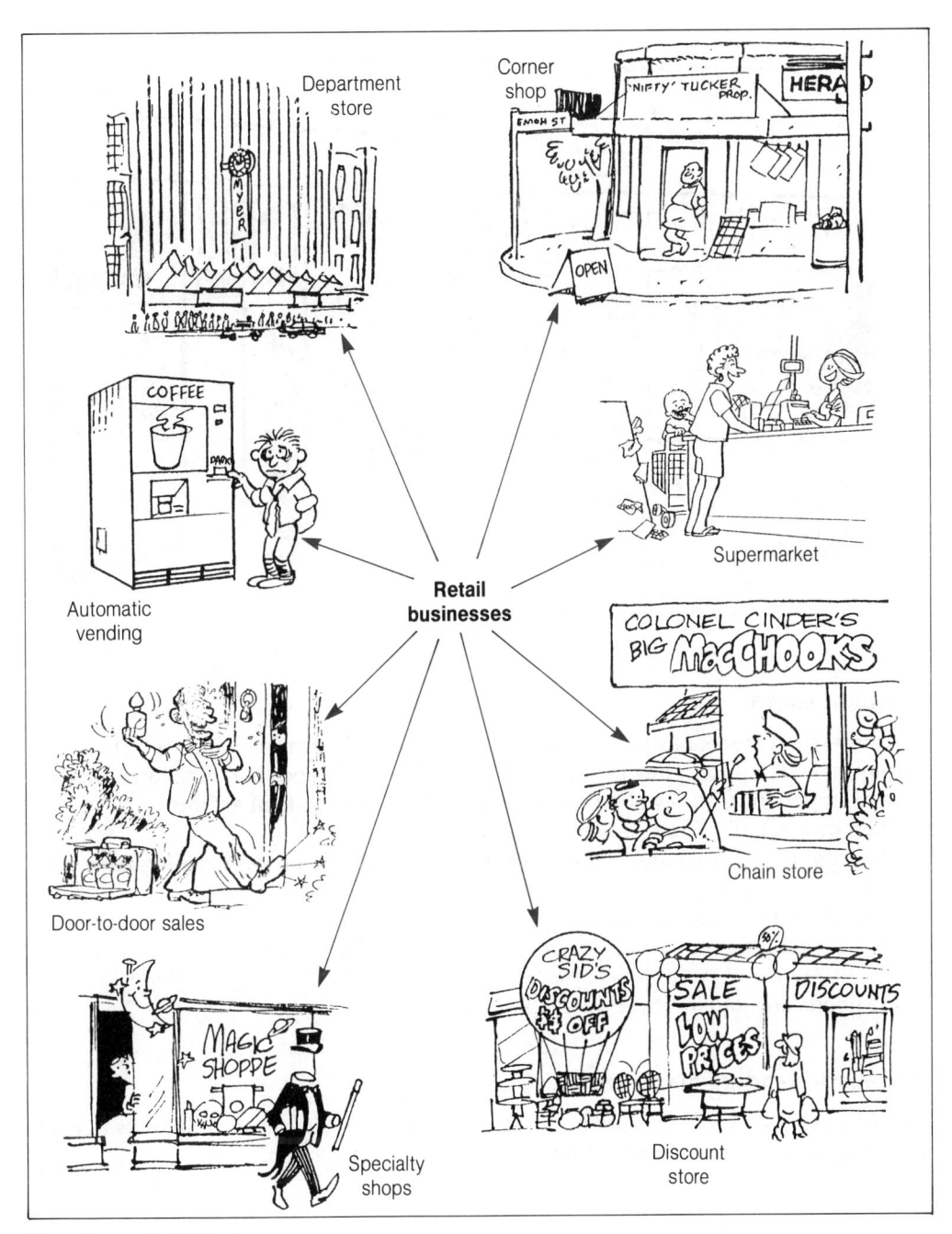

Some types of retail businesses

The one central office buys the stock for all the different branches. Goods are purchased in bulk, stored at a central warehouse and sent from there to all the branches. Bulk buying and centralised advertising either reduce prices for the customers or increase profits for the owners, or do both these things.

Why are specialty stores often located in shopping malls?

Discount stores

Discount stores are retail stores, usually located in suburban areas, which sell at less than the normal retail price. They mainly tend to sell electrical goods and furniture. There are several important features about the discount stores' methods of selling.
- They buy in bulk. They can get discounts for large orders.
- They aim to sell in volume. Discount stores have a quick turnover, selling large quantities at lower prices.
- They use self-service as much as possible to lower costs.
- They spend little on decorations for their stores to lower costs.

Some goods are sold in other ways apart from shops.

Automatic vending machines

These machines are widely used in the sale of chocolates, cigarettes and drinks in places such as railway stations, where there is a large passing custom.

Door-to-door sales

Some retailers bring their goods or services to the door. People selling cosmetics, cleaning materials, books and carpet cleaning services are examples. The representatives are trained to demonstrate and promote their products and usually get paid a commission. Working on a commission means that the representatives receive a percentage (say 10 per cent) of the sales price.

Buying from home is convenient, especially for people who cannot go shopping easily. The buyer must be careful that the seller has a good reputation, that the price is fair, and that he or she does not get talked into buying unwanted goods.

Mail order

Some firms send out catalogues to their customers with mail order forms which the customer completes. The order form, with a cheque or money order as payment, is returned to the firm, which then supplies the ordered goods. Other firms advertise in magazines with a coupon for the customer to complete.

Mail orders are important for people who live in isolated areas. They are also useful for people who find it hard to get to shops because of sickness, lack of transport or other difficulties. But it can be risky to buy goods 'sight unseen' or to send money to an unknown firm.

Exercise 3E

1. State the name and location of the corner shop closest to your home. List the type of goods it sells.
2. List the advantages and disadvantages of corner shops.
3. List the advantages of shopping in a supermarket instead of at the corner shop.
4. Name five supermarket chain stores.
5. Name one supermarket chain and list at least fifteen types of goods sold.
6. Name five department stores. List twenty different departments found in one of these stores.
7. Could all your family's shopping be done in a department store? Give a reason for your answer.
8. Name ten specialty stores in your shopping centre. Beside their names, state the type of product sold.
9. What advantage does shopping in a specialty store have over shopping in a department store?
10. What are chain stores? Name eight chain stores, two of which are
    (a) supermarkets
    (b) specialty stores
    (c) department stores
    (d) discount stores.
11. List the four main features of discount stores.
12. Name the type of place where vending machines are most common. List the main items they are used to sell.
13. List five items sold door-to-door.
14. List one possible advantage and one possible disadvantage for the customer of mail order selling.

Skills activities

Surveys

1. Ask three adults and three friends your own age whether they prefer to shop in a self-service or a counter-service store. Write the main reason they give for their choices. Is there a fairly common reason given? If so write this answer.
2. Ask two men and two women whether they prefer to buy petrol from a self-service station or a station with a driveway attendant. Write their reasons. Did the answers given by the men differ from those given by the women? If so, explain how.

Newspaper research

Find an example of an advertisement in a newspaper, magazine or catalogue in which a firm offers to sell a good by mail order. Paste this advertisement in your notebook.

Field survey

Select an area of your local shopping centre which includes twenty stores.

1. Draw a simple map to show the location of each store. Include a key (numbered 1 to 20) and name each store. Beside each name in the key write what kind of store it is, for example, a discount store. If a store is more than one kind, write each kind.
2. Write down any pattern you notice in the location of the stores (for example, are certain types of stores near or next to each other?). Briefly explain why you think this pattern exists.

Common methods of buying goods and services

Cash

Cash is the simplest way of buying goods and services. In a cash sale the customers pay the money and receive the goods in exchange. At the same time as they take possession, they also receive ownership. Some businesses insist on cash payments. Many corner shops, supermarkets, milk bars and school canteens deal only in cash. Some services must be paid for in cash—bus and train fares, cinema and ice skating fees. Where cash is demanded, the good or service offered for sale is usually inexpensive.

Common types of credit

Today it is possible to buy most goods and services on credit. That is, the seller allows the customer to go into debt in order to buy the goods or services. A debt is an amount owing. The buyer, who is in debt, is called the *debtor*. The seller, who has given credit and to whom the money is owed, is called the *creditor*.

Many goods are expensive and customers often have to buy these goods on credit. Large retail stores offer several means of buying on credit.

Store credit accounts

Customers 'charge' the goods they buy to an account. The store sends an account to the customer once a month. The account shows the amount owing.

Many stores give their credit customers a 'charge plate'

Bankcard

Many stores accept payment by customers using bankcard. The bank which issued the bankcard pays the store. Each month the bank sends the customer an account showing the amount owing.

Credit is a very convenient method of shopping, and the customers do not have to carry large amounts of cash with them.

Firms increase their sales when consumers buy, on impulse, goods they had not planned to buy and perhaps cannot really afford. Consumers who use credit must make sure they do not spend more than they can afford to repay.

Consumers who use a store credit card or a bankcard to buy goods have a certain amount of time in which to pay their account. If the account is not paid in full by the due date the card holder is charged interest on the amount still owing.

Lay-by

In many stores it is possible to pay a deposit on a good. The good is then set aside for the customer, who agrees to make regular payments to pay it off within a certain time. There are no extra charges such as interest to be paid by the customer.

The main advantage of lay-by is that consumers do not get the goods until they can afford them and so do not risk getting too deeply into debt. The main disadvantage is that they do not have the use of the goods while they are paying for them.

Exercise 3F

1. What is a cash sale?
2. List five goods and five services that are almost always paid for in cash.
3. What is a credit sale?
4. David Martyn purchased a trail bike for $600 on credit from Motor Cycles Pty Ltd. He must repay the firm over a period of two years, including interest of $200.
   (a) Who is the debtor?
   (b) Who is the creditor?
   (c) How much is the debt?
5. Name two methods of credit sale where the customer is sent a monthly account.
6. Name the extra cost a cardholder may have to pay when he or she buys goods or services on credit. Under what circumstances is this cost incurred?
7. State two advantages of lay-by as a method of buying goods. What is the main disadvantage?

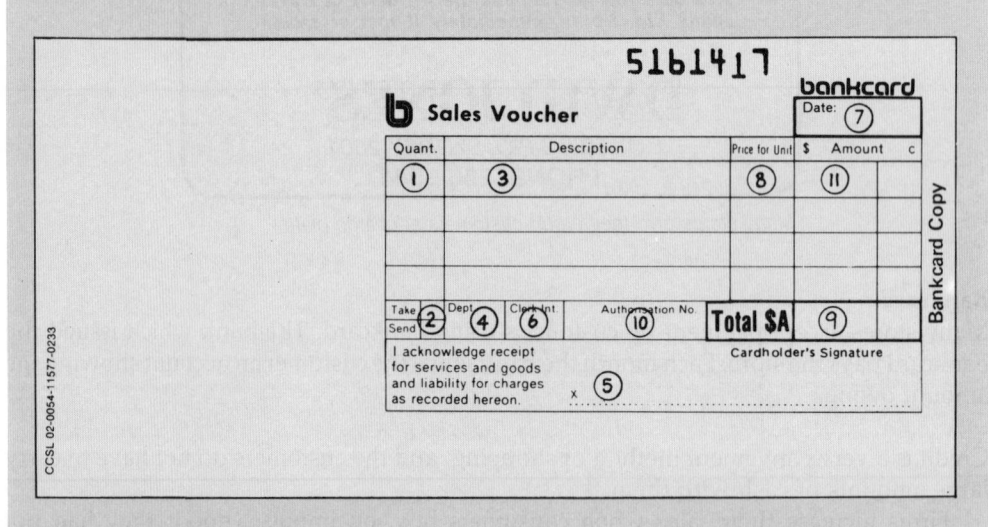

A bankcard sales voucher form

Skills activities

Research

Find out (for your local area if possible)
(a) which stores issue their own credit cards
(b) the names of five stores that accept bankcard
(c) the names of three restaurants that accept bankcard.

Interpret a document

1. The bankcard sales voucher on page 118 has its parts numbered. Copy the numbers 1–11 into your notebook and match the numbers with the descriptions given below.

   (a) The date the goods were purchased
   (b) The quantity of each item purchased
   (c) A description of the item purchased
   (d) The price of one item
   (e) The number of goods purchased multiplied by the price of one
   (f) The total value of all the goods bought
   (g) A number given over the phone by the bankcard centre to approve large payments
   (h) The shop assistant's initials
   (i) The number of the department or the checkout lane making the sale
   (j) Delivery instructions
   (k) The cardholder's signature

2. Look carefully at the copy of Minka Gillies' bankcard bill on page 120 and answer the following questions.

   (a) What is this bill's correct name?
   (b) When did Minka buy goods from Le Disc and charge them to bankcard?
   (c) What document would Minka have been given by Le Disc when she charged these goods to bankcard?
   (d) How should Minka use the documents given to her by Le Disc and the other merchants listed to make sure her bankcard bill is correct?
   (e) How much did Minka owe bankcard at the beginning of the accounting period?
   (f) How much did she owe bankcard at the end of the period?
   (g) On what date did Minka last pay bankcard?
   (h) What is the last day she can pay this bill without being charged interest?
   (i) What is the *annual* interest rate that she will be charged on money not paid by the due date? What is the *monthly* interest rate? What interest is charged on outstanding bankcard debts at present?
   (j) If Minka cannot pay her bankcard bill in full by the due date, how much must she pay?
   (k) What is the maximum amount Minka would be allowed to owe bankcard at any time?
   (l) How does Minka know which stores will accept payment by bankcard?
   (m) List three ways Minka can use her bankcard apart from paying for goods in a retail store.
   (n) List three ways Minka could pay this bill.
   (o) Which part of the form (that is, top or bottom part) should Minka keep for her own records? What details should she record on the part she keeps?
   (p) To whom does the *contract stamp duty* get paid?

THE WORLD OF COMMERCE

Secure Bank of Australia

Bankcard Statement
CARD SERVICES
GPO BOX 000
SYDNEY
NSW

bankcard

Minka C. Gillies,

56 Boronia Street,

LEICHHARDT

5690-6923-8980-6617
Account Number

Payment Due Date	Amount Paid
12/05/90	(Details on Reverse)

IMPORTANT: Payment must be received by Secure by Due Date and should be made through any Secure branch. If mailing, please detach and enclose top portion with payment. Retain bottom portion for your record. Cheques and money orders are to be made payable to Secure Bank Services of Australia Card Services.

For enquiries please call: (02) 26-1122

Please report lost and stolen cards to the telephone numbers shown on the reverse.

Opening Balance
381.64

Date	Description of Transaction		Amount
220390	KINGSFIELD PHARMACY	NORTH ROCKS	15.35
260390	AMPOL GALSTON	GALSTON	22.50
290390	LE DISC	NORTH ROCKS	18.00
040490	ALLENS PANEL&PNT RPS	DURAL	24.10
050490	PAYMENT RECEIVED THANK YOU		381.64C
060490	BP HORNSBY HGHTS EFT	HORNSBY HGHTS	26.00
090490	ALLENS PANEL&PNT RPS	DURAL	16.00
	CONTRACT STAMP DUTY		.11

INVESTMENT MANAGEMENT HAS BEEN NAMED INVESTMENT FUND MANAGER OF THE YEAR FOR 1989 BY MONEY MANAGEMENT. TO FIND OUT HOW   CAN SATISFY YOUR FINANCIAL NEEDS, CALL 008.26794 OR 02.220 585 TO ARRANGE AN APPOINTMENT.

'C' Indicates Credit

Statement Date	Closing Balance
17/04/90	122.06

Account Number	Credit Limit	Available Credit	Annual % Rate	Monthly % Rate
5690-6923-8980-6617	3000.00	2877.94	24.60%	2.050%

For Your Record	Payment Due Date	Past Due	Minimum Payment Due	Date Paid	Amount Paid
	12/05/90		6.00	/ /	

Secure Bank of Australia

bankcard

A bankcard customer statement

Documents and records kept by small businesses

Small businesses need to keep records of all transactions. Records help the owner or manager to keep control of the business and work out ways to reduce costs or increase income to make more profits. Shopkeepers, for example, need to know which goods are selling well so they can order more of them. The Taxation Department insists that records are kept. It needs to be able to work out the business's income and the tax owed. When there are several partners in a business they need to keep accurate records so that they can share the profits fairly. Firms need to know how much money they owe other people and how much money is owed to them.

Basic accounts may be kept by the firm's owner or manager, or by one of the partners. Usually firms employ an accountant to do the major accounting jobs such as the tax returns. The accountant is a specialist in this type of work. He or she gets the information from copies of the paperwork that should go with every transaction.

Cash sales

Most businesses give their customers a cash sales docket or at least a cash register slip with every sale. The firm keeps a copy of these dockets. It also keeps a record of the amount of money in the till at the start of the day's trading. The total value of sales recorded on the cash dockets added to the amount in the till at the start of the day should be the same as the total amount in the till at the end of the day. Any differences could be caused by theft by customers or staff. A more likely cause is incorrect change being given or a wrong amount being rung up on the cash register.

A cash register docket

```
              CUT PRICE DELI
                 27-04-00

             kg      $/kg           $
          BACON BONES
           0.954    3.99          3.81
          SOCCERBALL HAM
           0.218    12.99         2.83
          BACON BONES
           1.002    3.99          4.00

             TOTAL
                3 PC  $        10.64
           NO 004193    13:33    4
```

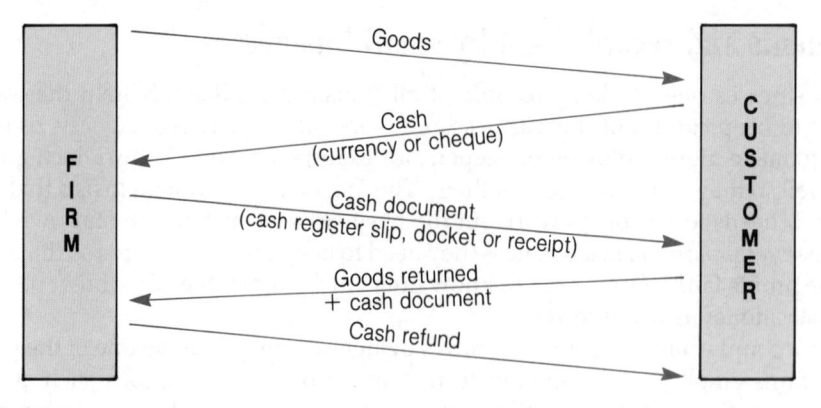

Cash sale

[Diagram: Firm ↔ Customer showing Goods, Cash (currency or cheque), Cash document (cash register slip, docket or receipt), Goods returned + cash document, Cash refund]

Credit sales

Credit sales *always* require an invoice. The invoice gives details about the goods sold and tells the firm how much the customer owes.

Invoice

Aust Pac Travel Pty. Ltd.
SUPPLIER OF TRAVEL GOODS

261 Trafalgar St., Annandale N.S.W. 2038 Australia
Telephone: (02) 60 3199 Telex: AA7487 Fax: No. 60 8662

A/c No ... 67032

Miss Emma James,
13 Darling Street,
Balmain. 2041

INVOICE N° 8785

DATE 7 November, 1991

3 Crestview suitcases at $102.00 each	306.00	
2 Leather wallets at $49.00 each	98.00	
4 Mohair travel rugs at $75.00 each	225.00	
		$629.00

TERMS 30 DAYS NETT:

Return of goods bought on credit

Customers sometimes need to return goods. Perhaps they were damaged or the wrong size or maybe too many were delivered. If a customer does return goods bought on credit he or she will be given a *credit note*. A credit note looks just like an invoice. It is often (although not always) on pink paper with red printing. The total amount on the credit note is *taken away* from the amount the customer owes.

```
             Aust Pac Travel Pty. Ltd.  [N]
                   SUPPLIER OF TRAVEL GOODS

            261 Trafalgar St., Annandale N.S.W. 2038 Australia
            Telephone: (02) 60 3199  Telex: AA7487  Fax: No. 60 8662

┌─                     ─┐           CREDIT NOTE

   Miss Emma James,                 No   1935
   13 Darling Street,
   Balmain   2041.
                                    DATE 15 November, 1991
└─                     ─┘

 2 Mohair travel rugs at $75.00 each    150.00



                                        $150.00




 TERMS 30 DAYS NETT:
```

Credit note

Statement

Each month a firm sends statements to the customers who owe it money. Some customers pay when they receive their invoices, but most wait for the statement. It records all their credit transactions over the month. The final balance on the statement is the amount owing. It is usually due (payable) within thirty days of the date on the statement.

Aust Pac Travel Pty. Ltd.
SUPPLIER OF TRAVEL GOODS

261 Trafalgar St., Annandale N.S.W. 2038 Australia
Telephone: (02) 60 3199 Telex: AA7487 Fax. No. 60 8662

Miss Emma James,
13 Darling Street,
Balmain. 2041.

STATEMENT FOR PERIOD ENDING: 30th November, 1991

DATE	INVOICE	DEBIT	CREDIT	BALANCE DUE
			BROUGHT FORWARD	250.00
nov 2	CHEQUE		250.00	0.00
7	8785 INVOICE	629.00		629.00
15	1935 CREDIT		150.00	479.00
			AMOUNT DUE	$479.00

Statement

Credit sale

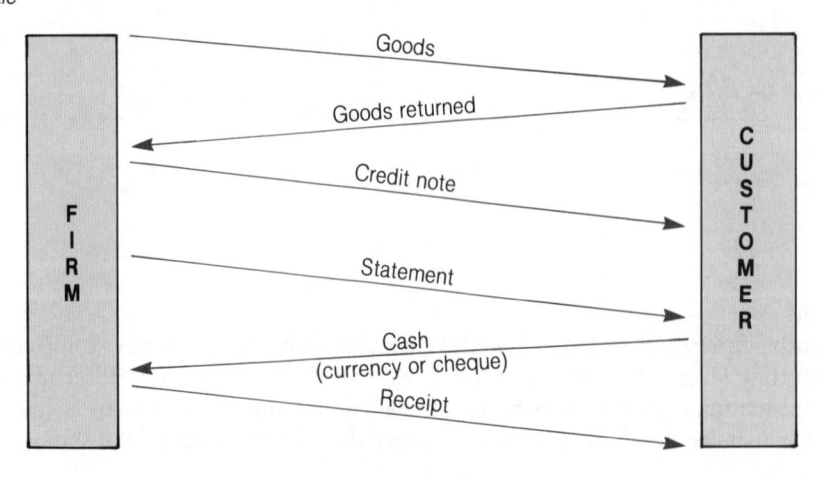

Computer records

Supermarkets, department stores and many other large and small businesses are making increasing use of computers. Many cash registers, especially in larger supermarkets, have been replaced by 'point of sale' terminals. The items in these supermarkets are not individually priced. The checkout operator passes the 'bar code' on the item over the scanner. The type of good, its size and price are recorded on the terminal. As well as adding up the total cost of the sale the terminal tells the operator how much change to give from the money received. The terminal feeds the central computer information about the sales. This information is used for restocking shelves and reordering goods. Management is able to find out which are the fastest selling lines.

A bar code contains information about the product, its manufacturer and the country where it was made and can be read by a 'light pen' or a scanner

Some shops use 'light pens' to read bar codes which are marked on a number of goods by the manufacturers. The computer has a file of all products and their prices in its memory, and the price and the description of the product is sent back to the terminal at the checkout. Both are printed onto the customer's docket along with, in many cases, the date, time of purchase, store number and checkout lane number. Prices on the shelves are not individually marked.

In McDonald's restaurants your order is recorded straight onto a computer terminal and it is then picked up by the central computer. The people responsible for purchasing meat, bread rolls, orange juice and other items on the menu can find out what items are needed and in what quantities. The advertising department can judge the success of a particular promotion. It is easy to find out when the stores are busiest and extra staff are needed.

Exercise 3H

1. Why do businesses need to keep accurate records of all their transactions? Write as many reasons as you can.
2. Where does the person who keeps a firm's accounts get the information he or she needs?
3. How does a firm know if the correct amount of money is in the till at the end of each day? What might cause the amount actually in the till to be different from the amount expected?
4. Name the document used to record
   (a) credit sales
   (b) the return of goods bought on credit.

5. What is a statement? What is the usual time allowed to pay a statement?
6. List the documents that would be involved if Mrs Cronk bought a gas barbecue from Mulhall's Hardware and paid by cheque.
7. List, in order, the documents that would be involved if Bell's Building Company bought $2000 worth of materials from Sam's Hardware, returned $300 worth of faulty material and paid the bill by cheque at the end of the next month.
8. How does a point of sale terminal differ from a cash register? List some of the additional information it records.
9. What use can the management make of the extra information it records?
10. What are some of the advantages to the retailer of using light pens and bar codes to help calculate the amounts customers must pay for their goods?
11. What advantages does the use of light pens and bar codes bring to customers?
12. What are the disadvantages of the use of light pens and bar codes at the checkout?

Skills activities

Collect documents

1. Collect as many as possible of the following documents and paste them in your notebooks:
   (a) a cash docket
   (b) a cheque butt
   (c) an invoice
   (d) a credit note
   (e) a statement.
2. Collect a sales docket from a store that uses a point of sale terminal at its checkout. Paste it into your notebook. Beside it paste an ordinary cash register slip. Underneath, list the additional information provided by the computerised system.
3. Collect a label which shows a bar code. Paste it into your notebook. Explain how a light pen or scanner can read this code.

Revision activities

New terms

In your notebook put the heading 'Important new terms and their meanings'. Copy the first word in List A into your notebook and select its correct meaning from the definitions in List B. Continue until you have listed each term and its meaning.

List A
Automatic vending machine, bonded store, cash purchase, chain store, consumer, creditor, credit purchase, debt, debtor, department store, discount store, door-to-door sales, interdependence, mail order, primary industries, producer, production, retailer, secondary industries, specialty shops, specialisation, supermarket, tertiary industries, wholesaler.

List B

1. The creation of goods and services to satisfy the wants of the community
2. The industry group which obtains or produces the materials largely supplied by nature and includes farming, grazing, mining, fishing and lumbering
3. The industry group which converts raw materials into semi-finished and finished goods
4. _____ _____ provide services and distribute goods
5. _____ is the concentration on one particular type of production or job
6. The way in which people and areas depend on each other for their goods and services
7. The buyer and user of goods and services
8. The person or firm which makes an article for sale
9. A firm that buys in large quantities from the manufacturer and sells in smaller bulk quantities to the retailer
10. Places for the storing of goods on which sales tax and import tax have not been paid; the taxes must be paid before the goods are removed from the stores
11. The _____ sells goods and services directly to the consumer
12. A store that has large or varied stocks of household goods, groceries, meat and vegetables; often facilities such as packing, delivery and parking are provided
13. A store that is divided into a number of areas, each of which provides a different good or service, for example men's clothing and furniture
14. Shops that are usually small and concentrate on providing a wide range of one type of good such as confectionery
15. Stores that operate under the same name in many different towns and suburbs: a central office buys the stock in bulk, stores it at a central warehouse and distributes it to all the branches
16. Retailers who sell at less than the normal price; they tend to concentrate on the sale of electrical goods and furniture
17. Equipment which is widely used in the sale of chocolates and cigarettes in busy places such as railway stations
18. The milk vendor and encyclopaedia salesperson may be involved with this; the salespeople are often trained to demonstrate their products and are usually paid a commission
19. A sales method important to people who live in isolated areas and to others who may find it difficult to get to shops; the firm sends a catalogue to the customer who sends back a completed order form with a cheque or money order to cover payment
20. The customer pays the money and receives the good or service in exchange
21. The customer receives the good or service and agrees to pay at a later date
22. An amount of money owed
23. The person or firm who owes money
24. The person or firm to whom money is owed

THE WORLD OF COMMERCE

Distributing goods

How goods reach the consumer

Primary producers
▼
Manufacturers
▼
Wholesalers
▼
Retailers
▼
Consumers

Stage 1 **Getting the raw materials**
The primary producer produces many foodstuffs and raw materials. They are called *primary products*.

The farmer grows wheat with the help of modern machinery.

Stage 2 **Manufacture**
Most primary products have to be changed into the goods we want. This task is done by secondary producers or manufacturers who make goods in their mills or factories.

At the mill the wheat is made into flour. At the factory the flour is used to make cake mixes which are put into packets.

Stage 3 **Distribution**
Finished goods may be taken where they can be sold to consumers. They may first be sold in large quantities to a 'middleman', a *wholesaler*, who sells in smaller amounts to *retailers*.

Packets of cake mix are transported to the wholesaler's warehouse from the factory.

Stage 4 **Consumers**
The retailer buys from the wholesaler and sells to the *consumer*. The retailer normally sells from a shop. Sometimes goods are retailed by automatic vending machines (e.g. drinks) or by door-to-door salespeople (e.g. soft drinks, bread).

A customer (consumer) buys a packet of cake mix in a retail store.

Study the diagram opposite and answer the following questions:
1. What is the general name for industries involved in Stage 1?
2. Give six examples of firms involved in getting raw materials for industry, e.g. Kim and Tran Nguyen's Egg Farm.
3. What is the general name for industries involved in Stage 2?
4. Give six examples of industries involved in processing raw materials. Choose examples from your local area where possible, e.g. Healthy Foods Fruit Cannery.
5. What is the general name for industries involved in Stage 3?
6. Give six examples of firms directly involved with the distribution of goods, e.g. Christina Pavlakis, Bread Vendor.
7. Name at least four other service industries indirectly involved with the distribution of goods, e.g. transport.

4 Labour

What is labour?

Labour refers to the role that workers play in production. It includes
- physical work, such as shearing and bricklaying
- mental work, such as management, accountancy and research
- skilled work, such as being a concert pianist.

This topic looks at labour's part in production. We see the reasons why people work, the different types of work they do and changes in the types of work available. We look at factors affecting the income people earn from their work. We also look at trade unions, the benefits they have gained for the people providing labour, the ways they have achieved their aims and reasons for the decline in union membership.

Labour's importance

Modern production is very mechanised. Machines help produce many goods and services, but workers still have an important role. They repair and maintain machines and supervise them at work. In some jobs machines will never be able to take over the more important tasks that people do. Computers, calculators and coffee machines can do some of the jobs that take up workers' time, giving people more time to do the jobs that humans do best, such as thinking about problems and making decisions.

Specialisation of labour

Labour *specialises* when workers do only one job or part of a job. Labour specialises to some extent in all societies. Among tribal Aborigines some jobs are done by children and others are done by adults. Tasks like hunting large animals are 'men's work' while others, like fishing and gathering food plants, are 'women's work'. In modern society people who are highly educated and trained have more specialised jobs than those with little education and training. For example, a person who leaves school with no formal qualifications may work stacking shelves in a supermarket. The person may leave that job and get another one on an assembly line in a factory or working as a labourer on a building site. However, people who get a full school and college or university education to become interior decorators or brain surgeons are likely to stay in their specialised field for most of their working lives.

Workers can specialise by working in primary industry, secondary industry or tertiary industry. Within each of these broad industry groups there are many jobs in which a person can specialise.

Primary industry

The raw materials for other industries are first collected in primary industry. Within primary industry a worker can choose to specialise in growing crops, grazing animals, fishing, cutting timber or mining. Workers can be much more specialised than this, however. They can be *wheat* growers, *sheep* graziers or *gold* miners.

Secondary industry

In secondary industry raw materials are processed into finished goods. There are many separate industries within the broad group called 'secondary industry' and there are many specialist occupations. There are many specialists in a furniture factory—cutting, shaping and assembling various items of furniture. Workers in steel mills, in textile factories, on car assembly lines and in fruit canneries are all specialists within secondary industry.

Think of two more examples of specialised jobs in each industry branch listed

SPECIALISATION OF LABOUR

Primary industry

Farming industry
e.g.
- market gardener
- fruit picker
- sheep shearer

Fishing industry
e.g.
- oyster grower
- deep sea fisher
- abalone diver

Mining industry
e.g.
- bulldozer driver
- geologist
- prospector

Secondary industry

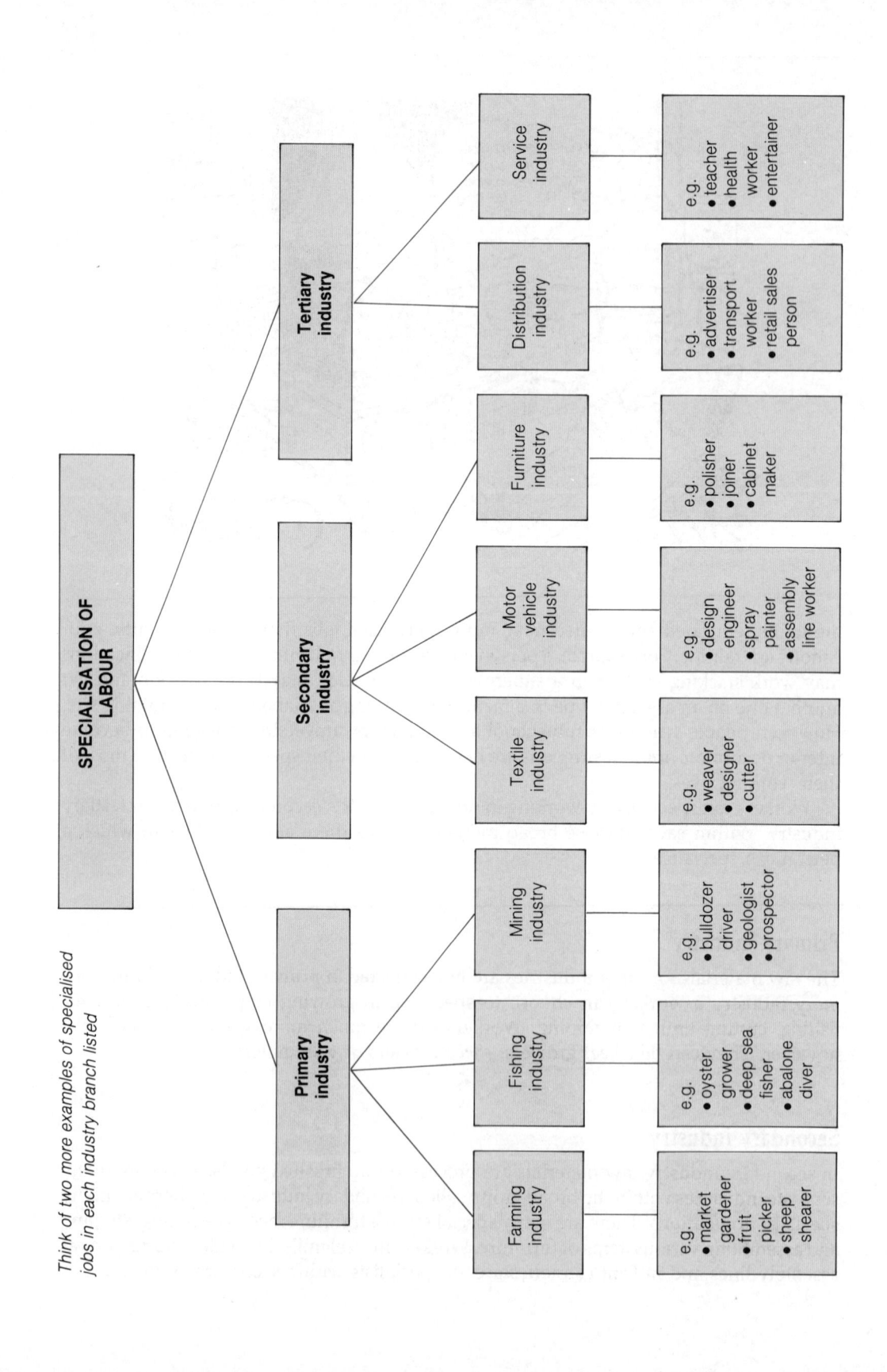

Textile industry
e.g.
- weaver
- designer
- cutter

Motor vehicle industry
e.g.
- design engineer
- spray painter
- assembly line worker

Furniture industry
e.g.
- polisher
- joiner
- cabinet maker

Tertiary industry

Distribution industry
e.g.
- advertiser
- transport worker
- retail sales person

Service industry
e.g.
- teacher
- health worker
- entertainer

Tertiary industry

Tertiary industry is made up of two quite different kinds of work. One kind involves distributing the goods that have been produced in primary and secondary industries. Packers, forklift drivers, clerks, sales people and managers in the wholesale and retail industries plus workers in advertising and transport are all specialists who play a part in *distribution*.

The other kind of tertiary workers provide customers with *services*. Teachers help provide education, doctors and nurses provide medical help, singers and television personalities provide entertainment.

Classify each of the workers into either providing services *or* distributing goods

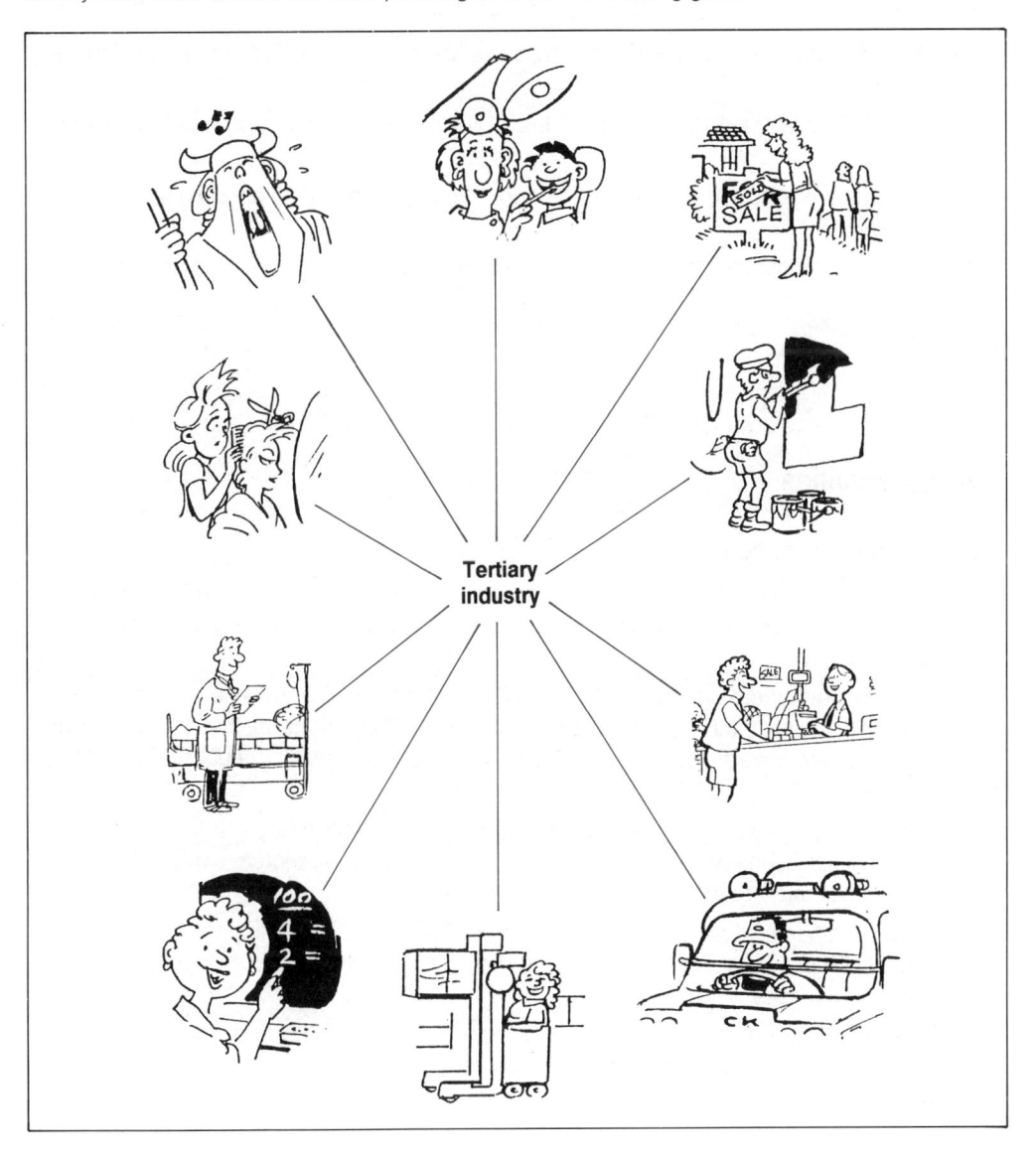

Exercise 4A

1. What is *labour*? Give three different examples of labour.
2. Give two examples of jobs that used to be done by humans and that are now done by machines.
3. Give two examples of jobs you believe will never be taken over completely by machines. Why do you think humans will continue to do these tasks?
4. What is meant by the expression 'labour specialises'?
5. What effect do education and training have on specialisation?
6. What is primary industry? List three examples of specialised jobs in primary industry.
7. What is secondary industry? List three examples of specialised jobs in secondary industry.
8. List three examples of specialised jobs involved with distributing goods and services.
9. List three examples of specialised jobs involved with providing services to customers.
10. Name the industry group involved with both distributing goods and providing services.

Skills activities

Apply your knowledge

1. Collect (or draw) some pictures of modern machines. Paste them into your notebook. Under each picture list the jobs that used to be done by labour and that are now done by these machines.
2. Collect at least three pictures that show jobs in primary industry. Paste them into your notebook. Under each picture write the job that labour does in that industry. For example, if you have a picture of trees being chopped down, write 'lumbering' below the picture.
3. Collect and paste into your notebook a picture showing secondary industry, such as a steelworks or people working on an assembly line. Under the picture explain the work that is done in that section of secondary industry.
4. Collect and paste into your notebook at least three pictures illustrating tertiary industry. Under each picture state whether the jobs are involved with distributing goods or with providing services.
5. Copy the following sketches into your notebook. Below each drawing write
   (a) the work done by each person (e.g. mining)
   (b) the industry group to which each belongs.

LABOUR **135**

6. Complete the table below to show the industry, one person's occupation and a machine involved in the production of each of the goods and services. The first one is done as an example.

Good or service	Industry	Occupation	Machine
Newspaper	secondary	journalist	word processor
TV commercial			
Bread			
Wool			
Sale of a motor bike			
Delivering bricks to a building site			
Fluoride treatment for teeth			

The results of specialisation

Increased output
The main *advantage* of specialisation is that specialists become very skilled at their job through constant practice. They can usually produce more, in the same time, than less experienced workers. An experienced tailor can cut and sew a garment more quickly—and with better results—than a person who just sews for a hobby.

Loss of some jobs
A problem with specialising is that workers might lose their jobs if new technology makes a job *redundant* (not needed any more). For example, firms with photocopiers need fewer typists.

Interdependence
Individuals, firms and industries which specialise depend on others. Workers who do only one job, say wait on tables in a restaurant, depend on others to produce all the other goods and services (such as food, clothing, entertainment, medical care and transport) they need. A waiter's *job* depends on many others as well:
- customers, to come to the restaurant
- the restaurant owner, to provide the job
- other workers in the restaurant, for example the chef, the receptionist and the cleaner
- other firms, to provide food, plates, power, etc.
- the government, to provide roads, postal services, street lights and other services to satisfy collective wants.

These groups also depend on the waiter. For example, the government depends on the waiter's taxes to help pay for the collective goods and services it provides.

The problem with interdependence
With interdependence, a breakdown in one area affects the others. For example, if the chef is ill and cannot cook the meals, the waiter will not be able to work either. If the train drivers are on strike, the waiter may not even be able to get to work.

Job satisfaction
Well-trained workers who specialise in interesting, well-paid jobs often get a lot of satisfaction from their work. They may enjoy it even more as specialisation gives them more experience and skill. Accountants may like helping their clients save money and doctors may get a lot of satisfaction from helping heal the sick. If they grow tired of their work, a high income lets them escape into interesting activities at weekends and during their holidays. However, some people, especially those who specialise in more boring, low-paid jobs, can find their work becomes very monotonous. They get little enjoyment from it and do not feel very involved in the task. For example, people who work on an assembly line tightening the nuts on the rear wheel of a certain model car day after day will not feel much pride in the finished car. They played a very small role in assembling it. In fact, they

LABOUR 137

List as many other people as you can on whom the fisherman in this picture depends

may get careless and the finished good may be worse, not better, than if there was less specialisation.

It is not always easy to change jobs in a highly specialised workplace. For example, computer technicians cannot easily change to another highly specialised job, such as raising stud horses, because they do not have the training or experience needed. Labour tends to be *immobile* (unable or unwilling to change jobs) in a highly specialised economy.

Exercise 4B

1. What is the main advantage of specialisation? Use an example to explain your answer
2. What is a disadvantage of specialisation? Give an example of a specialist job that you feel would have this disadvantage.
3. What is interdependence?
4. List at least ten people on whom the owners of a record bar depend in business and also to provide them with the goods and services they need.
5. What problem is caused by interdependence?
6. What effect do you think specialisation would have on workers' job satisfaction?
7. What effect does specialisation have on workers' *mobility*, that is, their ability to change jobs easily?

The workforce

A country's workforce is made up of
- all the people who have paying jobs, plus
- those who are out of work but who are looking for a job and would take one if it was available.

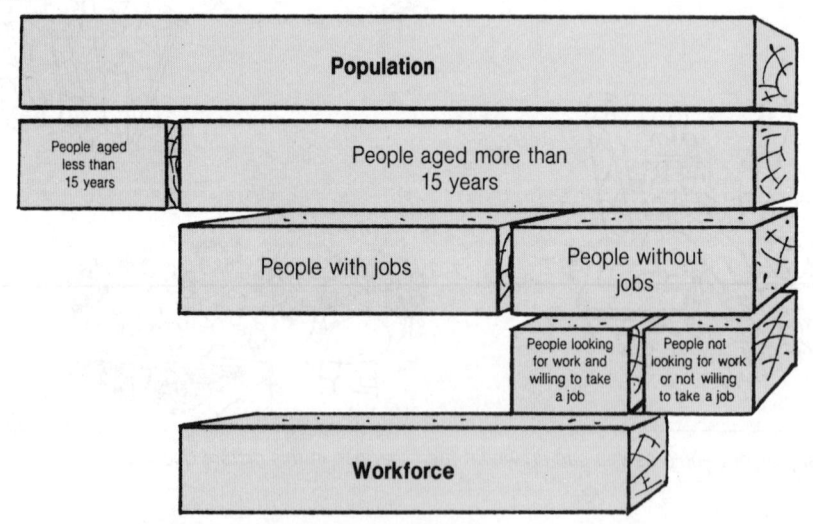

Give three examples of people who are not *in the workforce*

People who are retired, too young to work or not willing to get a job, are not part of the workforce. People in the workforce may be employees, employers, self-employed or unemployed.

Employees work for another person or a company. They are usually paid a wage or a salary.

Employers are people who pay others to work for them.

Self-employed people work for themselves. They do not get paid a regular wage. Their income varies from week to week, depending on the work they get. Many plumbers, electricians and gardeners are self-employed. They often advertise in the local paper and the *Yellow Pages* telephone book to get work.

Unemployed people do not have a job at present but they are looking for work and would take a job if they could get one.

Exercise 4C

1. Which people are counted as being in the workforce in Australia?
2. Copy the following list into your notebook and indicate which people are part of the workforce. The first has been done for you as an example.

Person	In the workforce? Yes No
Mr Holman, bus driver	X
Mrs Holman, homemaker	
Mr Marinelli, unemployed mechanic	
Mrs Marinelli, schoolteacher	
Mr Hollins, retired dentist	
Maeve McGovern, university student	
Mr Davidson, invalid pensioner	
Stefan Stacushen, school student	
Miss Ng, solicitor	

3. Describe a person you know who would be classed as
   (a) an employee
   (b) an employer
   (c) self-employed
   (d) unemployed
   (e) not in the workforce.

   (If you do not actually know someone in each of these groups, describe an imaginary person. For example, Kelly Jones who has her own hairdressing salon and has four people working for her is a/an . . .)

4. Write the following passage in your notebook after you first unscramble the words which are in capital letters.

   The OORWFCKRE is made up of people with jobs and people who are trying to get a job. People in the Australian workforce are PCLSEIISATS. One group of people in the workforce are EPOEMLESY who work for another person or MACPYON. The people who hire other people to work for them are SPORELYME. People who work for themselves are OEFMSEPLEYDL. The workforce also includes the NMLUEYEPOD people who would take a job if they were offered one.

Skills activities

Research

Using the library and newspapers, find out the number of people in Australia who are at present unemployed. What percentage of the workforce is officially counted as being unemployed? Is the percentage higher or lower than at this time last year?

Survey

Do a survey of your class. Of the members of their families over the age of fifteen years, find out how many are
(a) employees
(b) employers
(c) self-employed
(d) unemployed
(e) not in the workforce.

The workforce participation rate

The workforce participation rate is the percentage of the population aged fifteen years and over which is in the workforce. More than 62 per cent of the Australian population aged fifteen years and over is in the workforce. Nearly 78 per cent of all men over fifteen years are in the workforce and more than 50 per cent of all women over fifteen years.

People *not* in the workforce include full-time students, retired people, people on social security benefits (apart from unemployment benefits), full-time homemakers and people with other incomes who can afford not to work.

Do you expect the workforce participation rate for women to keep rising and for men to keep falling? Give reasons

Workforce participation rates

Rising for women
- Better education gives women more satisfying, better paid careers
- High housing costs often take two incomes
- Families want higher living standards, which take two incomes
- The rising divorce rate means more women need to support themselves and their children
- Smaller families and labour saving equipment make it easier than in the past for women to go out to work

Falling for men
- More young men stay out of the workforce to get higher education
- More men leave the workforce to retire early on superannuation

Changes in the participation rate

The participation rate for women is growing. More young women train for careers than in the past and they work for longer before having children. More married women with children return to the workforce too, these days, either because their income is needed to help with the family's finances or because they choose to work.

The participation rate for men is falling. Men are retiring earlier than they used to, mainly because more of them are now in private superannuation schemes. They do not need to keep working until they are sixty-five, when they can draw the age pension. As well, an increasing number of young men are staying on at school or doing tertiary studies instead of joining the workforce at an early age.

Distribution of jobs

Men and women are not spread evenly through all jobs. There are many more male miners and mechanics than female ones and many more female than male nurses and secretaries. There are many more men than women in management positions and professional jobs. Females are more likely than males to have part-time jobs.

The pattern is changing slowly. Some jobs, such as that of bank teller, which was once always held by men, are now more likely to be held by women. More girls receive higher education and qualify for a wider range of jobs. There are now many female doctors and lawyers. Some boys choose nursing and infant teaching as careers. In most jobs male and female workers receive 'equal pay for equal work'. It is against the law to discriminate against a worker on the grounds of his or her gender.

Think of other jobs now shared by males and females but which used to be done mainly by one or the other

142 THE WORLD OF COMMERCE

An apprentice shipwright—more women are choosing careers in areas once occupied only by men   JOHN FAIRFAX & SONS LIMITED

Exercise 4D

1. List the groups of people in the population who are not part of the workforce.
2. Suggest reasons why the proportion of all males over the age of fifteen years, who are actually in the workforce, is falling.
3. Suggest reasons why the proportion of all females over the age of fifteen years, who are actually in the workforce, is rising.
4. List six jobs which, in our society, are more likely to be staffed by men than by women. Why is this so?
5. List six jobs which, in our society, are more likely to be staffed by women than men. Why is this so?
6. List three jobs which were once done mainly by men but which are now frequently done by women.
7. How has the law been changed to help women get some jobs which were once done mainly by men?

Skills activities

Calculations

A country has a population of 20 million people, with 75 per cent of them fifteen years or older. Eight million people have jobs and another two million people are looking for work and would take a job if they could find one. Calculate
(a) the size of the workforce
(b) the workforce participation rate.

Survey, calculations and drawing conclusions

Do a survey of your school to find out the following information. Write the answers in your notebook.

1. How many teachers are there? How many are male? What proportion is this? How many are female? What proportion is this?
2. How many *executives* (that is, head teachers, deputy principal, principal) are there? What proportion of them are male? What proportion are female?
3. How many outside workers (such as caretakers) are there? What proportion are male? What proportion are female?
4. How many office workers are there? What proportion of them are male? What proportion are female?
5. Can you draw any conclusions about the *types* of jobs in which males and females are more likely to be employed? Can you suggest any reasons for this pattern?

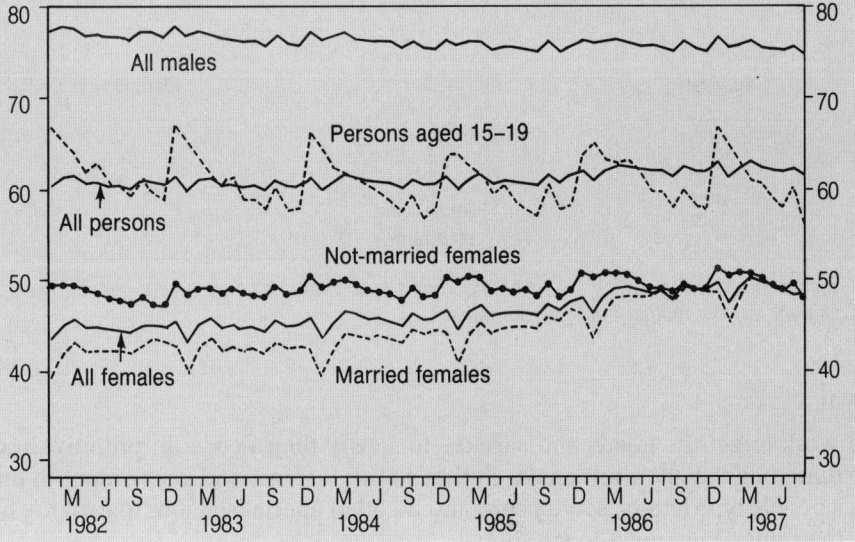

Graph interpretation

Labour force participation rates
(The labour force in each group as a percentage of the civilian population aged 15 and over in the same group)

144 THE WORLD OF COMMERCE

> Look carefully at the graph Labour force participation rates. Explain why, although the line showing male participation rates stays much the same all year, the participation rate for persons aged fifteen to nineteen *increases* around December each year, while the participation rate for married females falls around this time.

Why do people work?

Most people work for one of three reasons. These are survival, to improve their living standard, for self-satisfaction.

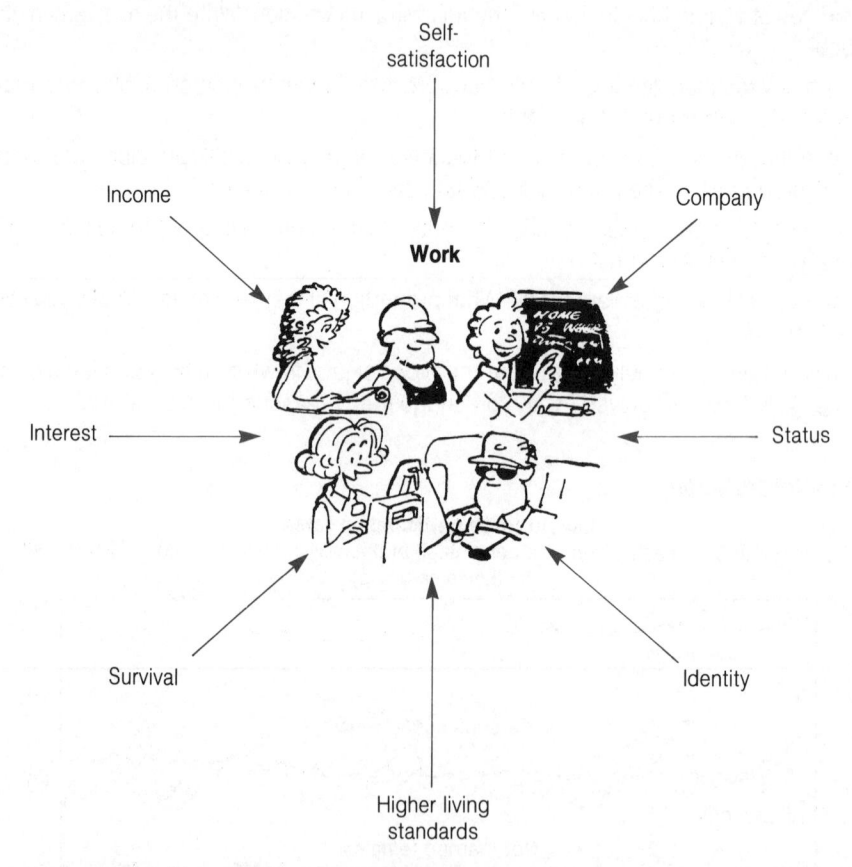

Of these reasons for working, which are most important to your parents? If both your parents work, are the reasons different for your mother than for your father?

Survival

People work to get the goods and services to satisfy their needs. In primitive societies people hunt, build shelters and make clothes so they can eat and keep warm. In modern societies people type letters, serve petrol and do other specialised jobs to earn the money to buy the things they need to survive.

People work to earn the income they need to survive

Improvement in living conditions

Most people want to do more than merely survive. They want a comfortable house, not just basic shelter. They like lots of fashionable clothes, not just enough to keep them warm and decent. They want to buy nice furniture and perhaps a swimming pool and holidays. These extra items often take a second income and the increased workforce participation rate often shows a family's wish to have a higher living standard. School students may take a part-time job to pay for concert tickets and other 'extras' they want.

Self-satisfaction

Many people work because they enjoy their jobs and the company of their workmates. People who inherit a lot of money or who win the lottery and people whose marriage partner earns a high income may still choose to work. Perhaps they would be bored or lonely without their job. They might like the feeling they get from doing a job well or from knowing they are doing something useful.

In our society a person's position and status depends a lot on his or her job. When people meet they usually ask 'What do you do?' or 'Where do you work?'. The answer helps them slot the person into a place in their minds. It gives them an idea of how wealthy the person is, how intelligent and how high or low on the social scale. A job helps give people an identity as well as an income.

Types of work

People do many different types of work. Those who work as labourers and on assembly lines in factories are usually called *unskilled workers*. Their jobs need little training and few special abilities. People whose jobs do need training or special abilities are called *skilled workers*. They include tradespeople, secretaries and lawyers. Some jobs can be grouped into the categories of trades, crafts, professions and paraprofessions.

People work for many different reasons

Trades and crafts

Tradespeople usually have to do an *apprenticeship*. Apprentices are given on-the-job training by someone who is already qualified and experienced in the particular trade. As well, apprentices have to go to a Technical and Further Education (TAFE) College for classes. Plumbers and carpenters are tradespeople.

Crafts need certain abilities and aptitudes as well as training. Craftspeople usually need a lot of experience to gain the special skills required. Pottery, glass blowing and jewellery design are crafts.

A carpenter is a tradesperson. Make a list of as many other trades as you can

Police officers are classified as paraprofessionals. Make a list of as many other paraprofessionals as you can

Professions and paraprofessions

The professions are jobs which need highly specialised training, usually at university or a college of advanced education. Accountants, lawyers and dentists are all classed as professional people. Paraprofessional jobs are those which involve theoretical knowledge and technical skills. They require on-the-job training as well as formal education. Examples of paraprofessionals are technicians, ambulance officers, police officers and community workers.

Exercise 4E

1. List the reasons why people work.
2. How important do you think each of the above reasons has been in your parent's (or parents') decision to work? Give reasons for your answer.
3. What is an unskilled worker? Give two examples of jobs done by unskilled workers.
4. What is a skilled worker? Give two examples of jobs done by skilled workers.
5. What is a tradesperson? Give two examples of jobs done by tradespeople.
6. What is a craftsperson? Give two examples of jobs done by craftspeople.
7. What is a profession? Give two examples of jobs done by professional people.
8. What is a paraprofession? Give two examples of jobs done by paraprofessional people.

Skills activity

Interview/report

Interview three people who do totally different types of work. You might choose a solicitor, a shop assistant and a carpenter, or an artist, a labourer and a nurse. Find out
(a) the reasons why they go to work
(b) the reasons why they work at those particular jobs
(c) whether they think their jobs will exist in ten years' time
Write a report on your findings.

Changes in the types of work

New technology has created many new jobs. Other jobs have disappeared. One hundred years ago there were no assembly-line workers in car factories. Sixty years ago there were no jet-aircraft pilots. Forty years ago there were no astronauts. But these days there are very few jobs for firemen in steam engines.

An assembly line in a General Motors-Holden factory. Assembly line jobs are constantly changing with the introduction of new technology GENERAL MOTORS-HOLDEN'S AUTOMOTIVE LIMITED

The costs and benefits of computers

Computers and other machines save labour. They do the work that humans once did, and cause changes in both the types of jobs available and the number of people doing different jobs. Some workers are worse off but others have benefited.

The loss of some jobs

Computers allow self-serve shops and petrol stations which reduce the need for sales people. Electronic banking needs fewer tellers. Robots and computers replace people on assembly lines. Computers can be programmed to do many of the routine jobs in factories and other businesses that were once done by unskilled workers. Some examples include working on the assembly line, marking prices on goods for sale and filing information.

Electronic banking needs fewer bank tellers. Name three other jobs that can now be done by machines

One of the first examples of automation occurred in 1801 when an attachment for a weaving machine was invented. A card punched with holes could control the machine and copy an intricate pattern almost exactly. Until then the looms for weaving cloth had all been hand operated. Silk weavers strongly opposed the invention as they felt their jobs were in danger. Workers who do highly specialised, well-paid jobs have a lot to lose if a machine takes their job. They need to retrain for other work and it could be a long time before they have the skill and experience to earn as much as before.

New jobs

Computers and other forms of mechanisation and automation also help to create new jobs. In the case of the silk workers, the punched cards led to an increase in employment in the factories. The cloth could be produced much more quickly, so it became cheaper and more people could afford to buy silk cloth. The increased sales caused the factory owners to employ more people, doing a variety of jobs.

While computers now do a lot of work once done by human labour, other people have jobs producing, selling, installing and programming computers. As well, computers allow firms to store and analyse a lot of information. Their businesses may become more successful and employ more people. Other people are needed to put the data into computers and make decisions on results.

Less interesting jobs

In some cases computers reduce the skill needed for a job. For example, sales jobs once involved a lot of responsibility. The sales assistant needed to know and understand the product, be able to advise customers, remember prices, keep track of the stock and reorder when necessary. Today, goods are scanned electronically at the checkout. The computer prices them and automatically adjusts stock records, reordering when they fall to a certain level. Customers choose their own goods. 'Selling' consists of simply taking the customers' money and giving them the change which has been calculated by the computer.

Explain how electronic scanners have reduced the skill needed to be a cashier

More interesting jobs

In many cases automation and the use of computers make it necessary for workers to increase their skills. Word processors have reduced the number of typists firms need, but their operators must be more skilled than an ordinary typist. Word processors have also freed some former typists from routine tasks, allowing them to do work that takes initiative and is more interesting. When machines do the boring, repetitive work people are freed to make decisions, solve problems and come up with new ideas.

Working hours and leisure time

A positive effect of mechanisation, automation and the use of computers has been a reduction in working hours and an increase in leisure time. As machines do more work, humans need to do less. Increased leisure has also changed the types of goods and services we buy. There has been a big growth in the fitness and tourist industries in recent years. Computers also control some of our leisure time. Think of the people who play pinball and poker machines.

Modern technology has changed the hours some people work. Computers can work day and night, so programmers, operators and technicians may have to do shift work. People who work at a computer terminal can have an office at home instead of going in to a central workplace each day. With more people doing shift work and more people working mainly from home, there will be fewer transport and traffic problems, especially in peak hours.

Exercise 4F

1. List five jobs that exist today that did not exist a hundred years ago. Why did people not do these jobs in the past?
2. List five jobs people do today that you think will probably disappear in the future. What changes would cause them to go?
3. List as many new jobs as you can that have resulted from the introduction of computers.
4. Explain how automation has given some people
   (a) less interesting jobs
   (b) more interesting jobs
   (c) more leisure time.
5. Give two examples of industries which have grown as a result of people having more leisure time.
6. Give two reasons why the increased use of computers may reduce transport and traffic problems.

Skills activities

Interview/report

Interview a person who uses a computer in the course of his or her work. Find out
(a) the qualifications needed to get this position
(b) how these qualifications were obtained
(c) the aspects of the job the person likes
(d) the aspects the person does not like
(e) the responsibilities of the job.
Write a report on your findings.

152 THE WORLD OF COMMERCE

Newspaper research

Find a newspaper advertisement for a position that involves working with computers. Paste it into your notebook. Underneath, write out the qualifications needed for the job.

Vocabulary exercise—crossword puzzle

Complete the following crossword in your notebook.

Clues

1. **(with 5).** This person has a job needing training or special abilities
2. This is needed to give workers special skills or qualifications
3. This person is given on-the-job training by a qualified person and also has to attend a college of TAFE
4. Most people work in order to satisfy these
5. See 1
6. This person is an unskilled worker
7. This is an important reason for people to work
8. These are needed by tradespeople, professional people and paraprofessional people
9. Most professional people have qualifications from this institution
10. A person working here would generally be classed as an unskilled worker
11. Shop assistants work in this industry

12. This describes the work done by labourers and assembly line workers
13. **(with 23).** Many families have two income earners because they want to improve this
14. These machines have taken the jobs of some workers but they have helped create many other jobs as well
15. The place where most clerical workers are employed
16. Many people like to go to work because they get this from their workmates
17. This machine can replace some workers doing repetitive tasks
18. Most people need to work to earn this
19. Plumbing, carpentry and electrical work are examples of these
20. Computers can be programmed to do this kind of work automatically
21. Changes in this have caused great changes in the work people do
22. Weaving, pottery and jewellery design are examples of this
23. See 13
24. Apprentices and many paraprofessionals get their qualifications here
25. Accountancy and dentistry are examples of this

Apprenticeship

Apprenticeship is a combination of employment and training. It gives on-the-job experience and college training. Apprenticeships are needed for trades and crafts. They usually last four years.

Training

Apprentices work for a practising, qualified tradesperson to get practical training and experience on the job. They also go to a TAFE college for a certain number of hours each week or month. There they receive training in the theory of their trade or craft. For example, a hairdressing apprentice will learn about the effect chemicals have on hair. An apprentice electrician will learn about the qualities of electricity and how to do the calculations needed in the work. Employers must give apprentices time off work, with pay, to go to technical college. The government may pay employers some money to help cover the costs involved in training apprentices.

Advantages of doing an apprenticeship

The main advantage of doing an apprenticeship is that apprentices get practical and theoretical training at the same time. They learn their trade very well and when they complete their apprenticeship they get a certificate. Skilled workers usually earn more money than unskilled workers and they can get jobs more easily.

Disadvantages of doing an apprenticeship

The main disadvantage of an apprenticeship is that *while they are training* apprentices often get paid less money than unskilled workers of the same age. Also, if they are *indentured* they are tied to the same employer for the four years of their apprenticeship.

THE WORLD OF COMMERCE

The apprenticeship contract

Indentured apprentices are under contract to their employers. Employers who take on apprentices want to be sure they will benefit from the time, effort and cost they put into training these people. They want to be sure the apprentice does not leave and go to work for someone else once he or she has been taught some skills.

A contract protects both the employer and the apprentice. In the contract the employer agrees to teach the apprentice the trade and pay him or her the proper wage. In return, the apprentice agrees to attend work and TAFE college and carry out the employer's instructions. The contract can only be cancelled if both the employer and apprentice agree or by a special apprenticeship committee. The apprentice cannot leave without the employer's approval, or be sacked. There is a three-month probation period before the contract is signed, to give the employer and the apprentice time to make sure they are happy with the arrangement.

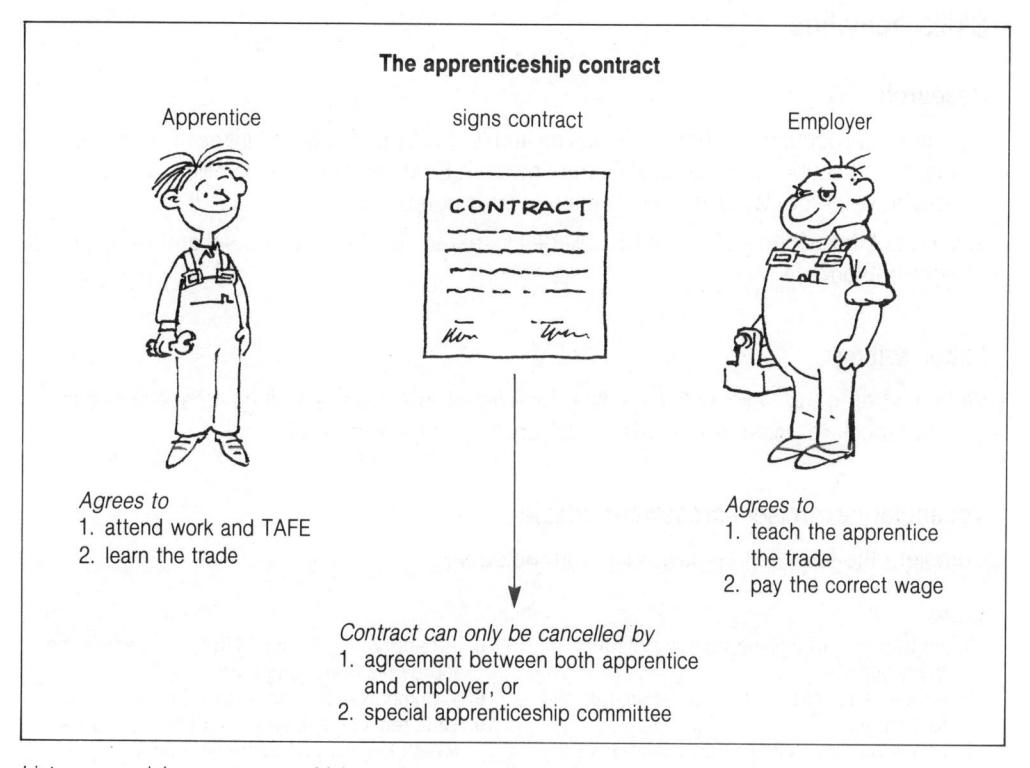

The apprenticeship contract

Apprentice — signs contract — Employer

Agrees to
1. attend work and TAFE
2. learn the trade

Agrees to
1. teach the apprentice the trade
2. pay the correct wage

Contract can only be cancelled by
1. agreement between both apprentice and employer, or
2. special apprenticeship committee

List as many jobs as you can which need an apprenticeship

Apprenticeships for girls

Apprenticeships for girls are not limited to the traditional areas of hairdressing and dressmaking. A number of girls now take apprenticeships in motor mechanics, painting and decorating, carpentry and other traditionally 'male' areas and sometimes win the 'Apprentice of the Year' awards in these fields.

Exercise 4G

1. What are the two distinct parts of apprenticeship training?
2. How long does an apprenticeship usually last?
3. What type of knowledge does the apprentice gain at TAFE college?
4. What help does the government sometimes give employers who train apprentices?
5. What are the advantages of doing an apprenticeship compared with going straight into unskilled work when you leave school?
6. What are the disadvantages of doing an apprenticeship?
7. Why does the *employer* want the apprentice to sign a contract?
8. What is the word used to describe an apprentice under contract?

Skills activities

Research

1. Choose an occupation that interests you and find out the training required. The careers teacher at school and the local Commonwealth Employment Service office should be able to help you. Write the information in your notebook.
2. Find out the address of the TAFE college closest to your home or school and write it in your notebook.

Letter writing

Write a letter to the TAFE college asking for a list of the courses it offers. Leave space in your notebook to paste in the letter or brochure you receive in reply.

Vocabulary exercise—crossword puzzle

Complete the following crossword in your notebook.

Clues

1. Apprenticeship training usually lasts this many years
2. It may be necessary to do an apprenticeship to learn this
3. It may be necessary to sign this in order to become an apprentice
4. This trade was once done by males only, but now a number of females are training for it
5. Apprentices have to attend TAFE college for a certain number of hours each _ _ _ _ or month
6. The apprentice gets this when he or she successfully finishes an apprenticeship
7. A training system which combines on-the-job training with studies at a TAFE college
8. An apprentice is trained in this aspect of the job by his or her employer
9. Commonwealth Employment Service (initials)
10. Until recently this was one of the few areas where females did apprenticeships
11. This term describes an apprentice under contract
12. This is usually lower for apprentices than unskilled workers the same age
13. Apprentices usually study here
14. This is the aspect of the apprenticeship course usually taught at TAFE college
15. The first three months an apprentice works with his or her employer

LABOUR

16 (with 20). A trade once traditionally followed by males only but which now has a number of female apprentices

17. People wishing to qualify in this area must do an apprenticeship

18. This body may pay employers an allowance to help compensate them for the costs involved in training apprentices

19. By doing an apprenticeship a person becomes _ _ _ _ _ _ _ _

20. See 16

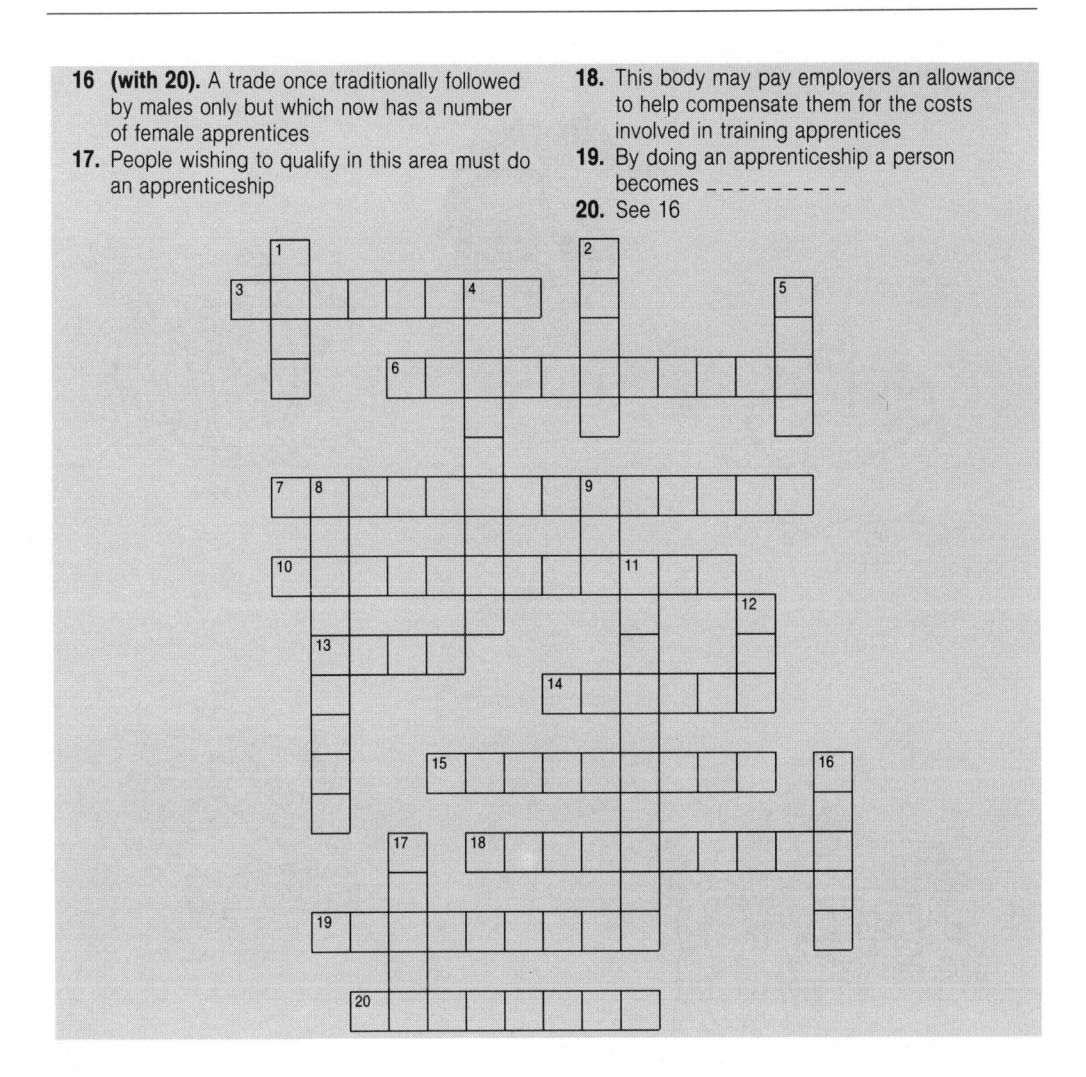

Incomes

In specialised societies, as we have in Australia, workers have one particular job. They depend on others to provide the hundreds of goods and services they must have to satisfy their wants and needs. Most workers exchange labour for a money income and then exchange the income for the other things they want.

Wages and salaries

Most people are paid wages for the work they do. Some work, such as charity work and jobs around the house, is unpaid, but most labour is paid. People who work for others usually get a wage or salary.

Wages are the amounts workers are paid for a regular working week, say $500 for a thirty-eight-hour week. People who work more hours than this are paid *overtime*. Over-

158 THE WORLD OF COMMERCE

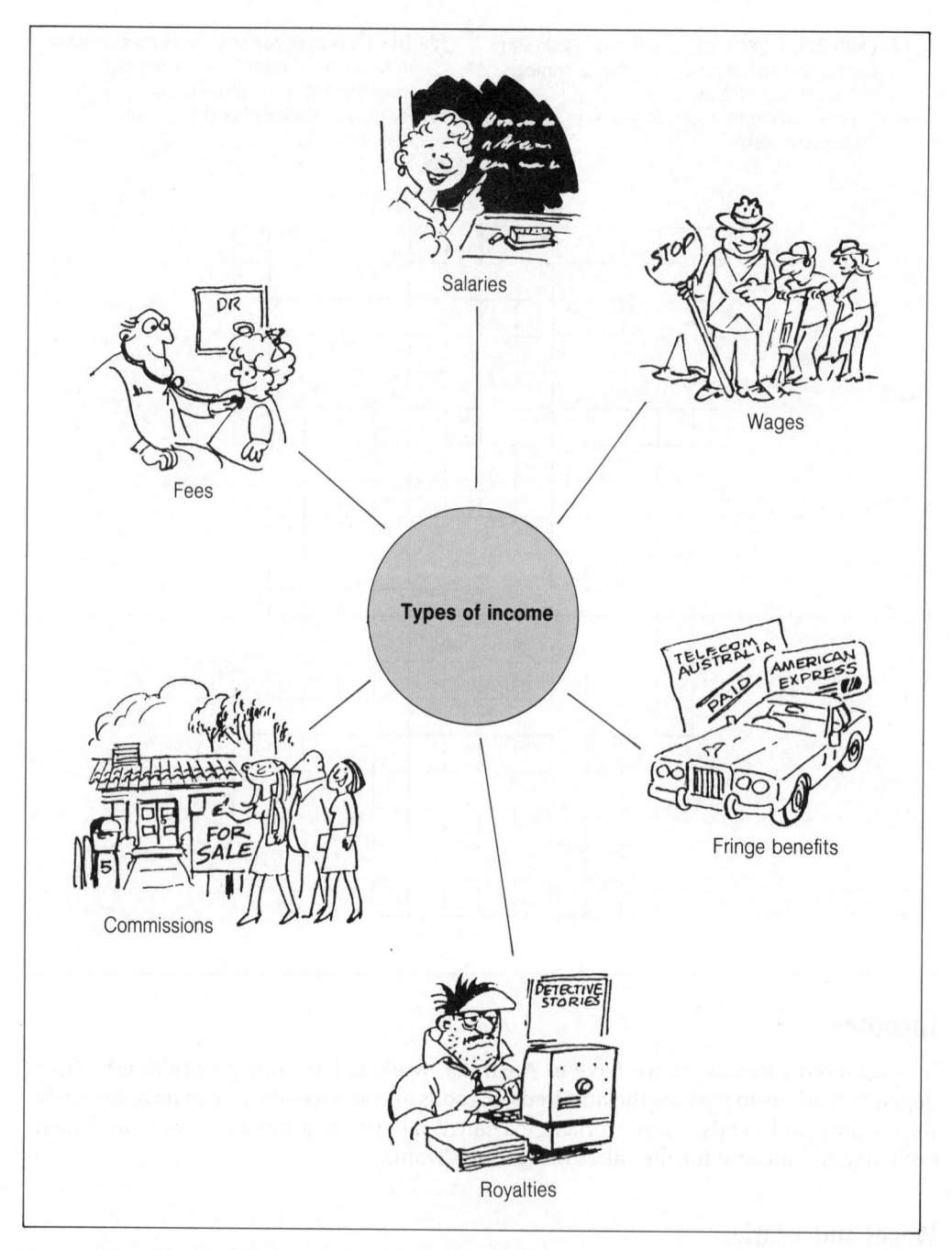

Types of income

- Salaries
- Wages
- Fringe benefits
- Royalties
- Commissions
- Fees

Name one type of worker who would earn income in each of the ways shown

time is paid at a higher rate than the ordinary wage, usually 'time-and-a-half', or one and a half times the ordinary rate. For example, if the ordinary rate is $12 per hour, the overtime rate will be $18 per hour.

A *salary* is the full amount a person will get paid for the year's work, say $26 000 per year. People on a salary do not get paid extra if they work longer hours. Managers, teachers and other workers who need to be flexible in their working hours are usually paid salaries.

Fees, commissions and royalties

Self-employed professional people (such as lawyers and accountants), tradespeople (plumbers, electricians) and entertainers usually charge *fees* for their work. Some sales people and most agents earn *commissions*, a percentage of the value of the item sold. People who write music or books and people who invent new products which are produced and sold by someone else earn *royalties*. Royalties are a small amount of money for each good sold.

Fringe benefits

In some jobs workers receive benefits in addition to their money wage.
- Shop and factory workers may get discounts on goods.
- Travel agents get cheaper holidays.
- Airline employees can travel at reduced fares.
- Bank employees get home loans at lower interest rates than the general public.
- People working for mining companies in remote towns are sometimes given housing at low rents.
- Sales representatives and people in management positions are often provided with a car which they are allowed to use for private purposes as well. The employer pays for the petrol, insurance and other costs involved in running and maintaining the car.
- Many firms pay for superannuation for their employees.

Fringe benefits are all a form of 'income', even if they are not paid in cash, because they add to the worker's standard of living. The travel agent can have a good holiday—and still have the money to spend on something else. Some people prefer to get fringe benefits instead of a pay rise because they would have to pay part of the pay rise to the government in higher taxes. The *employer* pays fringe benefits tax on many fringe benefits and in some cases the tax can be avoided altogether. Other people prefer to receive cash to spend in any way they choose. A beer allowance for workers in a brewery is of little use to people who do not drink alcohol.

Income from other sources

Most people get their income from wages but some people have other sources. Some have property (houses, shops, offices, factories) which they charge others to use. Their income is called *rent*. Some people lend money to others. They receive income called *interest*. Other people own their own businesses and earn *profits*. In 1989 more than half of all incomes earned were in the form of wages and salaries.

Why are there differences in incomes?

A few people in Australia earn very high incomes, many thousands of dollars each week. A few also earn very low wages, not much more than they would get in unemployment benefits. Others earn various amounts in between these two extremes. The amount people are paid reflects the value that others place on their labour.

Training, skill and experience make workers better able to do the job so others are willing to pay more for their services.
- Jobs that take a lot of training and which need high qualifications, like that of medical specialist, are usually better paid than jobs which need no special training, like labouring
- Highly skilled workers such as concert pianists are paid more than unskilled workers such as janitors.

More responsibility adds to a worker's value to his or her employer. People in management positions are paid more than those who simply carry out the tasks others set for them to do.

Competition for workers sometimes pushes up their wages. If there is a shortage of skilled secretaries, computer technicians or any other type of worker, employers will offer higher wages, better working conditions, extra holidays, more flexible working hours or other benefits to try to win them.

Community attitudes affect incomes. People receive what others will pay for their services. For example, a popular band can charge more to play at a dance than an unknown one. Dancers prefer the famous one. Doctors doing cosmetic surgery on film stars earn much more than scientists doing medical research into diseases in children. Film stars pay more than sick children!

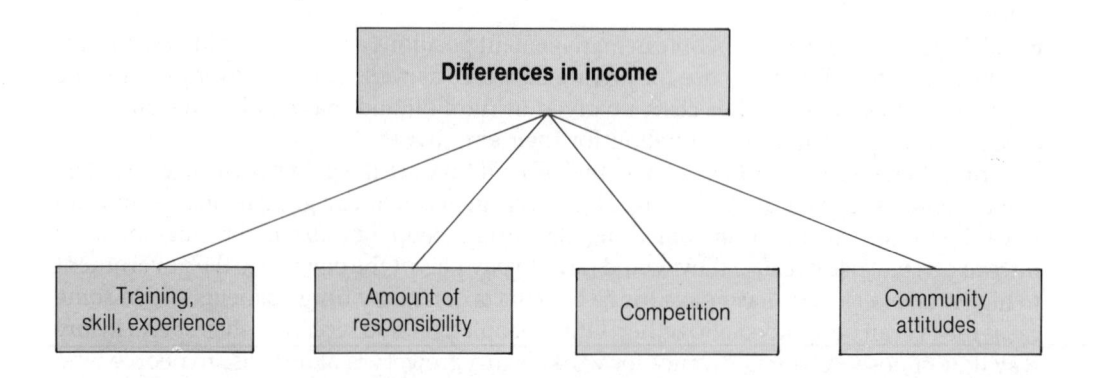

```
                    Differences in income
          ┌──────────────┬──────────────┬──────────────┐
    Training,        Amount of                       Community
  skill, experience  responsibility   Competition    attitudes
```

Exercise 4H

1. In modern societies like Australia, how do most people get the goods and services they want?
2. Name three forms of income different people are paid for work they do.
3. List five different fringe benefits available to workers in various jobs. Explain why fringe benefits should be counted as a form of income.
4. List three forms of income apart from wages.

5. Explain why the following workers earn different incomes:
   (a) an accountant and a labourer working on a road repair gang
   (b) a ballerina with a world-famous ballet troupe and a waitress
   (c) a factory manager and a worker on the assembly line in the same factory
   (d) a bricklayer during a building boom and a bricklayer at other times
   (e) a popular singer on a concert tour and a person giving public lectures on healthy eating habits.

Skills activities

Newspaper research

1. Look through the employment section of a newspaper. Find two job advertisements, one offering a much higher wage than the other. Paste them into your notebook. Under the advertisements give as many reasons as you can to explain why one job is so much better paid than the other.

2. Find a job advertisement which offers non-cash fringe benefits as well as a wage or salary. Paste it into your notebook. Under the advertisement list the fringe benefits being offered.

Calculation

Les Brown works for seven hours each day, five days a week for a weekly wage of $350. Last week Les was asked to work an extra one hour of overtime each day. Calculate Les's wage last week.

Incomes for people who cannot work

Some people cannot work to earn their living. They may be too old, too ill or physically or mentally handicapped. Others cannot work because there are not enough jobs available, or because they do not have the skills needed to do the jobs that are available.

Some members of the community are very critical of people who rely on the government or charities for support, but everyone needs some sort of income in order to survive. Most people would rather earn their own living, but if they cannot do that, for whatever reason, they need help.

In Australia the government provides an income for many people who cannot earn a living and who do not have other people to support them or enough of their own savings to support themselves. The government pays age pensions, unemployment benefits, sickness benefits, widows pensions and supporting parents benefits. These are all money payments. As well, some people can have meals delivered, free medical care, travel concessions and other *non-cash benefits*. Some private organisations also help people who cannot earn a living.

162 THE WORLD OF COMMERCE

Name as many pensions, benefits and allowances as you can that the government pays to people who cannot earn enough money to support themselves and their dependants

Government pensions and benefits

People must pass an *income test* or an *assets test* (or both) before they can get social security pensions or benefits such as the age pension or sickness benefit.

The income test means that pensioners cannot earn more than a certain amount from other sources, such as interest or rent, without the pension being reduced. In 1990 a single *age pensioner* could earn $40. Age pensioner couples could earn $70 per week. Every dollar earned above this level reduced the pension by 50 cents.

The assets test means that people on a pension cannot own assets worth more than a certain amount. The assets that are counted include money in the bank, jewellery and property, but not their family home. In 1990 an age pensioner couple who owned their own home could have $147 500 worth of other assets before their pension was affected. The pension would be reduced by $2 per week for every $1000 worth of assets above this limit.

Voluntary agencies

Some churches and charities help people who cannot earn their own living. They provide services such as sheltered workshops for handicapped people and nursing homes for old people. Sometimes they give clothing, household goods and money to people in need. The government sometimes gives grants of money to help these organisations and a lot of money is raised by donations. Some of the workers give their services free of charge.

Where does the money come from?

People with jobs pay taxes which help to provide income for those without jobs. Anyone who earns more than a certain amount of money in a year has to pay *income tax*. In most cases the tax is taken from the employees' pay before they receive it. The government uses some of the tax money to pay social security benefits. In 1990 about one-third of the federal government's income was spent on social security and welfare.

Exercise 4I

1. List five reasons why people may not be able to earn income to support themselves.
2. In Australia, who takes responsibility for most people who cannot earn their own living?
3. What is an income test?
4. What is an assets test?
5. Under what circumstances is a person entitled to receive the age pension in Australia?
6. List as many as you can of the types of help given to needy people by voluntary agencies.
7. How does the government raise the money to pay social security benefits?

Skills activity

Research project

Find out what assistance (financial, counselling, practical) is available from the government and private organisations for the following people. Consult the telephone book and the local papers. Your local member of parliament, school counsellor and minister of religion may have information.

1. A young man, eighteen, without a job
2. A family who are being evicted from their home because they cannot pay the rent
3. An unmarried girl, seventeen, who is pregnant
4. A deserted wife with young children (aged two and four) and no job
5. Teenagers and young children with violent parents
6. A widower with children below school age
7. A single girl of twenty who cannot work for six months because of injuries received in a car accident
8. A man of twenty-five who is permanently unable to work because he is mentally handicapped

Safeguarding against loss of income

Governments do provide income for those who cannot earn money themselves, but social service and welfare payments are not very high. They do not let people have as high living standards as they could with a full-time job. They would not cover many of the bills people already have, such as mortage payments. They would not cover the medical bills people would have if they became ill, or the travelling they might like to do in their retirement.

Some people do not want to rely on the pension when they retire. They want more than sickness benefits if they have an accident. It is possible to make private arrangements to receive an income if you have to give up work because of old age, illness or accident.

Superannuation

Superannuation is a scheme that allows workers and/or their employers to save money while they are working. The money buids up in a fund and it is invested to earn more money. The funds are then used to give members an income after they retire. Many firms make payments to superannuation funds as part of their workers' pay 'package'. Other workers join a scheme themselves and make their own payments to it.

Superannuation adds to or replaces the age pension. Age pensions are not paid until men reach sixty-five and women reach sixty. Superannuation can generally be paid from the age of fifty-five, or earlier if the person has to retire for health reasons. The government tries to encourage workers and employers to pay into superannuation funds.

LABOUR 165

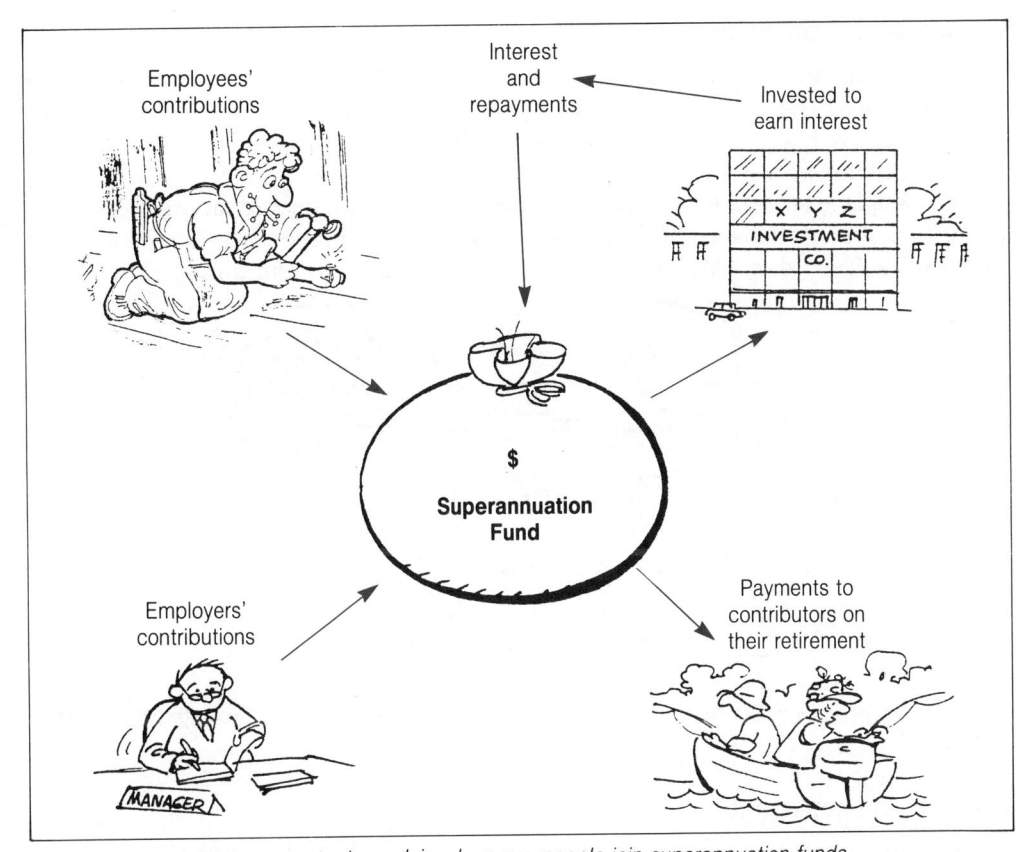

Give as many reasons as you can to explain why some people join superannuation funds

Superannuation helps reduce the amount that the government needs to pay in age pensions. The main way the government encourages it is to allow some superannuation contributions as tax deductions.

Many young people do not see superannuation as important. They would rather spend their money than save for their retirement, which is a long time off. The good thing about starting superannuation at a young age is that small amounts saved over a long period of time add up to a large sum of money in the end. A *portable* superannuation scheme is best for young people. It allows them to change jobs and still remain in the scheme.

Some women workers do not think superannuation is important for them. They expect to share in their husbands' superannuation. But women need income in retirement too. Some women never marry and some marriages end in divorce. Superannuation also gives married women some financial independence. Lower wages, part-time work and time out of the workforce (for example, to have children) may make it harder for women to pay superannuation. They should choose a fund which is flexible enough to allow them to vary their contributions as their work circumstances change.

Superannuation is not provided by employers for all workers in all jobs. People who can afford to do so may take out private superannuation cover. Employer-financed superannuation is one of the aims of today's trade unions.

Sickness and accident insurance

People who are injured or have a long-term illness which stops them from working still have many bills to pay. They might have rent and repayments on a car or stereo system. As well, they are likely to have extra medical expenses. People with families to support have even more expenses.

It is possible to take out insurance for sickness and accident. People choose the amount of money they want to be paid (weekly or in a lump sum) to cover their expenses if they cannot work. They then pay the premiums necessary to give them this level of cover.

How can people protect themselves against losing their income if they are off work through illness or accident?

Workers' compensation

People who cannot go to work because they have been injured at work, or in some way because of their work, are entitled to 'workers' compensation'. Self-employed people and people injured at home or in their leisure time are not entitled to workers' compensation.

People on workers' compensation are entitled to receive their full basic weekly wage for a certain time. They may also have any medical and hospital bills paid. If they are

Why would this man not be entitled to claim workers' compensation insurance if he is injured?

disfigured, say by losing an arm or having a badly scarred face, they may also receive a lump sum of money to help 'compensate' for the physical and mental suffering. If employees are killed in the course of their jobs, for example in an accident while operating a fork lift in a timber yard, their families will probably also be paid a sum of money in 'compensation' for the loss of earnings.

It is the law that employers must take out a workers' compensation insurance policy to cover all their employees in case they are injured at work, on the way to or from work, or doing something connected with their work. The employer pays *premiums* to the insurance company and the insurance company pays the injured employees. The premium a firm has to pay to cover its employees for workers' compensation depends on the type of work done and the risks involved, and also on the number of workers and the total amount of wages paid. Premiums are much higher for truck drivers and sawmill workers than for shop assistants because of the different risks. Most firms have to pay the first $500 of any claim themselves.

Some employees try to cheat on workers' compensation by claiming that other injuries were caused at work. For example, a person hurt playing sport on Sunday may claim that the accident happened at work on Monday. In other cases the person may claim to still be hurt long after he or she is fit to return to work. False claims have cost insurance companies a lot of money and made workers' compensation premiums very expensive. Firms and insurance companies try to reduce claims by *rehabilitating* injured workers, that is, getting them back to work as soon as possible.

Exercise 4J

1. Explain why some people make their own arrangements to safeguard themselves against loss of income.
2. What is superannuation?
3. Give two reasons why many people choose superannuation instead of relying on the age pension in their retirement.
4. Why does the government encourage workers to take out superannuation? How does it do this?
5. Explain the advantage of joining a superannuation fund at a young age.
6. Do you think superannuation is important for women workers? Explain your reasons.
7. Why should people consider taking out sickness and accident insurance?
8. Under what circumstances is an injured person covered by workers' compensation?
9. Peter Daniels lost the sight in one eye in an accident at work. He was off work for three months receiving medical treatment and then returned to his old job, packing shelves in a supermarket. List the various payments Peter would be entitled to claim from workers' compensation.
10. What determines the cost to the employer of covering his or her workers for workers' compensation?

Skills activities

Survey

Survey your friends and family to see if any of them have ever received workers' compensation. If so, find the following information and write the results in your notebook:
(a) what the injury they suffered was
(b) where the accident occurred
(c) what types of payment they received (for example, wages while they were off work, medical expenses, lump sum payment for a specific injury).

Newspaper research

Find two newspaper job advertisements which offer superannuation. Paste them in your notebook.

Trade unions

Trade unions began in Australia in the 1850s. Skilled tradespeople such as shipwrights, coachmakers and coopers formed unions to benefit workers in their particular trade or craft. They tried to limit the number of tradespeople competing for jobs, restricting the number of apprentices that could be trained and discouraging the employment of unskilled workers. They would not let unskilled workers join the union. In the 1890s the Australian Workers Union was formed to represent unskilled and semi-skilled workers. Later the trade unions formed the Australian Labor Party to represent them in parliament.

The basis of the trade union movement

Unions are based on the idea that there is 'strength in unity'. Workers speak and act as a united group. One worker alone has little influence with an employer. The employer can easily replace one worker who demands better working conditions and threatens to stop work if they are not granted, but if all the workers in a factory, or all the train drivers in the state threaten to stop work, it is a different matter. A trade union represents all its members and has a lot more power than individual workers.

Aims

Early trade unions were mainly concerned with shorter working hours. They also helped their members' families by providing sickness, unemployment and funeral benefits. Modern unions try to win benefits that will raise their members's standards of living. They want pay rises, shorter working hours, improved safety, child care for working parents and language classes for migrants. Unions also try to make sure that their members are not dismissed unfairly and that they are paid all money due to them when they leave a job.

Types of trade unions

Most trade unions in Australia are *craft* unions. They cover workers in particular occupations. For example, the Federated Clerks Union is for clerks working in any industry. *Industrial* unions have members doing a wide range of jobs in the same industry. The Metal Workers Union and the Transport Workers Union are examples of industrial unions.

Reasons why people join trade unions

In New South Wales it is not compulsory to join a trade union but in some industries employers must give a job to trade union members in preference to other applicants. When a lot of people are out of work, giving preference to union members is nearly the same as compulsory unionism. In some places where unions are very strong (for example, on many building sites), workers may refuse to work with someone who is not a union member.

Compulsory unionism and giving preference to union members are forms of *discrimination* against people who, for political, religious or other reasons, do not wish to join a trade union. However, many people feel that, since all workers get the benefit of the union's efforts to raise wages and improve working conditions, they should all support the union by their membership fees and, when necessary, by taking part in industrial action.

Hospital trade union members voting on a motion. Trade unions represent employees in many different areas of employment   VICTORIAN TRADES HALL COUNCIL; PHOTOGRAPH BY WENDY REW

What do trade unions do?

Unions' main role today is to bargain with employers for pay rates and employment conditions for their members. They do this either by collective bargaining or by going to arbitration. *Collective bargaining* means that the trade unions, representing employees, talk to representatives of the employers and try to reach an agreement on, say, a pay rise. If they cannot come to agreement between themselves, they must go to *arbitration*. Under arbitration, judges decide what will happen. Unions, employers and the government all argue for the pay rise they think is fair. Each party has the same amount of power and influence as the others. Judges listen to their arguments and then make a decision. Employers and employees must all obey the judges' ruling.

Unions can sometimes influence government policies. The trade union movement in Australia has close links with the Australian Labor Party.

How do trade unions achieve their aims?

Direct industrial action

Unions sometimes tell their members to go on strike or take some other form of *direct action* to try to make employers give in to their demands. There are many forms of direct industrial action.

- Workers *strike* when they refuse to work. Most strikes last less than two days. 'Stop work meetings' last for only a few hours. Workers do not get paid when they are on strike.
- In a *boycott*, union members refuse to handle goods from a certain firm or deliver goods to it, or unload a certain ship or use a certain product.
- A *black ban* is similar to a boycott.
- When unionists *work to rules* they do no more than the bare minimum. They don't do any task which is not specifically listed on their *job specification* and, in particular, they usually refuse to work overtime.
- In a *go slow* members attend work for the required number of hours each day but they do as little work as possible in that time.

An employer may also take direct action against employees by imposing a *lock out*. Employees are not allowed onto the premises to work until they agree to the employer's demands.

Reasons for industrial action

Industrial action can be triggered by one of a number of reasons.
- Demands for higher wages

- Demands for better working conditions, such as longer meal breaks or improved safety
- To show anger over management's policy, such as the dismissal of a fellow worker
- For political or environmental reasons. For example, a union may call its members out on strike to protest about high taxes or beach pollution
- For demarcation reasons—a *demarcation dispute* occurs when each of two or more unions claims that certain work should be done by its own members and by no others. Each union is trying to increase job opportunities for its own members.

What do trade unions hope to achieve by industrial action?

The effects of specialisation

Industrial action is very effective because our society is so specialised. Workers, firms and consumers all depend on many others to supply them with goods and services they need. One group of workers can affect many other individuals and industries. For example, if railway safety inspectors go on strike, drivers cannot take out the trains, many other workers cannot get to work and a lot of freight is delayed. The effects will be felt in most industries, yet only a small number of people will actually be on strke. In a society in which people satisfied most of their own wants and needs, strikes would not affect others.

The decline in trade unions

Australia has one of the world's highest rates of trade union membership. In 1990 about 40 per cent of the workforce belonged to a trade union compared with about 16 per cent in the United States of America. However, union membership is falling in Australia, as it is in many other countries.

- Part-time workers, female workers and workers from ethnic minorities are less likely than male, full-time workers (especially those of Australian or British background) to join trade unions. The workforce now has more people from these groups.
- 'White collar' workers (for example in the computer industry) and workers in service industries (such as the hospitality industry) are less likely to join unions than 'blue collar' workers in factories, mines and building sites. More workers in Australia are now employed in the white collar and service jobs.
- Workers on good wages and with high living standards see less need for a union to help improve their wages and working conditions.

Exercise 4K

1. When did the trade union movement begin in Australia? Why did skilled tradespeople form unions?
2. What is meant by 'strength in unity'? How does this idea apply to trade unions?
3. Compare the aims of the early trade unions with those of today's unions.
4. Distinguish between a craft union and an industrial union.
5. Describe the way unions try to win rises for their members.
6. What gives trade unions their political power?
7. List five forms of industrial action.
8. Distinguish between a strike and a lock-out.
9. List six reasons why workers may take industrial action.
10. What is a demarcation dispute?
11. Explain why industrial action is a lot more effective in a specialised society than in a society where people satisfy most of their own wants and needs.
12. Explain the reasons why union membership is falling in Australia.

Skills activities

Reasoned argument

Do you think all workers should join a trade union? On the blackboard, draw up lists of the benefits and disadvantages of joining a union, and arguments for and against compulsory unionism.

Newspaper research

Collect and paste into your notebook a newspaper clipping referring to a strike or dispute involving a trade union. Beneath the clipping, explain what the union was trying to achieve by its action.

Comprehension

Read the newspaper article 'The decline of trade unions in Australia' and answer the questions that follow.

The decline of trade unions in Australia

Bureau of Statistics figures show that trade union membership in the fulltime workforce fell from 49% in 1982 to 42% in 1988. Trade unionism has fallen in all states, across all age groups and in virtually all industries except mining.

During the six years concerned, private sector employment grew by 25% while trade union membership by workers in private industry rose by only 2%. In the public sector, employment grew by 3% and union membership fell by 5%. About 68% of workers in the public sector and 32% in the private sector are members of trade unions.

In spite of the growth in jobs, unions have not won many new members. The boom employment areas, such as computer work, cleaning, catering, tourism and retail and financial services, are using more contract labour and are increasingly non-unionised.

Women are increasingly entering the workforce but less than half join unions. Less than a quarter of part-time and casual workers and only 27% of teenage workers belong to unions.

Another reason for the fall in trade union membership is the decline in manufacturing industries. These were once the stronghold of trade unions. As well, a smaller proportion of factory workers belong to unions compared to the past. Closed shop practices ('no ticket—no start') once helped guarantee a steady stream of new members in unions, but such restrictions are much harder to enforce today.

Many workers see the unions as less relevant than in the past. Their leaders have become more involved in wider economic policy issues and pay less attention to the shop floor. For example, to try to raise employment levels they agreed not to press for higher wages.

---

1. What was the rate of trade union membership in Australia in
    (a) 1982   (b) 1988?
2. What has happened to trade union membership in
    (a) all Australian states   (b) most industries   (c) the mining industry?

3. Which of the following statements correctly complete the following sentence? (There is more than one right answer.) Between 1982 and 1988
   (a) trade union membership among workers in private industry grew faster than employment in private industry
   (b) union membership increased among government employees
   (c) employment in private industry grew faster than employment in government jobs
   (d) a bigger proportion of people in government jobs belong to unions compared with people employed in private industry.
4. Why is union membership not increasing in the growth areas such as computer work and financial services?
5. What proportion of the following groups of workers belong to unions:
   (a) women
   (b) part-time and casual workers
   (c) teenage workers?
6. List two more changes in the Australian workplace that have led to a fall in trade union membership.
7. Why do unions now seem less relevant to many workers?

Revision activities

Vocabulary exercise—crossword puzzle

Complete the following crossword in your notebook.

Clues

1. A system of training tradespeople involving on-the-job experience and formal study at a TAFE college
2. Income from the government to people who cannot earn their own living as a result of old age, ill health or certain other reasons
3. Commonwealth Employment Service (initials)
4. (with 28). People usually have to pass this before they can get a pension. It helps show if they really need help from the government
5. The initials of the political party which has close links with the trade union movement
6. (with 9 and 13). This shows the proportion of the population over the age of fifteen years that is in the workforce
7. A form of income available to people when they retire from work as a result of age or ill health. It is funded by the workers themselves or their employers
8. (with 18). A type of insurance that protects workers (and their dependants) from financial loss if the workers are injured in the course of their work
9. See 6
10. A group of workers who combine to try to improve their wages and working conditions
11. (with 16). A type of industrial action in which the workers go to work for the required number of hours but do as little as possible while they are there
12. In recent years trade unions have been more concerned with protecting this
13. See 6
14. The income earned by people who allow others to use land, buildings or other property they own
15. The name given to money, jewellery, and other property. Old people must calculate the value of these items to see if they qualify for the pension
16. See 11
17. The income earned from money in the bank or loans
18. See 8
19. (with 22 and 26). The trade union movement is based on this principle
20. Modern machines which have changed the nature of many kinds of work

21. The income received by many self-employed professional people and tradespeople
22. See 19
23. **(with 24).** Payments or other assistance some workers receive from their employers as well as their money incomes
24. See 23
25. The slang term for workers' compensation
26. See 19
27. The income of people whose payment is worked out on a yearly basis. People who are paid this way do not receive extra income if they work overtime
28. See 4
29. Technicians and nurses are in this classification of workers. They need theoretical knowledge and technical skills so they must have formal education as well as on-the-job training

New terms

In your notebook put the heading 'Important new terms and their meanings'. Copy the first term in List A into your notebook and select its correct meaning from the definitions in List B. Continue until you have listed each term and its meaning.

List A

Apprenticeship, arbitration, collective bargaining, demarcation dispute, fees, fringe benefits, interest, labour, paraprofession, pensions, primary industry, profession, profit, redundancy, rent, secondary industry, sickness and accident insurance, skilled workers, superannuation, tertiary industry, unskilled workers, wages, workers' compensation insurance, workforce, workforce participation rate.

List B

1. Money paid to employees in return for their labour
2. Money charged by professionals or tradespeople in return for work done
3. Benefits such as the private use of company cars and low interest loans given to workers instead of paying them a higher income
4. Money charged for the use of property
5. Income earned from lending money to others
6. The difference between the income earned and the expenses incurred in running a business
7. The work *people* do in the production process
8. The first stage in production. Raw materials are produced or gathered in this stage
9. The second stage in production. Raw materials are processed into finished goods
10. The final stage in production. Goods are distributed and services are provided
11. All people over the age of fifteen years who have jobs or are actively looking for a job and would take one if it were available
12. People whose jobs require little or no training
13. People whose jobs require training and/or special abilities
14. A combination of employment and training used to teach certain crafts and trades
15. Payments made by the government to certain groups of people who are unable to earn their own income
16. A policy taken out by employers to cover their employees in case they are injured at work, on their way to or from work, or doing anything connected with their work
17. A policy often taken out by self-employed people to provide themselves with an income if they cannot work due to illness or accident
18. A scheme which requires employers or employees (or both) to pay money into a fund; the fund provides an income for the employees when they retire
19. The situation when trade unions, representing the employees, talk with representatives of the employers, to try to reach an agreement and settle a dispute
20. The situation when a judge hears the points of view of the trade unions, the employers and the government and gives a ruling that all parties must accept
21. Loss of jobs because new technology means this type of work is not needed any more
22. The percentage of the population aged fifteen years and over which is in the workforce

23. A job which needs highly specialised training, usually at a university or college, for example accountancy

24. A job which needs theoretical knowledge and technical skills. It usually involves on-the-job training plus formal education, for example a technician

25. Industrial action that rusults from different trade unions each claiming certain tasks should be done by their members only

5 Law

The place of law in history

Laws are rules that are binding on the people in a certain community. Whenever people have lived together in groups they have made laws to govern their behaviour and activities. Laws set out the rights and duties of each person in the group. They help to create order in the society. They help each person to have a sense of security. Laws tell people what is expected of them and what they can expect from other people.

Laws in ancient societies were very simple. About 1800 BC the Babylonians were ruled by a powerful king called Hammurabi. He gave his people 282 laws inscribed on a pillar. The basis of Hammurabi's laws was 'an eye for an eye and a tooth for a tooth'. If a house fell down and killed the owner, then the builder was killed.

In Ancient Egypt trials were held with a judge, and a scribe who made notes of what was said. Egyptian punishments ranged from death for a serious crime to the loss of a limb or a hand for lesser crimes. The earliest laws were concerned mainly with the institutions of marriage and religion and the protection of personal property.

Aboriginal laws

Aboriginal laws were never written down. They were passed on by word of mouth from one generation to the next. Aboriginal laws were decided upon by the elders of the tribe. They were generally accepted by the members of the tribal community. When a law was broken, it was usual for the person who had broken the law to meet in public with the person who had been affected by the action. The rest of the tribe would witness the meeting. After the penalty was decided it was usually the tribe as a group that would carry out the punishment. Such punishments ranged from the withdrawing of a right to banishment from the tribe or even death.

When Captain Cook arrived at Botany Bay he took possession of 'The Great Southern Continent' for England. He imposed English law on the continent now named Australia. English law was to be obeyed by everyone who lived here. This included not only the

What type of punishments were given under traditional tribal law?

convicts, free settlers and soldiers but also the Aborigines who had been living in Australia for thousands of years. As far as the new settlers were concerned, the Aboriginal people had to accept English law. Conflicts between the new settlers and the Aboriginal people broke out.

Many Aboriginal people feel resentment towards 'white' Australians at the way in which their culture and system of law was undermined. In many Aboriginal communities in the outback the traditional system of law is still practised. In recent years some groups of Aborigines have claimed that they should not have to obey English law. They want traditional Aboriginal law to be used in cases involving Aborigines. Land rights cases have begun in which Aborigines have claimed sacred burial sites as tribal land. Some Aborigines have asked the Australian and state governments to give them back tribal lands and to let them live there under the government of Aboriginal tribal law.

Refer to the library and newspapers to find out what is meant by the term 'Aboriginal land rights'. Write a short explanation of the term in your notebook

GREINER to drop land rights Bill

The N.S.W. Government has made further concessions to Aborigines in its attempt to change land rights legislation.

The government has dropped plans to get rid of the Aboriginal Land Council and replace it with an Aboriginal Affairs and Land Rights Commission.

Exercise 5A

1. What are laws?
2. Name two ancient societies that had a system of laws.
3. Why was it necessary to have laws?
4. Who was Hammurabi? When did he live? Why is he remembered?
5. What is the meaning of 'an eye for an eye and a tooth for a tooth'? Explain how this system worked in Ancient Babylon.
6. Aboriginal law was never written down. Briefly explain it by answering the following questions:
   (a) How did Aborigines know what their laws were?
   (b) How did a 'trial' of an accused person take place?
   (c) What kinds of punishment were given?
   (d) How was the punishment imposed on a guilty person?
7. Briefly explain how the arrival of Captain Cook caused a conflict between the new settlers and the Aborigines.
8. Give two ways in which some Aborigines want conditions regarding their lifestyle changed.

Skills activities

Research

Consult a Bible and copy the Ten Commandments into your notebook. They are listed in Exodus, Chapter 20. Put a tick next to each commandment that is incorporated into the laws of modern-day Australia.

Class debate

'Aboriginal people should have the option of living in their tribal areas under traditional tribal law.'

An introduction to simple rules and laws

Every person in our community has to obey many rules and laws every day. You have to obey rules at home, on the sporting field and at school. Motorists have to obey traffic laws. There are regulations to stop people from smoking on public transport and in government offices.

Skills activities

Research

1. List ten rules you have to obey at your school. Beside each rule write the punishment given if you break the rule. Set out the information in a table as shown below. An example is given to help you.

Rule	Punishment if rule is broken
1. Wear full uniform	1. Pick up papers at lunchtime

2. Answer the following questions about the rules at your school:
   (a) Who made up the rules?
   (b) Who enforces the rules?
   (c) Do you have a student council at your school? If you do have one, then who elects it? What is the purpose of the student council?
   (d) Do you think school rules are needed? Give reasons to explain your answer.
   (e) Name one school rule you think is unfair or needs changing. Give the reason for your answer. State how you would change the rule.

Essay

Imagine life in a school that had no rules. Write an essay to describe what could happen in a normal day and how you think that day would pass.

Why we need laws

Laws are rules that must be obeyed by people living in a certain community. People who disobey laws may be punished. If people were free to act as they wish there would be no security for life, property or the rights of others. A state of *anarchy* (lawlessness and confusion) would exist.

Why do we need drink-driving laws?

Road laws are designed to safeguard car drivers as well as other road users
MIRROR AUSTRALIAN TELEGRAPH PUBLICATIONS

Protection

The law gives us protection against other people. Laws sometimes tell us what we *cannot* do. We cannot drive a car in the city faster than 60 kilometres per hour. We cannot drive while drunk. We cannot commit armed robbery or murder. Laws take away some of our freedom to act as we wish, but they also protect us from our own actions and protect us from other irresponsible people.

The law also provides us with the means to do many things. It gives us the means to marry, to divorce and to adopt a child. The law allows us to open and operate a business. It allows us to take legal action against someone who fails to pay back a debt.

The speed limit for trucks has been reduced

Why was a lower speed limit for trucks and coaches introduced?

Exercise 5B

1. What are laws?
2. What is anarchy?
3. Give one example of laws which protect us from our own, as well as other people's actions.
4. Name four things which the law says we cannot do.
5. Name four things we are able to do with the help of the law.

Skills activities

Research

Find and write in your notebook
(a) the speed limit in built-up areas
(b) the speed limit on the open road
(c) the maximum blood alcohol level that a person can have and still legally drive a motor vehicle
(d) the number of alcoholic drinks that brings the average person to the maximum blood alcohol level.

Research and essay

Refer to the newspaper headlines 'The speed limit for trucks has been reduced'. Use your library and newspapers to find out:
(a) what the speed limit for trucks is
(b) when the speed limit was lowered
(c) why the speed limit was lowered.
Use the information to write a short essay on 'How laws protect us'.

Vocabulary exercise

Rearrange the letters of the four scrambled words below to form four words associated with law. Write the answers in your notebook.

T T P R C E O

A A R N Y C H

S H P N T M U N E I

R K N U D

Print the numbered letters in your notebook.

Unscramble the letters to find a punishment common in the history of law.

Why we need to change laws

All societies change over a period of time. Most grow and develop. Some societies disappear. The laws that were used to rule the Ancient Egyptians or even the first white settlers in Australia would not be suitable for modern Australia, but our basic laws remain much the same. It is still illegal to murder, rob and assault other people. Many laws cease to exist, however. Others may be created to take their place. Sometimes punishments change even though the law against the action remains.

A more complex society

As society becomes more complex and values change, the laws need to change. We now need laws to stop air and noise pollution. We need to protect the environment. Many more laws are now needed to protect the consumer. We have laws against untrue advertisements and shady business practices. New laws have been made to protect people's privacy.

Why do we need new laws to protect the environment?

A more 'permissive' society

Australian society is now more 'permissive'. Language and activities that would once have landed the performers in gaol are now accepted on stage in this country. People's values have changed, so some laws have needed to be changed.

Exercise 5C

1. Name one recent change in society that has led to the need for new laws.
2. Name one recent change in our society that has allowed some laws to be less strictly enforced.

THE WORLD OF COMMERCE

Skills activities

Apply your knowledge

1. List some new laws that you think might have to be made to deal with:
   (a) a world fuel shortage
   (b) the impact of the 'greenhouse effect' on the Earth.
2. List any existing laws that you think will be changed in the near future.
3. Imagine that you live in the year 2050. List five laws you think would have been created to deal with the changes that have taken place in society since 1990.

Vocabulary exercise—hidden words

Find the word in the puzzle below which best fits each clue given. The words may be written in any direction, including horizontally, vertically, diagonally and backwards.

C	A	C	O	M	M	U	N	I	T	Y
O	W	E	G	A	U	S	A	L	R	L
N	W	A	R	D	R	U	N	K	E	A
V	A	I	L	O	D	E	A	T	H	N
I	P	E	A	C	E	E	R	U	I	I
C	R	A	N	B	R	A	C	E	S	G
T	O	L	D	E	N	S	H	O	T	I
S	T	H	G	I	R	A	Y	L	O	R
I	E	N	G	L	I	S	H	E	R	O
T	C	O	N	F	L	I	C	T	Y	B
E	T	E	G	A	I	R	R	A	M	A

1. Throughout _ _ _ _ _ _ _ people have always made laws to govern the behaviour and activities of the group
2. A rule that is binding on the people in a certain community
3. Something which the Aboriginal people are trying very hard to attain (two words)
4. It is illegal for a person to drive a motor vehicle while in this condition
5. Many members of this group of people in Australia wish to return to living under traditional law
6. Something which laws try to resolve
7. A condition of lawlessness which exists in a society which does not have laws
8. A crime which is outlawed in nearly every society
9. An action made possible by law
10. One of the things the law tries to do for us
11. The race of people who gave modern Australia her early laws
12. The law allows us to _ _ _ people who harm us
13. A group of people who live together, often sharing the same political, legal and social structures

The law in Australia

Law making and law enforcement

In Australia laws are made by the parliaments and by the courts. They are enforced (that is, people are made to obey them) by the courts and by the police. Some other people, such as customs officials and railway inspectors, have the power to enforce certain laws.

Legislature

The Australian government and each of the state governments has houses of parliament which *legislate* or make the laws. The Australian parliament makes laws which apply to all Australians. The state parliaments make laws which apply to residents of their states. Laws passed by parliament are called *statute law*.

Judiciary

The law courts which interpret statute law are known as the judiciary. The courts also decide disputes between individuals and 'try' people who are accused of having broken the law. The way that the courts interpret particular laws comes to be accepted as the law itself. Laws of this type are known as *common law* or judge-made law.

Why do you think a 'judge' is so named?

Administration

The people who administer the law, enforce it or carry it out are known as the administration. The police force is the main part of the administration.

Exercise 5D

1. Briefly explain the work done by
   (a) the legislature
   (b) the judiciary
   (c) the administration.

Skills activities

Research projects

1. Find a newspaper article which refers to a new law that has been passed (or is about to be passed) by one of the parliaments in Australia. Paste the article into your notebook. Write the answers to the following questions underneath the article.
   (a) Which parliament in Australia is responsible for the law?
   (b) Name the government department and the minister who were responsible for *initiating* the law (getting it started).
   (c) Explain why the new law was considered necessary.
   (d) Do you agree that the new law was necessary? Give reasons for your answer.
2. Find a newspaper article which refers to a recent court case. Paste the article into your notebook and write the answers to the following questions underneath the article.
   (a) Name the court in which the case was heard.
   (b) State the charge against the accused person (for example, armed robbery).
   (c) State the finding (result) of the court case.
   (d) Was a sentence or fine imposed? If so, state what the sentence or fine involved.
   (e) Do you agree with the final judgement of the court case? Give reasons for your answers.

The Australian Constitution   GOVERNMENT PHOTOGRAPHIC SERVICE

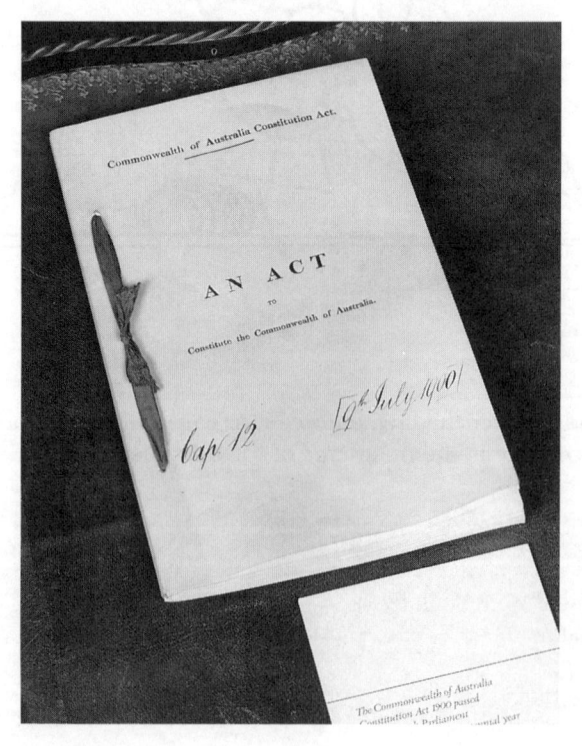

The parliaments

Australia has a written *constitution*. This sets out the basic laws within which the government can act. When a parliament in Australia passes a law it must be within the powers given to it by the constitution.

The laws made by the Australian government apply to all Australians. It makes no difference which state you live in. It is just as illegal for someone to commit bigamy in Queensland as it is for someone in Victoria. However, South Australian laws apply only to people in South Australia. Tasmanian laws apply only to people in Tasmania. Drink-driving laws and traffic rules vary from one state to another.

The table 'Some of the powers of each level of government' sets out the main areas in which each level of government is able to pass laws.

Some of the powers of each level of government		
Australian government	*State governments*	*Local governments*
Defence	Education	Local roads
Foreign affairs	Transport	Sewerage services
Currency	Health	Garbage collection and disposal
Trade	Police and justice	Parks and gardens
Social services	Local government	Health centres
Immigration		Health and building regulations
Marriage and divorce		Footpaths, street lighting
Postal services		

Exercise 5E

1. What is the constitution?
2. Why would the laws relating to social service benefits affect an invalid pensioner in Tasmania as much as an invalid pensioner in South Australia?
3. If you moved to the Northern Territory why may you be at a disadvantage, or an advantage, as far as your level of education is concerned?

4. Why is it not possible for the New South Wales government to have its own defence forces?

5. Complete the following table to show which level of government provides these services in your local area. Place a tick (✓) in the correct column.

Service	Australian government	State government	Local council
Education			
Post office			
Park			
Police			
Social services			
Health centre			

The courts

The *judiciary* consists of the courts and the judges which interpret the law. Most courts in Australia handle *civil* and *criminal* cases.

Civil cases

A civil case involves a dispute between individuals and/or between business firms. It aims at settling a dispute. It does not aim to punish anyone. However, damages in the form of a financial payment can be awarded to one person against another person. Civil cases include divorce proceedings, a claim for a debt and a dispute involving a contract, among many others.

Criminal cases

A criminal case involves the breaking of a law. It may end in a punishment such as a fine, imprisonment, or both. Criminal cases include theft, assault, failure to pay taxation and driving an unregistered motor vehicle.

Open courts

Most courts in Australia are 'open' courts. This means that anyone may enter the court and listen to the case being heard.

Closed courts

The legal phrase used to describe a 'closed' court is the term 'in camera'. This means that the case is to be heard in private. A Children's Court may be closed to outsiders. Only the child, his or her parents and legal representatives may be allowed to attend.

An appeal

Different types of cases are heard in different courts. There is a hierarchy of courts so that some hear more serious types of cases. When a person is found guilty of a crime he or she is sometimes able to 'appeal' to a higher court for the judgement to be reversed. To be granted the right to appeal the convicted person must be able to show that he or she has a reasonable chance of being able to prove his or her innocence.

The High Court of Australia can hear appeals against decisions made by the lower courts. It is located in Canberra, ACT   NATIONAL CAPITAL PLANNING AUTHORITY

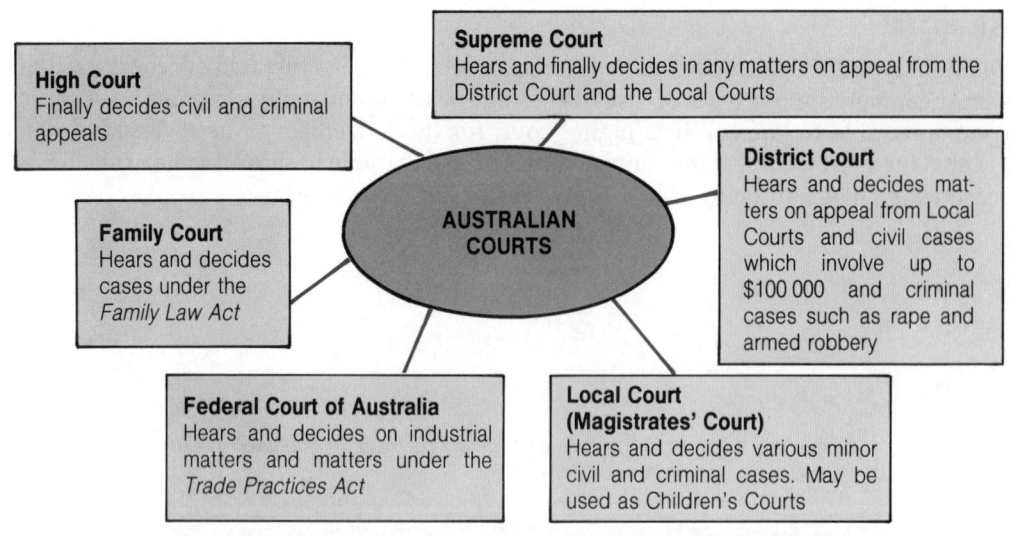

192 THE WORLD OF COMMERCE

AUSTRALIAN COURTS

High Court
Finally decides civil and criminal appeals

Supreme Court
Hears and finally decides in any matters on appeal from the District Court and the Local Courts

Family Court
Hears and decides cases under the *Family Law Act*

District Court
Hears and decides matters on appeal from Local Courts and civil cases which involve up to $100 000 and criminal cases such as rape and armed robbery

Federal Court of Australia
Hears and decides on industrial matters and matters under the *Trade Practices Act*

Local Court (Magistrates' Court)
Hears and decides various minor civil and criminal cases. May be used as Children's Courts

Australian courts—a simplified version of the court system in New South Wales, Queensland and Victoria. The system in other states is very similar but they do not all have District Courts or Local Courts

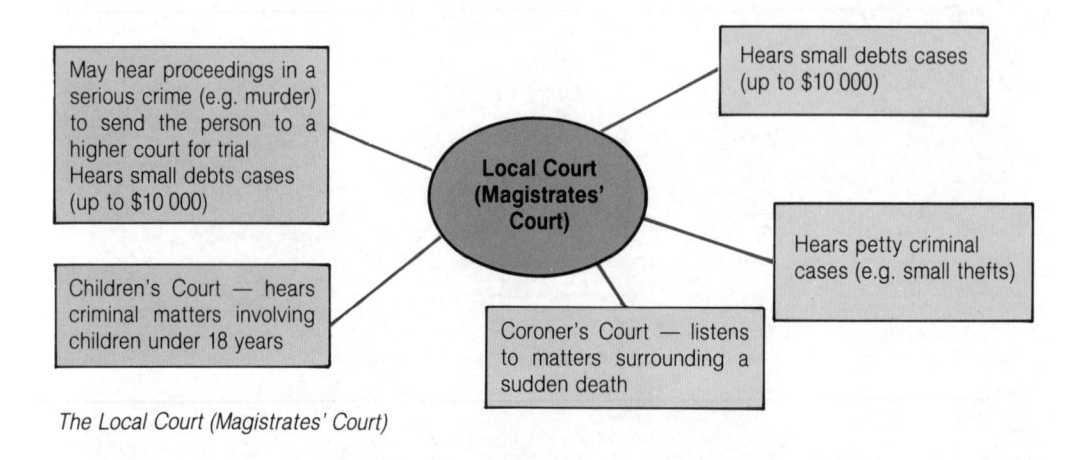

Local Court (Magistrates' Court)

- May hear proceedings in a serious crime (e.g. murder) to send the person to a higher court for trial. Hears small debts cases (up to $10 000)
- Children's Court — hears criminal matters involving children under 18 years
- Hears small debts cases (up to $10 000)
- Hears petty criminal cases (e.g. small thefts)
- Coroner's Court — listens to matters surrounding a sudden death

The Local Court (Magistrates' Court)

The District Court

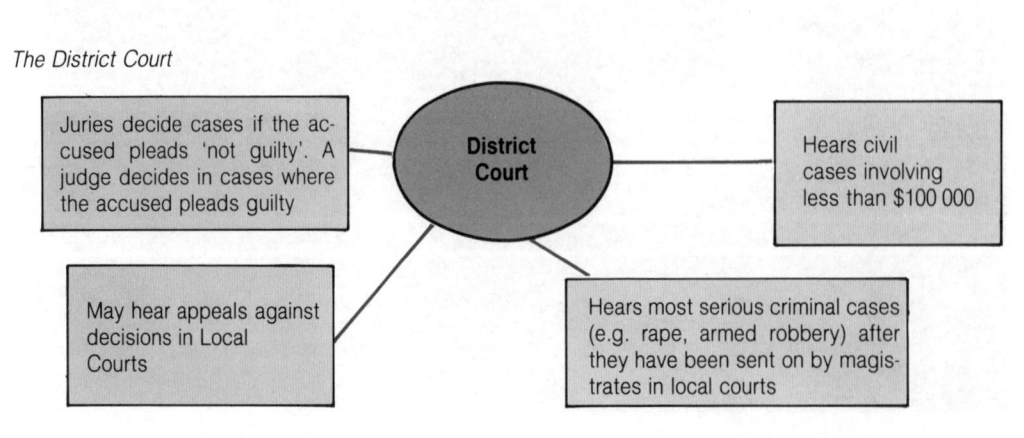

District Court

- Juries decide cases if the accused pleads 'not guilty'. A judge decides in cases where the accused pleads guilty
- May hear appeals against decisions in Local Courts
- Hears civil cases involving less than $100 000
- Hears most serious criminal cases (e.g. rape, armed robbery) after they have been sent on by magistrates in local courts

LAW

The Supreme Court

- Several judges may sit together as the Court of Criminal Appeal
- Hears civil cases involving any amount of money
- Several judges may sit together to hear appeals against one Supreme Court judge
- Highest state court
- Decides civil and the most serious criminal cases
- Hears appeals against Local Court and District Court decisions

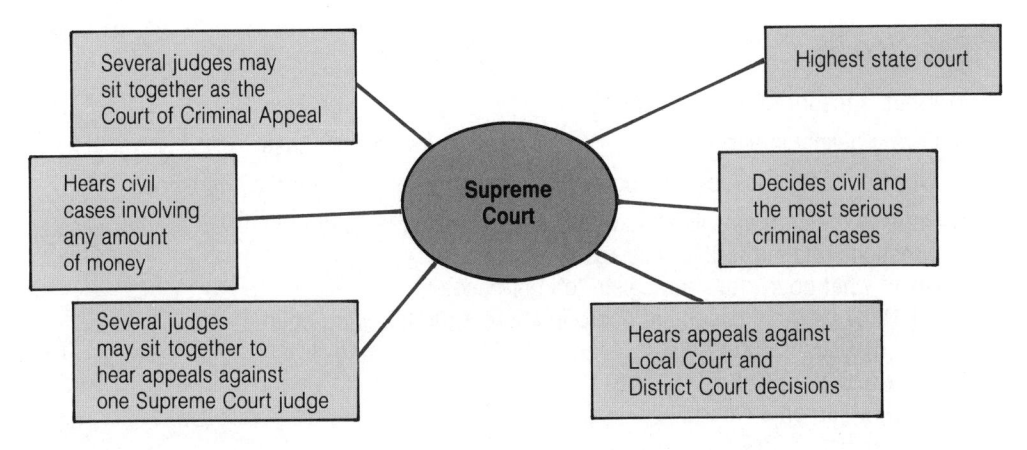

The Supreme Court

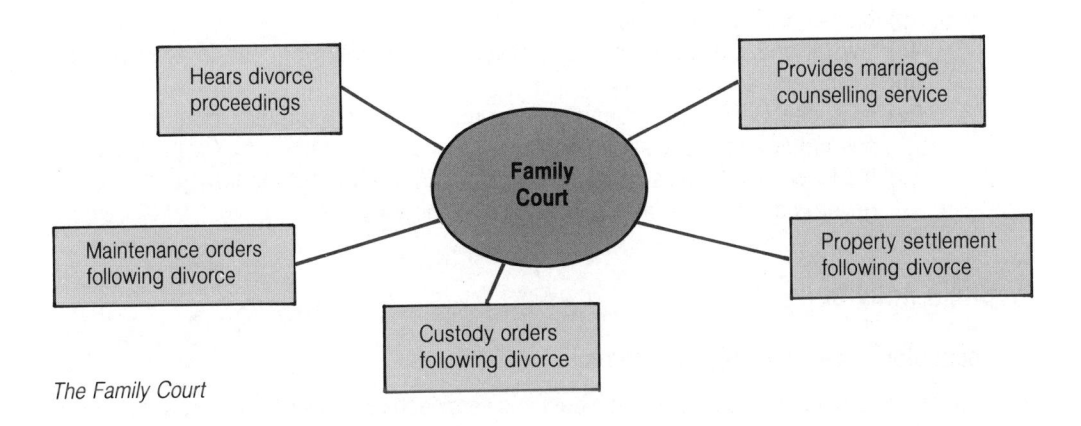

The Family Court

- Hears divorce proceedings
- Maintenance orders following divorce
- Custody orders following divorce
- Provides marriage counselling service
- Property settlement following divorce

The Family Court

The High Court

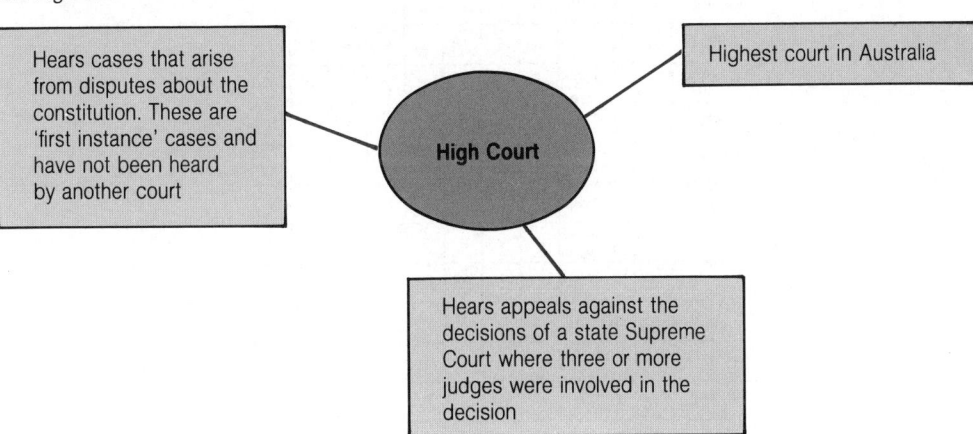

- Hears cases that arise from disputes about the constitution. These are 'first instance' cases and have not been heard by another court
- Highest court in Australia
- Hears appeals against the decisions of a state Supreme Court where three or more judges were involved in the decision

Exercise 5F

1. What is meant by the judiciary?
2. Give a definition and example of a civil case and a criminal case.
3. What is meant by a 'closed' court? For what type of case are they common?
4. Refer to the diagrams illustrating the Australian court system to answer the following questions relating to the judiciary.
   (a) In what court does a magistrate hear cases?
   (b) What types of cases are heard in each of the following courts:
      (i) Local Courts
      (ii) District Court
      (iii) Supreme Court
      (iv) Family Court
      (v) High Court?
   (c) Which court is *never* a court of appeal? Why not?
   (d) In which courts would the following matters be heard:
      (i) theft of $1500 (name the lower court involved)
      (ii) lawsuit of $20 000 against a newspaper (name the lower court involved)
      (iii) truancy by a 12-year-old
      (iv) an appeal by someone found guilty of murder in the Supreme Court, in which one judge and a jury sat in judgement
      (v) the New South Wales government disputing the right of the federal government to pass laws concerning off-shore oil?

Skills activities

Vocabulary exercise—hidden words

Find the word in the puzzle below which best answers each clue given. The words may be written in any direction, including horizontal, vertical, diagonal and backwards.

C	R	I	M	I	N	A	L	X	A	B	N
P	O	F	D	G	S	R	B	E	A	H	O
D	C	L	O	S	E	D	O	M	H	F	I
E	E	E	K	D	I	S	T	R	I	C	T
M	C	G	F	E	A	T	L	E	S	S	U
E	I	I	D	Y	L	I	M	A	F	B	T
R	L	S	S	H	I	G	H	K	I	O	I
P	O	L	E	R	V	D	E	T	L	I	T
U	P	A	R	L	I	A	M	E	N	T	S
S	E	T	A	C	C	A	D	E	I	G	N
G	H	E	T	U	T	A	T	S	O	F	O
D	I	P	O	N	B	F	R	E	S	W	C

Clues

1. The Australian government and each of the state governments has houses of parliament which _____ or make laws.
2. Laws passed by parliament are called _____ law.
3. In Australia laws are made by the _____ and by the courts.
4. A _____ lists the rules by which a government will be run.
5. A _____ case involves an offence against the law and is punishable by a fine, or imprisonment, or both.
6. A _____ case involves a dispute between individuals which a court seeks to settle.
7. A Children's Court may be _____ to the public.
8. The best-known law enforcement officers are the _____.
9. The _____ Court hears most serious criminal cases and any civil cases involving less than $100 000.
10. The _____ Court hears divorce proceedings and makes custody, property and maintenance orders.
11. Cases that arise from disputes about the constitution are heard in the ____ Court.
12. The highest state court is the _____ Court.

Newspaper research

Refer to newspapers to try to find a selection of cases which have been heard in a variety of courts. Paste these articles into your notebook. Underline the parts which show

(a) the type of case involved
(b) the court involved
(c) whether it was a civil or criminal matter
(d) the court decision
(e) whether or not there will be an appeal.

Research

Find the address of your closest Magistrates' Court (Local Court) and the closest Family Court. Write them in your notebook.

Class visit

Try to arrange a class visit to a court house. You may be able to see a case being 'heard'.

Law enforcement

The best-known law enforcement officers are the police. Each state in Australia employs police to enforce its own local laws. Federal laws, such as those on taxation, customs and immigration, are enforced by the Australian federal police, who are employed by the federal government.

The rights of the police

The police have the right to stop anyone and ask questions, although in most cases the person does not have to answer. In certain cases the police have the right to stop and search people in the street, for example if they suspect the person has broken a customs regulation or is carrying prohibited weapons or stolen goods.

When do police have the right to search people in the street?

The police do not have a general right to search private property. They can get search warrants to look for a particular item, however, and they are also entitled to search the premises in which a person is arrested. Motor vehicles usually cannot be searched without the owner's consent. The exception is if the police officer suspects that the vehicle contains firearms, drugs, stolen goods, goods on which customs duty should be paid or similar illegal goods.

The police also have the right to keep as evidence items they have found in their searches. They are even able to keep items which belong to other innocent people. A car which was stolen and then used as the getaway car in a robbery can be kept and used as evidence at the trial.

The rights of an arrested person

Anyone being questioned by the police is not necessarily allowed to make a phone call. People who go voluntarily to the police station to 'assist with inquiries' should call their solicitor *before* going to the police station, just in case they are refused permission to contact their solicitor. The person arrested must be told by the police officer

Why do police have the right to confiscate items they have found in their searches?

- that he or she is under arrest
- exactly on what charge he or she has been arrested.

If you have not been told by the police that you are under arrest, then you do not have to give any information apart from your name and address. You cannot be forced to go to the police station if you have not been arrested.

If the person arrested is under sixteen years special conditions apply. Before the police ask any questions they must ensure that the child's parents, guardian or another idependent witness is present.

Other law enforcement officers

Other law enforcement officers include customs officials, local council inspectors such as health and building inspectors, and state government officers such as parking police and railway inspectors.

Exercise 5G

1. Who are the main law enforcement officers in our society?
2. Give two examples of law enforced by the Australian federal police.
3. Under what circumstances do police have the right to stop and search people in the street?

4. Under what circumstances do police have the right to search your home?
5. Why would you be wise to ring your solicitor *before* going to the police station to 'assist with inquiries'?
6. What information *must* you give the police if you are arrested?
7. What special right does a child under the age of sixteen years have when he or she is arrested?
8. List four types of law enforcement officers apart from the police.

Skills activities

Research

Find out the address and telephone number of your closest police station. Write them in your notebook.

Class visit

Arrange a class visit from a member of your local police force. Ask him or her to give your class a talk on topics such as the following.
1. What you should do if you are arrested
   (a) when you are innocent
   (b) when you are guilty of whatever you have been accused of.
2. What you should do if you are fairly sure a neighbour is doing something illegal.
3. Life is so bad at home you feel you have to leave.
4. How you go about reporting a crime.
5. What happens at a police station when a person is arrested and/or brought in for questioning about a serious crime.
6. Ways to safeguard yourself from attack by someone else.
7. Training for the police force.
8. Any other topic that interests you about law enforcement.

Write a report

Watch an American police show on television. In your notebook write a short report pointing out the differences between American and Australian police methods.

A court case

People who are arrested for breaking the law often have to go to court. Depending on what type of court it is, the case is heard by a magistrate, a judge or a judge and jury. The *defendant* (person accused of a crime) is found either guilty or not guilty. If the defendant is found guilty, a punishment is given. The punishment is usually either imprisonment or a fine, or a combination of both.

If you were accused of a crime and were under the age of eighteen years you would be tried in a Children's Court. When a proper Children's Court is unavailable, a Magistrate's Court or Local Court (formerly called a Court of Petty Sessions) is used. When the Magistrate's Court is used as a Children's Court it becomes a 'closed court'. Members of the public and the press cannot enter. The police in the court do not usually wear their gun or their uniform.

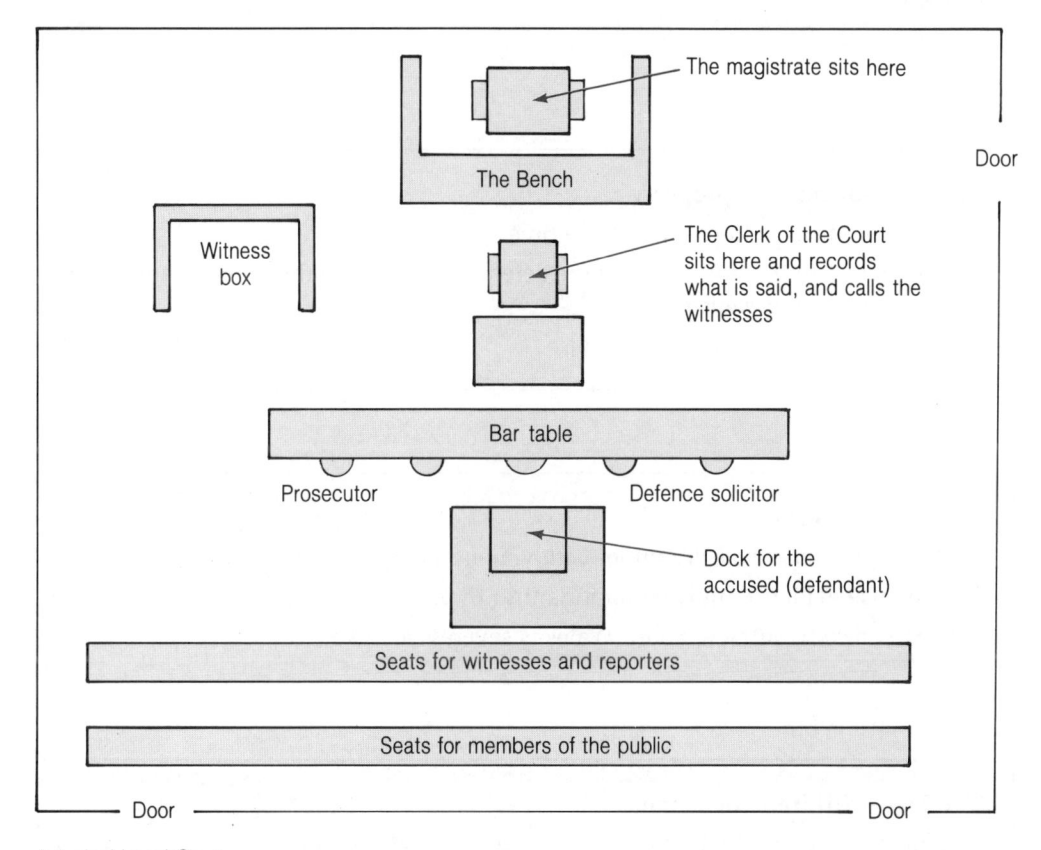

A typical Local Court

Skill activity—a mock trial

You will need to set up your classroom like a Children's Court. The outline of the story is below. The laws relating to the case are explained. Choose members of your class to play the roles. The class members who are not given a role can assist the main players in the trial.

Only an outline of the trial is given. Each player will need to build up his or her role by working out relevant questions to ask and so on.

The story

Two twelve-year-olds stayed back at school and spray-gunned the principal's office. They sprayed graffiti over the walls and desk and smashed several windows. The caretaker saw the students leaving the hallway of the administration block at 5 p.m. and was suspicious. When he checked the area he found the damaged office. Having recognised the students he then telephoned the local police station. The police went to the students' homes and interviewed them. They were later arrested and charged with malicious damage to property.

The law—damage to property

1. *Malicious damage* to property is a crime.
2. The prosecutor has to prove that the defendants damaged the property and did it *intentionally* and *maliciously*.

Maximum penalty is seven years gaol

The law—perjury

1. If you give *false evidence* under *oath* you are guilty of perjury.
2. The false evidence must be important to the case.

Maximum penalty in New South Wales is seven years gaol

The law—children and crime

1. Children younger than ten cannot be charged with an offence.
2. The law *presumes* that children between the ages of ten and fourteen cannot *intend* to commit a crime because they do not know when they do wrong.
3. If the *prosecution* can present evidence to prove that a young person knew that what he or she was doing was wrong then the presumption can be overturned.

Before you begin to plan your mock trial you will need to list each of the *italicised* words (from the text above) in your notebook. Use a dictionary to find precise meanings of these terms. Write the meanings next to the terms.

Below is the information you will need for each person appearing in the mock trial. Remember to give each person an assistant to help them in their preparation for the trial.

The magistrate

1. Decides if, on the evidence, the young people charged
   (a) have damaged the property
   (b) intended to damage the property
   (c) maliciously damaged the property
   (d) knew that their actions in damaging the property were wrong.
2. Considers each young person separately.
3. Decides the penalty as set down by law.

The police prosecutor

1. Presents the evidence of what took place to the court. You will need to call the witnesses (the principal, the caretaker and the police constable) to the witness box and question them about what happened. For example you may ask the police constable to describe the condition of the principal's office when he or she was first called to the school.
2. Sums up the prosecution's case.

The defendants' solicitor (or solicitors)

1. Explains the clients' point of view. You will need to:
   (a) Cross-examine each witness called by the prosecution. This means that you have to question witnesses about what they have told the police prosecutor. For example, you may ask the police constable whether the defendants had told him or her that they intended to damage the office.
   (b) Present their own witnesses, including character witnesses for the defendants.
   (c) Sum up their clients' case.

The defendants

1. You are very scared as you have been in trouble at school for the last six months.
2. You really intended to make a huge mess in the principal's office.
3. You have decided to claim that as you are both only twelve years old you didn't know that you were wrong to enter the principal's office and cause damage. You also claim that you went to the office to talk to the principal but found his door unlocked. You happened to have the paint with you (left over from an art lesson) and got carried away.

The police constable

1. You were telephoned at about 5.10 p.m. by the caretaker.
2. When you arrived at the school the caretaker gave you a description and the names of the two young people he had seen leaving the hallway of the administration block.
3. You then went to the homes of the two young people and interviewed them.
4. You asked each of them if he or she had damaged the principal's office.
5. One young person didn't answer and the other mumbled that he did do it but that he didn't mean to.
6. You arrested the two young people and charged them with malicious damage to property.

Witness no. 1—the principal

1. You are the principal of the school.
2. You left your office at 3.45 p.m.
3. When you left the office the desks, walls and windows were in good order.
4. When you were called back to the school by the caretaker and the police constable at 6 p.m. you found that graffiti had been sprayed on the desk and walls and that windows had been smashed.

Witness no. 2—the caretaker

1. You saw the two young people running from the hallway of the administration block at about 5 p.m.
2. You saw the two people clearly and identified them.
3. You then checked the administration block and found the damage done to the principal's office.
4. You telephoned the police.

Character witnesses for the defendants

It is your job to provide a character reference for one or both of the defendants. You may be the local newsagent who employs one of them doing a newspaper run, perhaps a minister of the church attended by one or both of them and so on.

The court case

The people in attendance at the court include:
- the magistrate
- clerk of the court
- court constable
- police prosecutor
- police witnesses
- the young people (defendants)
- their solicitor/solicitors
- their parents
- their character witnesses.

The procedure of the court case

1. The names of the young people (defendants) are called outside the court. This is usually done by the court constable.
2. The defendants and their parents then go into the court. The court constable tells the magistrate who is present.
3. The charge is read by the magistrate and the defendants are each asked if he or she admits or denies the charge. In other words each is asked if he or she is guilty or not guilty.
4. Both defendants plead not guilty.
5. The prosecution witnesses are called in turn. Each gives evidence under oath. They are cross-examined by the defendants or their solicitors.
6. The magistrate has to decide whether or not there is a case for the young people to answer. If it is decided that there is not, the charge is dismissed and the defendants are allowed to go free. If, on the other hand, the magistrate decides there is a case, the defendants tell their side of the story.

7. The defendants may decide to say nothing. If they do decide to give evidence they must do so under oath.
8. The defendants' witnesses are called to give their evidence under oath. They are then cross-examined by the prosecutor.
9. The magistrate then listens to addresses (speeches) from the prosecution and the defendants (or their solicitors). These addresses are to remind the magistrate of the positive evidence of each side.
10. The magistrate must then decide if he or she is convinced *beyond reasonable doubt* that the defendants committed the offence. Remember that the magistrate must also be convinced that the defendants *intended* to damage the property and that they *maliciously* damaged the property. If the magistrate is not satisfied with the prosecution's case, the charge is dismissed and the defendants are freed.
11. If the magistrate finds the defendants guilty, he or she will consider any reports about the young people and will listen to what they have to say. The magistrate may then make one of the following orders regarding the defendants:
    (a) release on probation
    (b) commit to the care of a person willing to accept the responsibility
    (c) commit to the care of an institution
    (d) commit to a wardship (the young people become wards of the state)
    (e) commit to an institution and then suspend the committal (this means that the young people are placed on a bond and don't have to go to an institution unless they come before the court again)
    (f) deal with the young people as if they were adults—in other words according to the law for the crime.

Revision activity

New terms

In your notebook put the heading 'Important new terms and their meanings'. Copy the first term in List A into your notebook and select its correct meaning from the definitions in List B. Continue until you have listed each term and its meaning.

List A
Administration, anarchy, appeal, civil case, 'closed' court, common law, constitution, criminal case, District Court, Family Court, High Court, judiciary, laws, legislate, Local Court, statute law, Supreme Court.

List B
1. Rules that are binding on the people in a certain community
2. The absence of government in society—a condition of lawlessness and confusion exists

3. The basic laws within which the government can act
4. Make laws in a house of parliament
5. Laws passed by parliament
6. Law courts which interpret the laws made by parliament, decide disputes between individuals and 'try' people accused of a crime
7. Decisions of a court which have come to be accepted as laws
8. The people who enforce or carry out the law
9. A dispute between individuals which is settled in a court
10. An offence against the law which is heard in a court and is punishable by a fine, imprisonment or both
11. A court which is not open to the public
12. When a case is heard again in a higher court with the aim of reversing the earlier decision
13. The court which hears and decides minor civil and criminal cases
14. The court which hears and decides matters on appeal from Local Courts, civil cases which involve up to $100 000 and criminal cases such as rape and armed robbery
15. The highest state court which hears and decides the most serious civil and criminal matters and hears appeals against Local Court and District Court decisions
16. The court which hears divorce proceedings and makes decisions about the custody of children, maintenance and property settlement
17. The highest court in Australia, which hears cases that arise from disputes about the constitution and appeals against some Supreme Court decisions

6 Government

Every group of people needs law and organisation. This is true of a playgroup, a church youth group, a family, a school, and a whole country. Societies need rules. They need people with authority to see that the rules are obeyed.

The government makes laws which set limits on the way we behave. It has set up a system to *enforce* the law. Police officers, local council inspectors and customs officials make sure we obey the laws. The government has set up a court system with judges and juries to decide whether the law has been broken and to impose punishments.

In Australia we *elect* people to govern us. This type of government, elected or chosen by the people who will be governed, is called *democracy*. Some countries have a system of government in which one person rules or governs. This is a *dictatorship*.

Many Eastern European countries have replaced their communist dictatorships with democracies in recent years. This has been done by allowing more political parties to be formed. These new parties can oppose the communist party in elections.

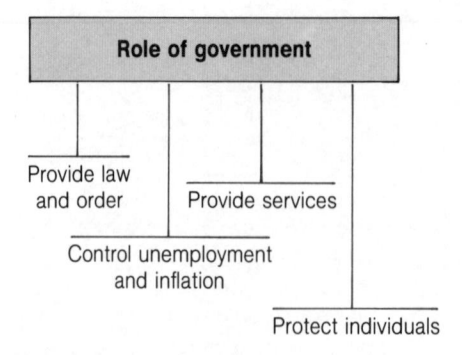

Role of government
- Provide law and order
- Provide services
- Control unemployment and inflation
- Protect individuals

The role of government in Australia

Governments have traditionally provided the services of law and order and defence. As communities have grown their wants and needs have become greater. Sometimes we

The government makes laws and has set up a system to enforce the law

want the government to go into competition with private firms and run its own businesses. The old and the ill need to be protected. Consumers need to be protected in their dealings with business firms. Pollution and traffic congestion need to be reduced. We now look to the government to do these things for us.

Law and order

In any society the government has always provided a system of law and order. In today's modern Australian society we have many laws that have existed for hundreds, even thousands of years. Individuals are not allowed to murder or to steal. The law allows us to marry, to divorce, to sue another person and to make a will. Other laws are newer. We have laws to make sure that workers are paid a fair wage. There are laws to cover the rights and duties of people and firms who enter into contracts. Laws cover the way in which businesses operate so that, for example, it is an offence for them to empty toxic waste products into rivers.

Controlling unemployment and inflation

The government tries to make sure most people can get work and that prices do not rise too quickly. Prices must be kept under control so we can afford to buy goods and services without needing large pay rises.

Providing services

Business firms cannot provide some services because they cannot charge for their use. Some examples are defence, parks, roads, dams and bridges. The government taxes people and uses the money to provide these services.

Sometimes the government competes with private firms to provide goods and services. Competition often helps to improve standards, raise quality and lower prices. The New South Wales state government runs the Government Insurance Office in competition with private insurance companies and the federal government runs Qantas in competition with overseas airlines. State governments run hospitals and schools as services, but private and church schools and hospitals compete with the government institutions. We have a *choice*.

Sometimes the government has a monopoly. It is the *only* producer of some goods or services. Most railways in Australia are run as state government monopolies.

Protecting individuals

In our society the government protects people who are in need of help. Some old people and invalids receive special help in the form of a money income (pension), free hospital and medical treatment, public transport fare concessions, cheaper telephone rentals and reduced council rates.

Laws prevent firms from making false claims for their goods

Laws protect the consumer from certain actions by firms. Firms cannot make false claims for their goods when advertising them. They cannot continue to sell certain goods such as toys which are proven to be dangerous. In other cases the goods may have to carry a warning, for example, that the product is a health hazard or highly flammable.

Protecting the environment

Governments have brought in laws to help control pollution. Firms may not dump toxic waste products into rivers or seas. Noise pollution controls save people from having to suffer from excessive noise made by their neighbours or nearby industries. New cars must use lead-free petrol.

Noise levels cut back

The company in charge of construction work on the Happy Harry site in Balmain has agreed to reduce the number of hours during which heavy equipment is used. The company has agreed to work to conditions set down by Leichhardt Council.

The company has agreed to restrict jack hammering and rock breaking to 7.30am to 9.30am and 11.30am to 3.30pm until the work is finished. The site is beside Birchgrove Public School.

The construction company applied to build a sound barrier along the borders of the site. Council deferred this plan to allow engineers to look at other ways of solving the noise problem. Council felt the wall would not solve the problem, would block views and would be an eyesore. The Project Manager for the site said the company was happy to agree with the conditions set by council.

Exercise 6A

1. Why do all societies need a government?
2. What is meant by democracy? Name three democracies other than Australia.
3. Why does a modern society such as Australia need the government to supply more than just the traditional services? Name three 'roles' of the government that could be regarded as newer roles.
4. Give two laws made by the government to control
   (a) individuals
   (b) business activities.
5. Some laws prevent us doing things. Others allow us to do things. Write down two things that laws *allow* us to do.
6. Why is it important for the government to control unemployment and inflation?
7. Why is it better for the government (rather than private businesses) to provide some services? List five of these services.
8. Why does the government sometimes compete with private businesses? List three examples of businesses with which the government is in competition. Set your answer out in a table, as shown.

Government business	Private business
1.	
2.	
3.	

9. What is a monopoly? List three government monopolies and find out whether each is owned by the Australian government, a state government or local government.

Government monopoly	Level of government
1.	
2.	
3.	

10. List six ways in which the government helps age pensioners.
11. List three pollution controls imposed by the government. Why are they needed?

Skills activities

Library research

1. Use the library to find the names of three countries that are or have until recently been ruled as dictatorships.
2. (a) Find out the figures for unemployment and inflation
    (i) in March this year
    (ii) in March last year.
   (b) Briefly explain what these figures mean.
   (c) Have conditions improved?

Newspaper research

Find a newspaper clipping which discusses a new law which has recently been or is going to be introduced by a government in Australia. Paste it into your notebook. Explain why the law has been introduced and what it hopes to achieve.

Interview and lecturette

Read the newspaper clipping entitled 'Noise levels cut back'. Appoint two or three members of your class to meet with the building inspector for your local council. The members are to interview the inspector about the work he or she does for the council. In particular they should find out how the council works to enforce building codes and noise pollution controls.

To prepare for the interview the class should help make up a list of questions for the members to ask the inspector. After the interview the members are to prepare and give a talk to the class about the information they obtained.

Specialisation in government

Specialisation means that an individual, a firm, an industry, a region or a government concentrates on one type of activity. Government in Australia is divided into three levels. Each level specialises in the areas to which it is best suited.

The federal system

Australia's government is organised on a federal system. This system is also used in the United States of America, Canada and the Federation of Malaysia. Under a federal system the country is divided into states. The power to govern is shared by the federal (or Australian) parliament and the state parliaments. In Australia each of the states is divided further into local council areas.

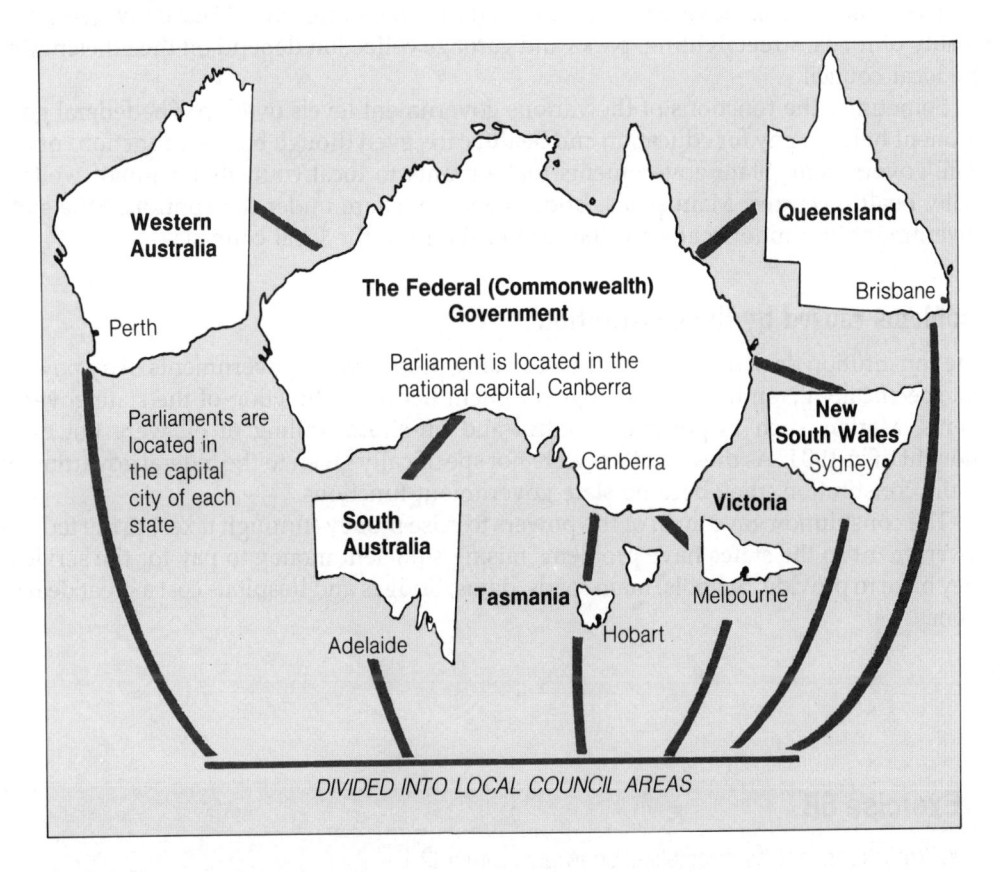

The federal system of government

The constitution

When Australia received self-government from Britain on 1 January 1901, a constitution was drawn up. The Australian constitution is a list of rules for governing Australia. Certain responsibilities were given to the federal government. The state governments took over all the powers not actually given to the federal government. Each of the states has its own constitution.

The tasks of each level of government

The main idea behind a federal system, with one national government and several state governments, is that each level deals with the matters it is most suited to handle. The federal government controls matters which affect everyone equally, whatever state they live in. Examples of these matters are defence, immigration and currency.

Each state has its own parliament. It can make laws on the matters it controls. States control hospitals, education, transport, police, water supply and electricity.

The local councils have power in the matters which most affect our daily lives. The quality of roads, street lighting, parks and garbage collection depend on the efficiency of the local council.

Sometimes the functions of the various government levels overlap. The federal government helps to pay for education and health care, even though both are functions of the state government. State governments make grants to local councils for infant welfare (baby health) centres. Main roads, bridges and dams are under the control of the state government but minor roads are the responsibility of the local council.

Problems caused by the constitution

The constitution drawn up in 1901 causes many problems for governments. Any powers not specifically given to the federal government became a function of the state governments. Matters such as pollution control and off-shore drilling of oil were not even thought of in 1901. As these matters were not specifically given to the federal government in the constitution, they became state government functions.

The constitution gave most of the powers to raise money (through taxes) to the federal government so the states have problems raising sufficient money to pay for the services they have to provide. Schools, main roads, dams, bridges and hospitals cost a great deal of money.

Exercise 6B

1. What is meant by specialisation in government?
2. What is meant by a federal system of government? Name four countries which use this system.
3. What types of matters are controlled by the federal government? Give four examples.
4. What types of matters are controlled by the state governments? Give four examples.
5. What types of matters are controlled by the local governments? Give four examples.
6. Give two examples of areas where the functions of the federal government and state governments overlap.
7. Give two examples of areas where the functions of the state governments and local governments overlap.
8. Why does the Australian constitution cause some problems to governments?

Skills activities

Newspaper research

1. Find a newspaper clipping which refers to a matter that is the responsibility of the federal government. Paste it into your notebook and next to it write the names of
   (a) the government department responsible for this matter
   (b) the government minister responsible for it.
2. Find a newspaper clipping which refers to a matter that is the responsibility of the state government. Follow the same procedure as in Activity 1.
3. Find a newspaper clipping which refers to a matter that is the responsibility of the local government and paste it into your notebook. Does this function overlap with a state government function? Write your answer in your notebook and explain why they overlap.

Local government

New South Wales is divided into 176 city, municipal and shire councils. In 1919 the New South Wales parliament drew up a list of rules (or laws) for local councils. It is called the *Local Government Act*. The Minister for Local Government is the member of the state parliament responsible for making sure that councils obey these laws.

Local councils

City and municipal councils

City and municipal councils are similar. City councils look after the large cities such as Sydney, Newcastle and Wollongong. Municipal councils look after larger country towns such as Moree, and the suburbs surrounding the cities. Municipal councils around Sydney include Leichhardt, Marrickville, Drummoyne and Waverley.

A municipality is divided into a number of areas called *wards*. Each ward elects *aldermen* to the local council. The term aldermen is used for both male and female representatives. The aldermen who have been elected usually choose the *mayor*. He or she becomes the head of the council.

Shire councils

Shire councils usually govern the outer suburbs of large cities and the rural areas of the state. Many shires are sparsely populated, although some of them do have large numbers of people. Shire councils near Sydney include the Sutherland Shire and the Baulkham Hills Shire. Country shires include the Boomi Shire and the Boolooroo Shire, both of which border the Moree Municipality. Shire council areas are usually much larger than municipal council areas.

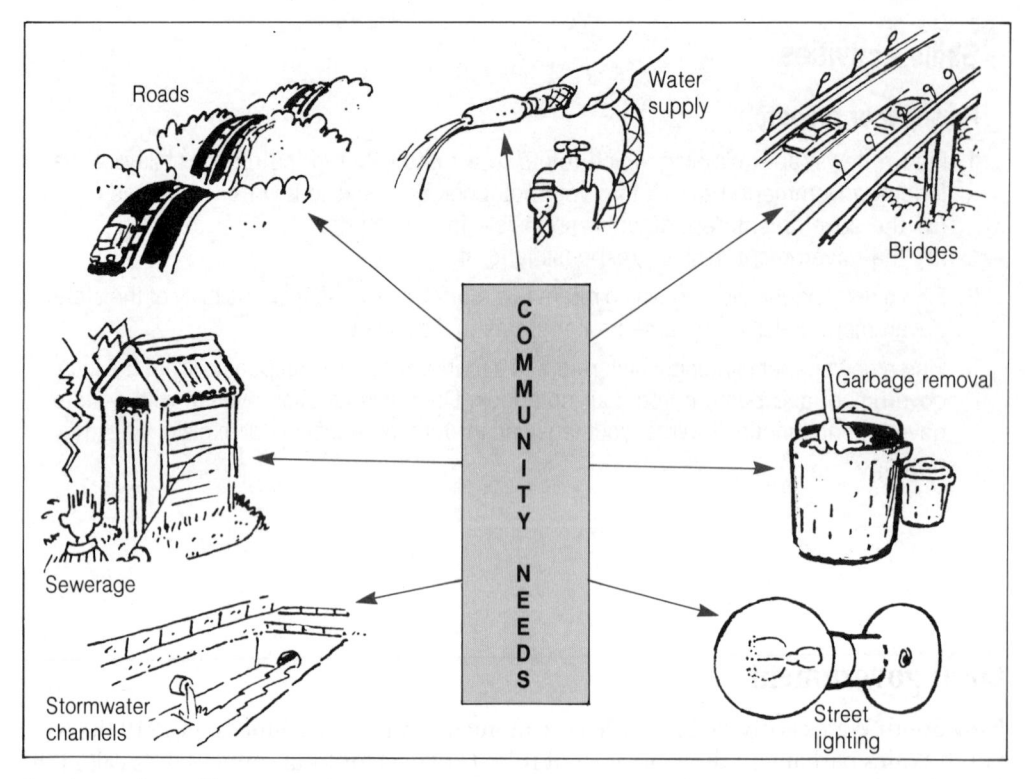

Local councils provide many services

Shires are divided into *ridings*. Residents and landowners in the riding elect *shire councillors*. The shire councillors usually choose a *shire president* to head the council. Sometimes the shire president (or the mayor, in a municipality) is chosen directly by the voters at the time of the election.

Some council services

Councils provide many services. The most important ones are shown in the diagram above.

Examples of council services	
■ litter control ■ tree planting ■ tree preservation ■ immunisation services ■ waste disposal ■ dog control ■ social workers ■ school holiday activities	■ home help for sick people ■ child care centres ■ meals on wheels ■ senior citizens centres ■ library services ■ baby health centres ■ buildings for use by local groups ■ sports facilities, e.g. ovals

Council wants to ban bull terriers

Leichhardt council has announced that it will try to ban cross breed bull terriers from the municipality. This action follows a report to council of a vicious attack by a cross breed bull terrier on a family cat.

The council asked its chief health and building inspector to find out whether it could ban them. He reported back to council last week. Apparently the council does not have the power to exclude any dog from registration. But the council was not satisfied.

Council plans to lobby the State Government to have the animals banned. Some residents have expressed anger and concern over the council proposals. They have claimed that many other breeds of animals are also dangerous.

Other residents have suggested that all dogs over 5kg. should wear muzzles outside their yard to protect other animals and children.

Local government elections

Every three years elections are held in New South Wales to choose the members of councils. Voters include all people over eighteen years old who own property in the area (and are therefore *ratepayers*) and all *residents* over eighteen years old. It is compulsory for residents to vote at council elections. People who are eligible to vote and who fail to do so may be fined.

All government elections in New South Wales are by *secret ballot*. Voters are given a ballot paper which has a list of all the people seeking election to the council. Voters choose the candidate (or candidates) they would like elected. Candidates' supporters often give voters pamphlets to show them how to vote for their people.

Voters fill in their ballot paper in a *polling booth*. No other person can see how they mark their papers. They then place them in a *ballot box* which is kept locked until the end of voting.

Exercise 6C

1. List five services provided by modern councils.
2. What is the difference between a shire and a municipality?
3. What is the difference between a shire president and a mayor?
4. How often are local government elections held?
5. Who is entitled to vote in local government elections?

'How to vote' card

OPEN COUNCIL

How to Vote for Tom Dan

- [1] **Tom Dan**
- [ ] W. Goodman
- [3] Dianne Minnis
- [ ] P. Murphy
- [2] Sue Stock
- [ ] C. Vecchio-Nepita

Authorised by T. Archibald 64 Johnston St Annandale, and printed by AVIWEB 181 Glebe Point Road Glebe.

Skills activities

Research project
The following questions refer to your own local council. Use your library, visit the council chambers, interview your aldermen or shire councillors and/or read the information booklets put out by the council to find the answers.
  (a) What is the name of your local government area?
  (b) What is the name of the ward or riding in which you live?
  (c) Name the alderman/councillor who represents your ward/riding.
  (d) Name your mayor/shire president.
  (e) What is the address of the council chambers?
  (f) What does the local council do to improve your area?
  (g) Where do people cast their votes for your local council elections?

Class discussion
Read the newspaper clipping entitled 'Council wants to ban bull terriers'. As a class discuss the rights of dog owners to enjoy the company of their animals as opposed to the rights of other residents who want to enjoy a safe and clean environment.

Local government income

Councils receive most of their income from rates. People and firms who own property in the council area pay rates on the value of their land. All land has a 'land value' placed on it by the Valuer General's Department. The value of any buildings, fences or other improvements is not taken into account. Each year the landowner has to pay a few cents for each dollar of the land value as rates to the council.

Example
The council has set a rate of 1.5 cents in each dollar of the land value. A property has a land value of $50 000. The rates are 50 000 × 1.5 cents, or $750.

Other council income is obtained by charging entry fees to swimming pools, renting out halls and other council property, and charging property owners for council work such as kerbing and guttering. Councils also borrow money, and they are given grants of money by the state and federal governments.

Are rates just?
Rates are paid by *landowners* in the council area. People and firms who rent property in the municipality or shire do not directly pay anything towards council costs of supplying services, yet they get the benefit of these services. On the other hand there are many landowners who live outside the council area who pay rates but do not benefit from the council services.

Many people believe that there is no justice in the way rates are worked out. The land value depends, to a certain extent, on where the land is located in the municipality or

SHIRE OF BROOKSHAM - RATE NOTICE FOR YEAR 1990

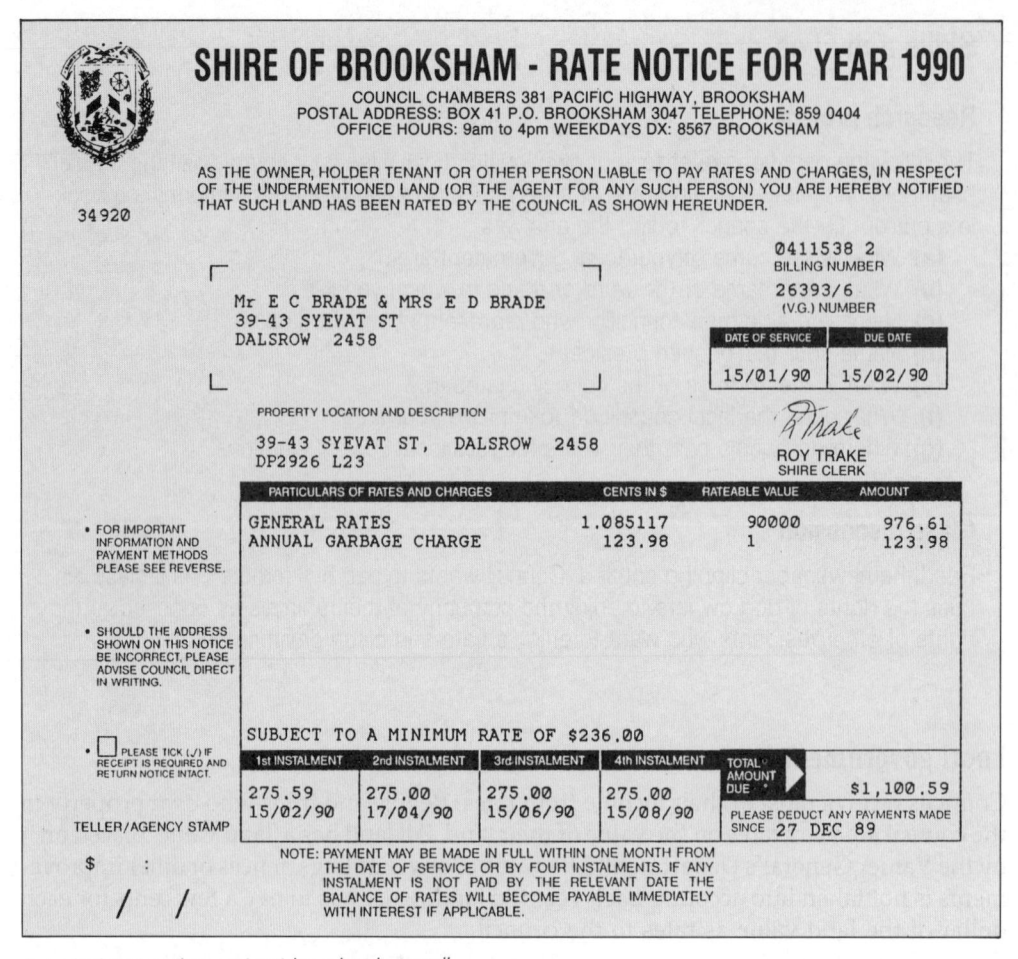

COUNCIL CHAMBERS 381 PACIFIC HIGHWAY, BROOKSHAM
POSTAL ADDRESS: BOX 41 P.O. BROOKSHAM 3047 TELEPHONE: 859 0404
OFFICE HOURS: 9am to 4pm WEEKDAYS DX: 8567 BROOKSHAM

AS THE OWNER, HOLDER TENANT OR OTHER PERSON LIABLE TO PAY RATES AND CHARGES, IN RESPECT OF THE UNDERMENTIONED LAND (OR THE AGENT FOR ANY SUCH PERSON) YOU ARE HEREBY NOTIFIED THAT SUCH LAND HAS BEEN RATED BY THE COUNCIL AS SHOWN HEREUNDER.

34920

Mr E C BRADE & MRS E D BRADE
39-43 SYEVAT ST
DALSROW 2458

BILLING NUMBER: 0411538 2
(V.G.) NUMBER: 26393/6
DATE OF SERVICE: 15/01/90
DUE DATE: 15/02/90

PROPERTY LOCATION AND DESCRIPTION
39-43 SYEVAT ST, DALSROW 2458
DP2926 L23

ROY TRAKE
SHIRE CLERK

- FOR IMPORTANT INFORMATION AND PAYMENT METHODS PLEASE SEE REVERSE.
- SHOULD THE ADDRESS SHOWN ON THIS NOTICE BE INCORRECT, PLEASE ADVISE COUNCIL DIRECT IN WRITING.
- PLEASE TICK (✓) IF RECEIPT IS REQUIRED AND RETURN NOTICE INTACT.

TELLER/AGENCY STAMP

PARTICULARS OF RATES AND CHARGES	CENTS IN $	RATEABLE VALUE	AMOUNT
GENERAL RATES	1.085117	90000	976.61
ANNUAL GARBAGE CHARGE	123.98	1	123.98

SUBJECT TO A MINIMUM RATE OF $236.00

1st INSTALMENT	2nd INSTALMENT	3rd INSTALMENT	4th INSTALMENT	TOTAL AMOUNT DUE
275.59 15/02/90	275.00 17/04/90	275.00 15/06/90	275.00 15/08/90	$1,100.59

PLEASE DEDUCT ANY PAYMENTS MADE SINCE 27 DEC 89

NOTE: PAYMENT MAY BE MADE IN FULL WITHIN ONE MONTH FROM THE DATE OF SERVICE OR BY FOUR INSTALMENTS. IF ANY INSTALMENT IS NOT PAID BY THE RELEVANT DATE THE BALANCE OF RATES WILL BECOME PAYABLE IMMEDIATELY WITH INTEREST IF APPLICABLE.

A typical rate notice sent out by a local council

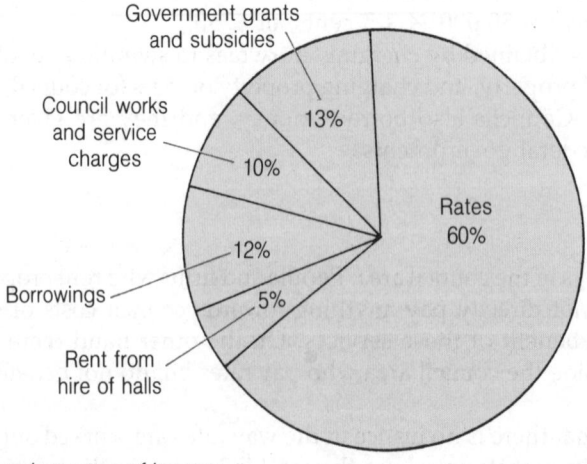

- Rates 60%
- Government grants and subsidies 13%
- Council works and service charges 10%
- Borrowings 12%
- Rent from hire of halls 5%

A council's main sources of income

shire. Land with a water view will have a higher value than land located near a noisy, dirty factory. The owners of these two properties will pay different amounts in rates yet they receive the same services from the council.

Alternative ways to raise money

There are three other ways open to council to raise funds.

1. Everyone who *lives* in the municipality, as well as landowners, could pay a tax towards financing the council. One problem is that it would be difficult to keep track of all residents, especially those who stay only for a short time. It might also be hard to force them to pay the money they owe.
2. Rates can be worked out according to how many adults live in a house. A household shared by five adults would pay five times the rates that a house with only one adult would pay. This system assumes that a house with five adults would use five times the services that a house with only one adult would use. England tried to introduce this method of working out rates. It was called a *poll tax*. It was a very unpopular tax and it was soon abandoned.
3. An extra charge, called a *surcharge*, could be added to income tax and then passed on to the councils. In this way all employed people would share the cost of council services.

Local government expenditure

Municipal and shire councils spend their money on providing many services. The most important ones are shown below.

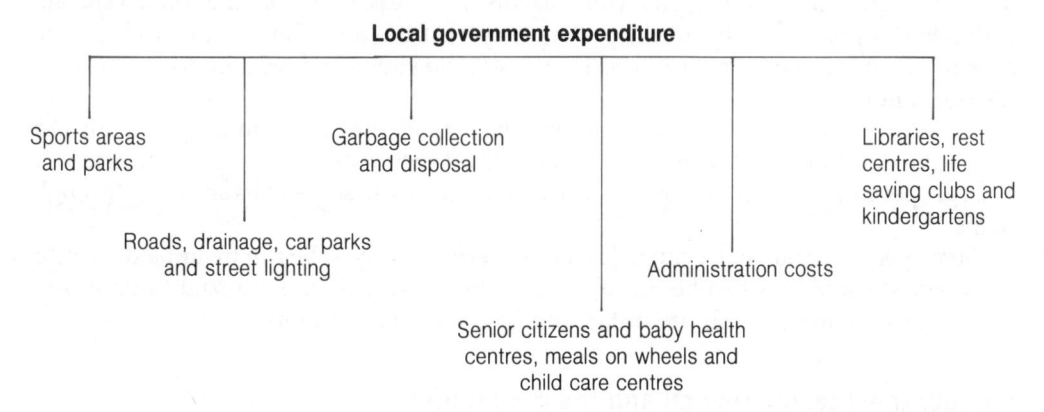

Local government expenditure

- Sports areas and parks
- Roads, drainage, car parks and street lighting
- Garbage collection and disposal
- Senior citizens and baby health centres, meals on wheels and child care centres
- Administration costs
- Libraries, rest centres, life saving clubs and kindergartens

Some of the administration costs incurred by council involve providing the following services:
- giving permission for new buildings, to make sure builders obey all the building laws
- controlling town planning
- providing services such as health inspection of shops and restaurants to make sure conditions are hygienic for serving food
- paying council staff.

Welfare services

Some of the services provided by council are welfare services. Most councils now provide home nursing services and meals on wheels for elderly residents. They provide clinics and preschool kindergartens. They usually provide immunisation against diphtheria, whooping cough, tetanus and polio.

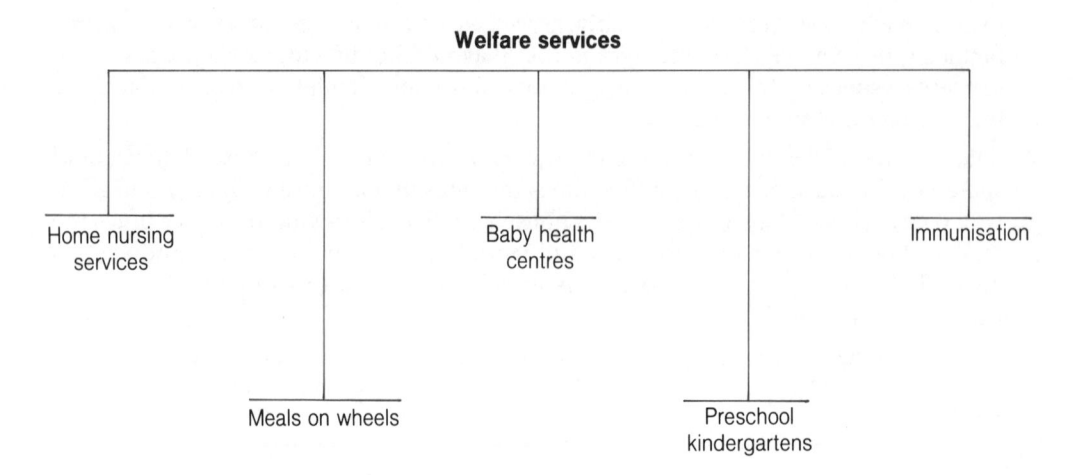

Welfare services

- Home nursing services
  - Meals on wheels
- Baby health centres
  - Preschool kindergartens
- Immunisation

Local government power

The local council has a lot of power in the community. If you wish to extend your home or build an in-ground swimming pool you must first put the plans before the council and get permission. Council and health inspectors may visit boarding houses to check on the cooking, washing and toilet facilities. They visit food shops and restaurants to check on the cleanliness.

Through its powers over town planning the council may zone an area for high-rise home-unit development. If you wish to open a travel agency or a shop in a certain area you must get permission from the council. The council can close some of its streets to through traffic.

Some people argue that a council is too powerful a body to be run by unpaid, elected aldermen. It should instead be run by 'expert' businessmen who are paid to do a professional job. Some councils are in fact run by paid administrators.

Interdependence: the council and the community

The work of the council is vital in ensuring a well-organised, attractive community. It provides many services for local residents and business firms. They depend on the council for good roads and a clean local area. The council in turn depends on ratepayers for its income. It employs many people: health and building inspectors, engineers, librarians, garbage collectors, gardeners and office staff.

The council is also a large user of goods and services. It buys them from businesses both in and outside the municipality. Car dealers, nurseries, building suppliers and office equipment manufacturers all sell products to the council.

GOVERNMENT   221

Local council responsibilities

Recreation
Name your closest public swimming pool. How much do you pay to go in? What happens to this money?
What other public sporting facilities are available in your local area?

Roads, footpaths, gutters
Name three roads your council is responsible for. Name three roads it is not responsible for.

Building
Who are these men? Explain what they are doing.

Health
What local government service is shown here? How often is this service provided in your area? Find the yearly cost of this service.

Name the services shown here. Do you have to pay for these services? How are they financed?

Parking
Are there parking meters in your main shopping centre?
Is there a council car park? Where is it?

THE WORLD OF COMMERCE

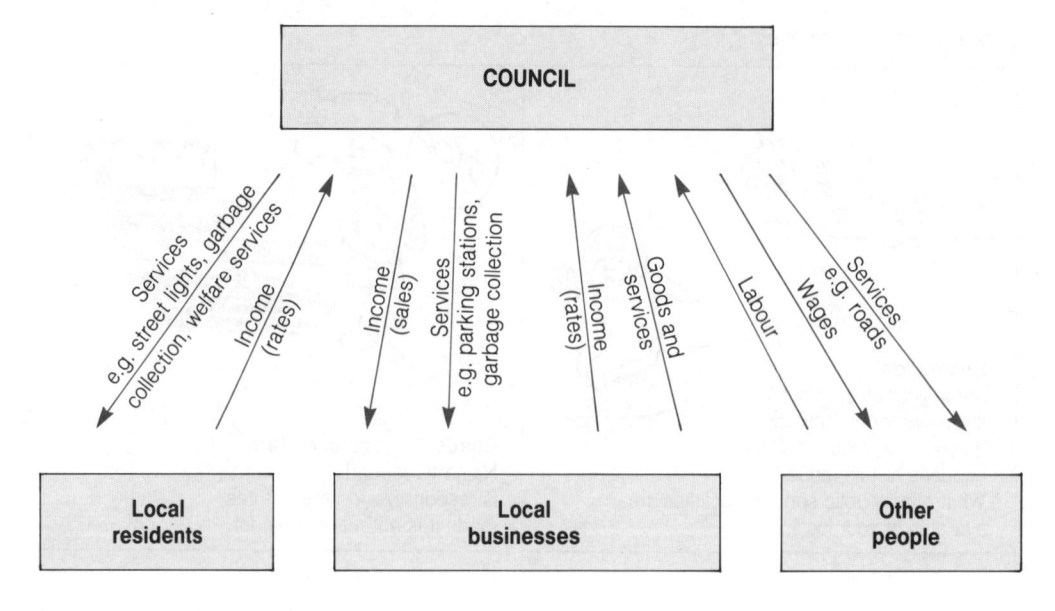

Interdependence between the council and the community

Exercise 6D

1. What is the largest single item of income for councils?
2. Explain what is meant by land value.
3. Explain how rates are worked out.
4. List five sources of income for the local council other than rates.
5. Do you think that the present system of charging and working out rates is just?
6. Suggest three other possible ways that councils could raise the money they now get from rates.
7. Copy into your notebook the diagrams which illustrate the responsibilities of local government. Answer the questions under each diagram.
8. List the services provided by councils that are *not* shown in the diagrams.
9. List five welfare services provided by the council.
10. List three ways in which the local council is able to exercise power over
    (a) individuals in the community
    (b) businesses in the community.
11. List ten occupations whose workers depend on the council for employment.
12. List ten types of businesses which supply goods and services to the council.

Skills activities

Interpreting a document

Study the rate notice on page 218 and answer the following questions in your notebook.
1. Name the council that issued the rate notice.
2. Name the person who is liable to pay the rates.
3. What is the total amount of rates which has to be paid to the council?
4. State the two different methods by which the ratepayer may pay.
5. What happens if the ratepayer chooses to pay by instalments and fails to make a payment on time?
6. Find out why some people may only have to pay the minimum rates stated on the rate notice. Write the answer in your notebook.

Newspaper research

From your local paper cut out any articles that refer to the council *controlling* someone or something. Paste these articles into your notebook. Under each cutting write whether individuals, business firms or some other community groups are being controlled.

Collecting notices

Collect and paste into your notebook as many council notices as you can. Some suggestions are notices advising about a 'council cleanup', dog registration, bottle collection, vaccination, rates.

Vocabulary exercise—crossword puzzle

Complete the following crossword in your notebook.

Clues

1. A person who is eligible to vote in local government elections and does not do so may have to pay a _ _ _ _
2. (with 5). Zoning laws are the responsibility of _ _ _ _ _ _ _ _ _ _ _ _ _ _ _
3. Ratepayers and _ _ _ _ _ _ _ _ _ are eligible to vote in local government elections
4. The number that you put next to your first choice when you vote using the preferential system
5. (with 2). Zoning laws are the responsibility of _ _ _ _ _ _ _ _ _ _ _ _ _ _ _
6. (with 21). The right to vote in private is called _ _ _ _ _ _ _ _ _ _ _ _ _
7. These allow people to choose their representatives in government
8. The age at which a person is allowed to vote
9. Local government elections are held every _ _ _ _ _ years
10. The name given to councils which look after large cities such as Sydney and Wollongong
11. The term used in the United States for *railway*
12. You do this to choose which candidate you would like to represent you
13. The name given to councils which look after larger country towns and the suburbs surrounding cities
14. Local governments can raise money by charging people _ _ _ _ to use their halls and sports grounds
15. To vote in government elections you mark your ballot paper and place it in the ballot _ _ _
16. The place where you mark your ballot paper is called the polling _ _ _ _ _
17. Local and state governments share responsibility for these
18. The name usually given to local government

224 THE WORLD OF COMMERCE

19. Local government is responsible for providing and maintaining these
20. Shires are divided into these
21. (with 6). The right to vote in private is called _ _ _ _ _ _   _ _ _ _ _ _
22. Rates are worked out on the value of the _ _ _ _
23. The name given to councils in charge of the outer suburbs of large cities and the rural areas of the state
24. Local governments' main source of income
25. Local governments provide baby _ _ _ _ _ _ centres
26. Municipal council areas are divided into _ _ _ _ _ for voting purposes
27. Australian Capital Territory (initials)
28. Local Government Act (initials)
29. One way to make more people share in the cost of providing local government services would be to put a _ _ _ _ _ _ _ _ _ on income tax

State government

Representation

It would be impossible for all citizens to vote on all new laws the government wants to introduce. Instead, New South Wales is divided into ninety-nine areas called *electorates*. The voters in each electorate elect one person to represent them and vote on their behalf. Parliament is made up of these *representatives*.

Electorates

Each state is divided into a number of electorates. Each electorate is supposed to contain about the same number of voters. As a result, electorates in cities may be quite small in area while electorates in country areas may be very large in area. Each electorate is represented in the state parliament by the person who received the most votes for that electorate in the previous election. Each electorate is given a name, for example Bathurst or Parramatta. The person elected to represent the Parramatta electorate is known in parliament as the Member for Parramatta.

Secret ballot

All government elections in Australia are by secret ballot. The voter fills in a ballot paper privately in a booth and places it in a locked ballot box. The ballot paper does not have the voter's name on it. Nobody need ever know how any person voted.

In Australia all government elections are by secret ballot

The houses of parliament

There are two houses of parliament in New South Wales. They are the Legislative Assembly and the Legislative Council. The Legislative Assembly is also called the 'lower house'; it has more power than the Legislative Council. Most laws begin in the Legislative Assembly. The Legislative Council is the 'upper house' and its main job is to review laws framed in the Legislative Assembly.

In Australia we have a 'party' system. After an election the governor, representing the queen, sends for the leader of the political party which gained the most members in the Legislative Assembly. The governor asks him or her to form a government. The leader of the party which forms the government becomes the *premier*. The other major party is called the *opposition*. If no one party has an outright majority on its own, two or more parties with fairly similar views might combine to form a *coalition government*.

Responsible government

The premier selects *ministers* from among the members of his or her own (or the coalition) party in parliament. The premier gives each minister a special job or *portfolio*. A minister given the portfolio of education becomes the Minister for Education. Another minister will become the Minister for Police and so on. Each minister is responsible or 'answerable' to parliament for all the actions and decisions made by his or her department.

The ministers form the *cabinet* which works out the policies that the government will follow. It usually drafts new *bills* which, if passed by parliament, become laws (or Acts).

The members of parliament who are not chosen to be part of the cabinet (or the 'shadow cabinet' if they are in the opposition) are called *backbenchers*.

Exercise 6E

1. What is an electorate?
2. Why are city electorates much smaller in size than country electorates?
3. How many people represent each electorate in parliament?
4. Name the house or houses of parliament in your state.
5. What does the governor do after the results of an election for the lower house are known?
6. What is a portfolio? Name two portfolios in your state government.
7. What is the cabinet? Why is it important?
8. What is a backbencher?

Skills activities

Research

1. Refer to the 'Government New South Wales' section at the front of the telephone directory white pages. List six departments in the New South Wales government. Either telephone those departments or refer to newspapers to find the names of the ministers in charge of those departments. Write the name of the relevant minister next to each of the departments.
2. Use the library and newspapers to find the answer to these questions for your state. Write both the questions and the answers (or form sentences) in your notebook.
   (a) Which party forms the government at present?
   (b) Which party forms the opposition at present?
   (c) Who is the premier?
   (d) Who is the deputy premier?
   (e) Who is the treasurer?
   (f) Who is the leader of the opposition?
   (g) Who is the deputy leader of the opposition?

(h) Who is the governor?
(i) When was the last state election?
(j) Was there a change of government in the last state election? Explain why or why not.
(k) Where is Parliament House located?
(l) Name the state electorate in which you live.
(m) Who is your local member in state parliament?
(n) What is the address of his or her electoral office?

3. Find photographs of the following people, paste them into your notebook and label them clearly. Daily and Sunday newspapers and your local paper are good places to look or you could write to their electoral offices and ask for a photograph, explaining why you want it.
    (a) The premier
    (b) The deputy premier
    (c) The leader of the opposition
    (d) The deputy leader of the opposition
    (e) Your local member in state parliament

Organise an excursion

Contact the member of parliament for your school's local area. If you attend school in or close to Sydney ask him or her to arrange for your class to visit state parliament. You should be able to see both houses of parliament and have their workings explained to you. Ask your local member to describe the work he or she has done for your area. If you attend school in a country area invite your local member to visit your school and talk to your class about the same matters.

State government income

State governments obtain their money from
- grants of money from the federal government
- payroll tax (a tax on the wages that employers pay to the people they employ)
- motor registration fees
- taxes on Pools and Lotto, profit on lotteries
- racing taxes and income from the Totalizator Agency Board (TAB)
- stamp duty on financial transactions such as buying a car
- tax on deposits in financial institutions such as banks
- loans
- income from government businesses such as the railways, buses, the State Bank and the Government Insurance Office.

State government expenditure

State governments spend their funds on providing the following services:
- education
- justice (police, state law courts)
- hospitals and health care services
- child welfare
- public transport and main roads
- water resources—dams and reservoirs
- Department of Housing homes.

The states have a major problem in supplying services. They never have enough money! The state governments have very few 'growth' taxes—their income increases very little each year, but the costs of supplying services grow quickly. On the other hand, the income of the federal government, particularly income tax and sales tax, increases greatly each year.

Welfare services

The state governments provide some welfare services. They give pensioners 'concession' fares on public transport. They make payments to deserted wives for the first six months. After six months, deserted wives receive a widows pension from the federal government. The state governments run children's homes and orphanages. State governments subsidise 'meals on wheels' services.

State government power

The state government has passed many laws that affect the community. New laws are constantly being drawn up. The Department of Consumer Affairs may ban the sale of toys that it feels are dangerous. Speed limits on the open road may be changed. Trading hours for hotels may be altered. State pollution control authorities have placed limits on the amount of noise we can make. Motor lawnmowers may not be used on Sundays before 8 a.m. Musical instruments and amplified sound equipment cannot be used in private homes between midnight and 8 a.m. if they can be heard in other houses or home units. State government laws are enforced by the state police force.

Interdependence: the state government and the community

The state government relies on many people and firms to provide it with goods and services. It employs many people—large numbers of teachers, nurses, police officers, train drivers and power workers—to provide necessary services to the community. In turn, these people rely on the government for their income. Governments buy goods (such as computers, stationery and transport equipment) from private firms. Individuals and firms all benefit from state government services such as roads, railways, power supply and education.

State government responsibilities

Education
Name three state schools in your local area.

Public transport
Name the railway station closest to your home.
Where does the railway line go?

Police
Name the police station closest to your home. What is the telephone number?

Child welfare
Name the state government department in charge of child welfare. Give three examples of things it does.

Health
Name the public hospital closest to your home. Name three sections of the hospital that specialise in a particular service.

Justice
Name the courthouse closest to your home.

Water resources
Name two dams in your state.
Name the reservoir which supplies water to your area.

Main roads
Name two main roads in your area. What state government department is responsible for them? Why are they not financed by the local council?

230 THE WORLD OF COMMERCE

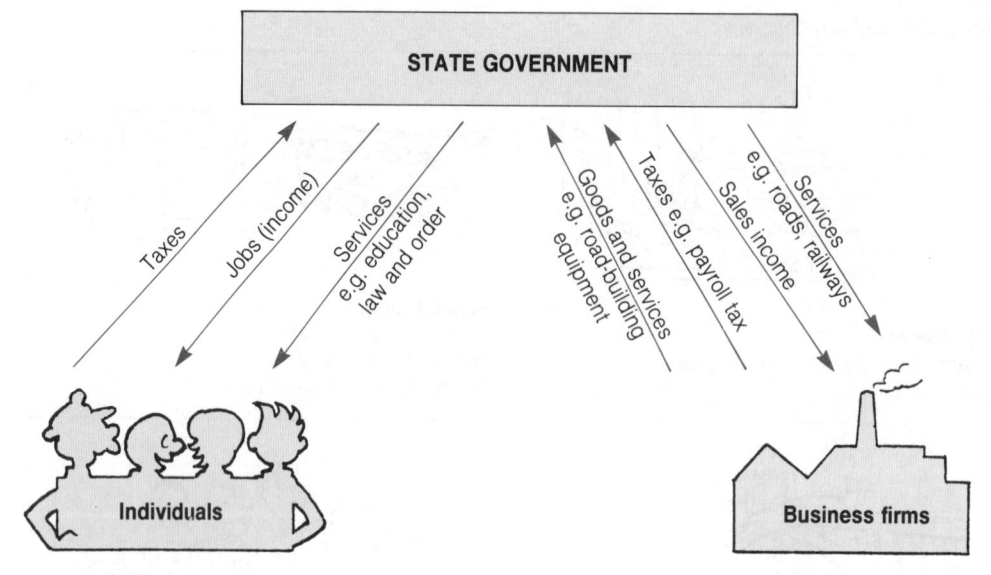

Interdependence: the state government and the community

Exercise 6F

1. List six sources of income for the state government.
2. List the main services provided by the state government.
3. Why does the state government often have a problem providing these services?
4. List three welfare services provided by the state government.
5. List three ways in which the state government exercises power over the community.
6. Name five groups of workers who rely on the state government for employment.
7. Copy into your notebook the diagrams which illustrate the responsibilities of the state government. Answer the questions below each drawing.

Skills activities

Newspaper research

1. Collect five newspaper clippings which refer to work done by the state government. Paste these into your notebook. Next to each write the name of the government department and minister involved.
2. Collect a newspaper clipping reporting a statement by a member of the opposition in state parliament. Paste it into your notebook. Underneath, explain why the opposition likes to keep in the news.

Vocabulary exercise—crossword puzzle

Complete the following crossword in your notebook.

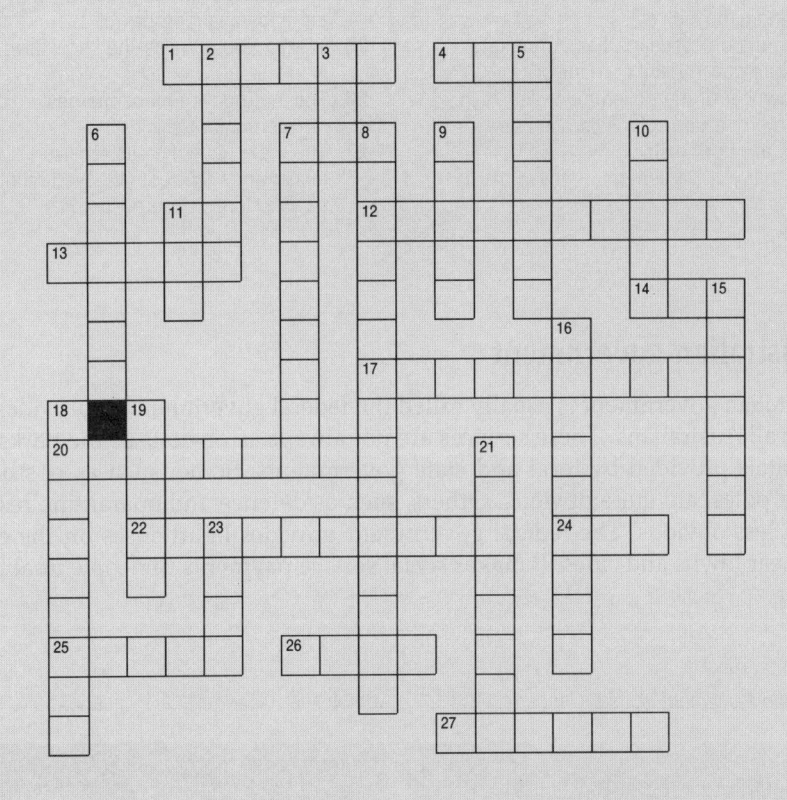

Clues

1. Members of the Opposition whose job is to take a particular interest in a certain portfolio are called _ _ _ _ _ _ ministers
2. The Legislative Assembly and the Legislative Council are the two _ _ _ _ _ _ of the New South Wales state parliament
3. The number you put next to your first choice when you are voting under the preferential system
4. Australian Labor Party (intitials)
5. The state government receives some revenue from the _ _ _ _ _ _ _ of its own businesses
6. The committee made up of more senior government ministers who usually work out the policies the government will follow
7. **(across).** For each
7. **(down).** The special responsibility given to a minister is called his or her _ _ _ _ _ _ _ _ _
8. Members of parliament are the _ _ _ _ _ _ _ _ _ _ _ _ _ _ _ of the people in their electorate
9. The system of government in which the members of parliament are usually members of one group or another, depending on their political views
10. This person is represented in Australia by the governor or the governor-general
11. **(down).** Member of the Legislative Assembly (initials)
12. The body of all the elected representatives in state or federal politics
13. If these are passed by parliament they become laws
14. National Country Party (initials)
15. The name given to the leader of the government party in state government
16. If one party does not win a majority of seats in the lower house in an election two or more parties with similar views may form one of these to become the government
17. The people in an area who choose a particular politician to represent them in parliament

18. The state government raises some of its funds by charging _____ _____ (two words) on financial transactions such as buying a house
19. One of the political parties in Australia
20. A state government responsibility
21. A member of the government who is in charge of a particular field such as education or health
22. The party or parties *not* in government
23. The government's welfare services try to help _____ people
24. The state government raises some of its funds by charging payroll _____
25. In New South Wales the Legislative Council is the _____ house
26. The state government charges _____ to register motor vehicles
27. The state governments receive _____ of money from the federal government to be used for special purposes

The Australian government

The Australian government is usually called the federal government. It provides services to benefit all Australians. These services are not always as obvious as the parks, schools and hospitals provided by local and state governments. Some, such as postboxes and telephone poles, are quite obvious. Others, such as defence and quarantine restrictions, are much less obvious. The federal government provides lighthouses on the coast and airports near towns and cities. It makes social service payments to people unable to earn an income.

The Australian Parliament House, Canberra, ACT MIRROR AUSTRALIAN TELEGRAPH PUBLICATIONS

Basic features of the Australian government

House of parliament
There are two houses in the Australian parliament, the House of Representatives and the Senate.

The House of Representatives is the 'lower' house. It is sometimes called the people's house as its members are chosen directly by the people. Each member represents about the same number of voters. After each election the party which wins more than half the seats in the House of Representatives forms the government and its leader becomes the *prime minister*. The other major party becomes the *opposition*. If no single party wins more than half the seats, two parties with similar ideas may join together to form a *coalition government*.

The life of the House of Representatives is limited to three years from the time it first meets after an election. However it may be dissolved sooner by the governor-general acting on the advice of the prime minister.

The Senate is the 'upper' house. It is meant to be a 'house of review', checking over the bills (proposed laws) which the House of Representatives wishes to pass. To become a law, a bill must be agreed to by *both* the House of Representatives and the Senate. The Senate can ask for amendments (changes) to a bill and it can reject bills. The Senate was also designed to protect the interests of the smaller states.

Electorates
Australia is divided into 148 federal electorates for the House of Representatives elections. Each electorate is represented by one man or woman in the lower house of the Australian parliament in Canberra.

Australia is divided into eight electorates for the Senate elections, corresponding to the states and territories. Each state elects twelve members to the Senate. The Northern Territory and the Australian Capital Territory each elect two members to the Senate. As the Senate was designed to protect the interests of the smaller states, each state is equally represented, regardless of its population.

One vote one value
The electorates for the House of Representatives vary greatly in area. However, each electorate is supposed to contain about the same number of voters. Each chooses one person to represent it in the House of Representatives. Rural electorates are much larger in area than city electorates. The average number of voters in each electorate in 1988 was about 68 000. The vote of each person in any electorate has about equal influence on which candidate is elected.

In elections for the Senate the principle of 'one vote one value' is not used. Each state and territory is a single electorate. Each state is represented by twelve senators and each territory by two senators. This system of representation gives the smaller states a greater influence in parliament and helps to protect their interests.

Responsible government
The prime minister selects ministers from among the members of his or her party (or the coalition parties) that were elected to parliament. Ministers can be chosen from either the House of Representatives or the Senate. Each minister is given a certain area of responsi-

bility called a portfolio. The ministers form the cabinet which is responsible or answerable to parliament. Individual ministers are responsible for the actions of their department. Cabinet is responsible for the policies of the government.

Compulsory voting
Voting is compulsory for both the House of Representatives and the Senate. Anyone who is registered on the Electoral Roll and who fails to vote can be fined.

Secret ballot
The elections for both the House of Representatives and the Senate are held by secret ballot. Secret ballot is explained in the section on state government.

Exercise 6G

1. Name five services provided by the federal government.
2. Name the two houses of parliament in the federal government.
3. Explain how an election for the House of Representatives decides which political party will form the government and which party will form the opposition.
4. How is the prime minister selected?
5. How long is the life of the House of Representatives? How can this term be shortened?
6. Describe the work done by the Senate.
7. What is meant by the term 'electorate'? What is the difference between the size of the electorates for the House of Representatives and the Senate?
8. Explain why each state has the same number of members elected to the Senate.
9. What is meant by 'one vote one value'? For the election of which house of parliament is this principle used?
10. Explain why the principle of 'one vote one value' is not used in elections for the Senate.
11. Write a sentence to explain the meaning of each of the following terms: responsible government, minister, portfolio, cabinet, compulsory voting, secret ballot.

Australian government income

The main sources of income or *revenue* for the federal government are taxes, loans and income from government businesses.
- *Income tax* paid by individuals and companies provides well over half the federal government's income from taxation.
- *Customs duty* is a tax paid on some goods imported into Australia.
- *Excise duty* is a tax paid on some goods produced in Australia. Goods on which excise duty must be paid include petrol (refined in Australia), beer, cigarettes and tobacco.

- *Sales tax* is a tax paid both on goods produced in Australia *and* on goods imported into Australia. The tax is paid on many goods, ranging from hair clips to motor vehicles.
- *Loans* are obtained by the government both from within Australia and from overseas. Loan money is usually used for the construction of public works such as reservoirs, hospitals and railways.
- *Income* also comes from profits of federal government businesses which include Qantas, Australian Airlines, Telex and Australia Post.

Australian government expenditure

The federal government spends most of its income on providing these services:
- payments to the states—this money is used by the state governments to provide schools, hospitals, roads and so on
- defence
- postal services and telecommunications
- foreign affairs
- social services, such as welfare payments to aged and invalid pensioners and to the unemployed, family allowance payments and so on
- repatriation or veterans' affairs—caring for returned servicemen and their families
- immigration and quarantine services
- civil aviation and shipping, providing airports and wharves
- Aboriginal affairs.

The federal government also controls a number of other matters, including banking, currency issue, overseas trade, marriage and divorce laws, taxation, statistics and bankruptcy laws. The federal government pays the expenses of running the departments that control these matters.

Australian government power

The federal government has a lot of power over very important matters. Through immigration it can control the numbers and type of people coming to Australia to live. The government can choose to allow in only people who are qualified in certain fields, such as nurses, engineers and so on. Refer to the diagrams showing the responsibilities of the federal government on pages 236 and 237.

Welfare services

The most important welfare service provided by the federal government is pensions to people unable to earn an income. These people include the aged, invalids, supporting parents, widows and the unemployed. The government also provides many pensioners with benefits such as free medical services and reduced telephone rentals.

Interdependence: The Australian government and the community

The federal government employs many people to help it provide services and fulfil its other functions. The government employs pilots, customs inspectors, soldiers, postal officers and clerks, among many others. The government relies on them and they depend on the government for their jobs and their wages.

Federal government responsibilities

1. Customs	2. Currency
Name one item that you may not import into Australia.	Where is the mint located?
3. Defence	4. Immigration/emigration
Where is the nearest army base?	From which country do most of our immigrants come?
5. Aboriginal affairs	6. Foreign affairs
Name the Minister for Aboriginal Affairs. What types of things does this department do?	Where are foreign embassies located?
7. Social security	8. Marriage and divorce
Name five types of social security payments.	How much notice do you have to give before you can get married?

GOVERNMENT   237

Federal government responsibilities

9. Statistics

What is a census?

10. Overseas trade

Name the shipping port closest to your home.

11. Quarantine

Why do we have quarantine restrictions in Australia?

12. Banking

What is the address of the Commonwealth Bank closest to your home?

13. Taxation

Where is the closest office of the Taxation Department?

14. Civil aviation

Name the aiport closest to your home.

15. Post/telecommunications

Where are GPOs located?

16. Veterans' affairs

Who are the people cared for by the Department of Veterans' Affairs? Give an example of a service provided by this department.

Business firms supply the government with many goods and services such as planes and helicopters, office supplies and stationery and painting and building services. Any cutback in government spending will lead to reduced production and employment in many businesses.

State governments rely on the federal government for a large part of their income. An increase in the amount of money given to the states can lead to more teachers and nurses being employed, more roads being built and an improvement in the amount and quality of services offered by the states.

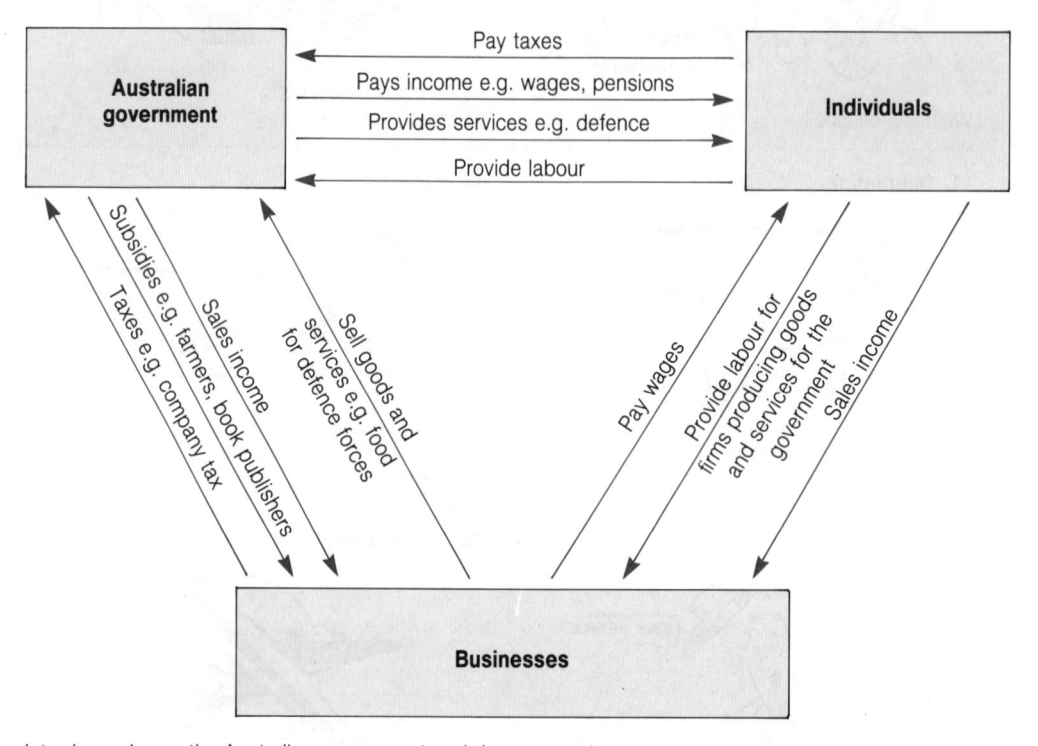

Interdependence: the Australian government and the community

Many businesses rely on the federal government for *subsidies*. Subsidies are payments which do not have to be repaid. Subsidies help some firms stay in business. Some exporters receive payments to help them increase exports.

Exercise 6H

1. What is the main source of income for the federal government?
2. List five other important sources of income for the federal government.
3. What is the main difference between excise duty and customs duty?
4. Name four businesses run by the federal government.
5. List five important services provided by the federal government.

6. Name five other matters controlled by the federal government.
7. How can the federal government affect the level of employment in Australia?
8. What is the most important welfare service provided by the federal government?
9. Name five groups of workers who rely on the federal government for employment.
10. Name three types of businesses that rely on the federal government to buy their goods and services.
11. How does the state government rely on the federal government?
12. What is a subsidy?
13. Copy into your notebook the diagrams which illustrate the responsibilities of the federal government on pages 236–7. Answer the questions under each drawing.

Skills activities

Mapping

Obtain a map of your local area. The map could be obtained from a street directory (by photocopying and then pasting the pages together), a real estate agent or a newsagent. Complete the following tasks:

1. Draw in the boundaries of your local council area. Underline the names of the suburbs which are included in the council area.
2. Mark in the location of your house and the school you attend.
3. Name and locate a primary school, park, library, public swimming centre, public hospital, railway station, government bus stop, post office, town hall, police station, law court, ambulance station, government-owned bank and the local council chambers. (The best way of showing these services is to draw a key on the bottom of the map. Write down the name of each of the services. Beside each name draw a small picture to represent it, for example, beside 'Balmain Post Office' draw a letter box. Draw each of the pictures on the map to show their location in the local area.)
4. Draw straight lines from your home to each of the services marked on the map. Draw red lines to show local council services, green lines to show state government services and blue lines to show federal government services. Include these coloured lines in the key to show their meanings.

Research project

Use the library and newspapers to find the answers to the following questions. Write both the question and answer in your notebook.

1. Which party forms the government in the Australian (federal) parliament?
2. Which party forms the opposition?
3. Who is the prime minister of Australia?
4. Who is the deputy prime minister?
5. Who is the leader of the opposition in the federal parliament?
6. Who is the deputy leader of the opposition?

240 THE WORLD OF COMMERCE

7. Who is the governor-general of Australia? What person does he or she represent?
8. Where is the Parliament House for Australia located? Why was that location chosen?
9. List the names of the ministers of the following federal government departments:
   (a) Defence
   (b) Social Services
   (c) Foreign Affairs
   (d) Post and Telecommunications
   (e) Attorney-General's
   (f) Transport
   (g) Aboriginal Affairs
   (h) Immigration
   (i) Trade.
10. What is the name of the federal electorate in which you live?
11. Who is your local member in federal parliament?
12. What is the address of his or her office?
13. List the names of the twelve senators who represent your state in the Senate. To which party does each senator belong?
14. Collect five newspaper articles which discuss work done by the federal government. Paste these in to your notebook. Underneath each write
    (a) the name of the department involved
    (b) the minister responsible for that department.

Vocabulary exercise—crossword puzzle

Complete the following crossword puzzle in your notebook.

Clues

1. Money received by the government
2. Slang name for unemployment benefits
3. Commonwealth Employment Service (initials)
4. Electoral Claim Form (initials)
5. We do this to elect our members of parliament
6. The group of ministers who work out the government's major policies
7. A vote or an election
8. A member of the upper house in the federal parliament
9. National Country Party (initials)
10. The age at which a person can vote in a federal election in Australia
11. Within thirty days of turning eighteen a person must register on the _____ roll
12. The term used when the political leaders and ministers give up their positions to allow all the places to be voted on or reappointed
13. The number of senators representing each state in Australia
14. One of the areas for which the federal government is responsible
15. A minister's area of responsibility is called his or her _____
16. Member of the House of Representatives (initials)
17. The upper house in federal parliament
18. The place where you go to mark your vote on the ballot paper is called the polling _____
19. The time when we choose the people to represent us
20. The Australian or Commonwealth government is also called the _____ government
21. The main form of federal government income
22. The former name of the federal government's interstate airline (initials)

23. The group of people represented by a particular politician
24. The initials of the territory in which the federal parliament is located
25. The name of the pension paid to men over sixty-five years and women over sixty years
26. The member of parliament responsible for a particular portfolio or department
27. The number you write next to your first choice when voting under the preferential system

Revision activity

New terms

In your notebook write the heading 'Important new terms and their meanings'. Copy the first term in List A into your notebook and select its correct meaning from the definitions in List B. Continue until you have listed each term and its meaning.

List A
Backbencher, bill, cabinet, coalition, constitution, democracy, dictatorship, electorate, federal system, government, House of Representatives, Legislative Assembly, Legislative Council, minister, opposition, preferential voting, premier, prime minister, rates, secret ballot, senate, taxes.

List B

1. The type of government in which the people choose the representatives to govern them and in which the representatives are answerable to the people who elected them
2. The type of government in which one person is the absolute ruler
3. The type of government in which the country is divided into states and the power to govern is shared by the national government and the states
4. A set of rules for governing Australia
5. A voting system in which the voter numbers the candidates in the order in which he or she prefers them
6. The main source of income for local governments, paid by owners of property in the local area
7. The group of people who choose someone to represent them in government, *or* the area in which they live and which the government member represents
8. The right to vote in private
9. The lower house in the New South Wales state parliament
10. The upper house in the New South Wales state parliament
11. The leader of the party in government in state parliament
12. The party or parties which do not have a majority in the lower house of parliament and so cannot form a government
13. Two or more parties with similar views, combined to form a government or opposition
14. A government member who has been given responsibility for a particular department such as health
15. A group of senior ministers responsible for forming the government's policy
16. A proposal that is put before the parliament and if it is approved (passed) it will eventually become law
17. An ordinary member of parliament without any special area of policy under his or her control except for the general needs of the electorate
18. The lower house in federal parliament
19. The upper house in federal parliament
20. The party that wins most seats in the lower house of parliament
21. The leader of the party in government in federal parliament
22. A payment people must make to the government and for which they do not get anything of equal value directly in return—the main way the government gets its income.

Index

A
Aboriginal law, 178–9
administration, 187
advertising, 6, 19–20
age and wants, 4
anarchy, 181
appeal, 191
arbitration, 170
assets test, 163
Australian Consumers' Association, 22
Australian Government, 189, 232–8
Australian Standardsmark, 22
automatic vending machines, 35, 114
award wage, 65

B
backbenchers, 226
ballot box, 215, 225
bank reconciliation statement, 76–8
bank statement, 75–6
bankcard, 117
banknotes, 53
bar codes, 125
barter, 45
bonded stores, 110
boycott, 170

budgeting, 83–6
business, 91–129
   distribution of goods, 109–11
   environment and industry, 100–101
   industry groups, 91–2
   interdependence, 106–7
   location of industry, 97–100
   methods of buying goods and services, 116–17
   records kept by small businesses, 121–25
   types of retail businesses, 111–15
Business and Consumer Affairs, 23

C
Cabinet, 226, 234
capital good, 10
cash buying, 15, 116
cash docket, 38, 121
cash register slip, 38, 121
cash sales, 121–2
caveat emptor, 17–18
chain stores, 112–13
changes
   in law, 184–5
   in types of work, 148–51

   in workforce participation rate, 141
characteristics of money, 56–7
cheques, 73–5
Children's Court, 199
choice, 12–14, 208
Choice Magazine, 22
circular flow of income, 46
city council, 213
civil case, 190
closed court, 190, 199
coalition government, 225, 233
coins, 52
collective bargaining, 169–70
collective wants, 2
commission, 65, 159
competition, government, 208
compulsory voting, 234
computers
   and cheques, 75
   costs and benefits, 149–51
   and filing, 41
   and records, 125
Constitution, 189, 211, 212
consumer, the, 1–44
   documents and records, 38–40
   durables for, 10
   goods for, 10
   help for, 22–3
   non-durables for, 10

power, seller's influence on, 19–21
rights, 18
Consumer Affairs, Department of, 228
consumption
 changes, 6–8
 patterns, 4–6
contracts, 155
corner shop, 111–12
court case, 198–204
courts, 190–3
crafts, 146
credit accounts, 117
credit buying, methods of, 116–17
credit cards, 54, 78
credit note, 123
credit transactions, 15, 122
creditor, 54, 86
criminal case, 190
crossed cheques, 74
culture and wants, 5
currency, 49–50, 51–2, 73
customs duty, 234

D
debts, 86
defendant, 198, 202
demarcation dispute, 171
democracy, 206
department store, 29, 112
dictatorship, 206
direct marketing, 35
discount store, 29, 114
discrimination, 67, 169
distribution
 of goods, 109–11, 128
 of income and wealth, 67–70
 of jobs, 141
District Court, 192
dividends, 66
door-to-door sales, 33–4, 114–15
Door-to-Door Sales Act, 34

E
EFTPOS, 79–80
Egyptian law, 178
elections, 215, 225, 233, 234
electorates, 224, 225, 233
electronic scanning, 150
employee, 138
employer, 139

enforcement, law, 187, 195–7, 206
environment
 and government, 208–9
 and industry, 100–1
 and wants, 4
excise duty, 234
expenditure
 Australian government, 235
 local government, 219
 state government, 228
expenses, personal, 84

F
family and wants, 6
Family Court, 192, 193
fashion and wants, 5
federal system, 211–12
fees, 65 159
filing, 40–1
financial institutions, 53–4
fringe benefits, 159

G
garnishee order, 86
general store, 31
goods, 10, 91
 methods of buying, 116–17
 where to buy, 28–36
government, 206–42
 Australian, 232–8
 local, 213–21
 role of, 206–9
 specialisation in, 210–12
 state, 224–30
gross income, 24

H
habits and wants, 6
Hammurabi's laws, 178
High Court, 192, 193
home shopping, 35
House of Representatives, 233
Houses of Parliament, 225, 233

I
impulse buying, 13
income tax, 163, 234
income test, 163
incomes, 4, 24, 46, 157–67
 for Australian government, 234–5
 budgeting, 83–6
 for local government, 217–19

 for people unable to work, 161–3
 for state government, 227
 types of, 64–6, 157–9
industrial action, 170–1
industry groups, 91–2
 primary, 91, 97–8
 secondary, 91, 98–9
 tertiary, 91–2, 100
inflation, 207
interdependence, 26, 46, 106–7, 136, 220, 222, 228, 230, 235, 238
interest, 60, 66, 159
invoice, 40

J
job satisfaction, 136–7
judiciary, 187, 190

L
labour, 130–75
 and apprenticeship, 153–5
 and incomes, 64–5, 157–67
 specialisation of, 130–7
 trade unions, 168–72
 types of work, 145–7
 why people work, 144–5
 workforce, 138–41
land rights, 179
law, 178–205
 in Australia, 187–204
 courts, 190–3
 enforcement of, 195–7
 in history, 178–9
 need for, 181–2
 need to change, 184–5
 parliaments, 189
law and order, 206
layby, 117
legal tender, 54
Legislative Assembly, 225
Legislative Council, 225
legislature, 187
leisure time, 151
light pens, 125
Local Court, 192, 199
local government, 189, 213–21
location of industry, 97–100

M
magistrate, 201, 203, 204
mail order sales, 35, 115
measure of value, 61
media, 23

INDEX

ministers, 226
money, 45–90
  budgeting, 84–6
  characteristics of, 56–7
  functions of, 60–2
  how we get, 64
  in Australia, 51–4
  motives for wanting, 63
  need for, 45–6
  ways of making payments, 73–80
monopoly, government, 208
motives for wanting money, 63
municipal council, 213

N

need for law, 181–2
need for money, 45–6
need to change laws, 184–5
needs, 1, 14
net income, 24
non-cash benefits, 161
not negotiable, 75

O

obsolescence, planned, 21
open court, 190
opposition, 225, 233

P

packaging, 20–21
parties to a cheque, 74
party sales, 34
perjury, 200
police, 195–7
police prosecutor, 201
polling booth, 215
pollution control, 228
portfolio, 226, 234
power, 220, 228, 235
premier, 225
premiums, 167
primary industry, 91, 93, 97–8, 131
prime minister, 233
production, 91–2

professions, 147
profit, 60, 66, 159

R

rates, 217–19
receipt, 38
records
  business, 40–41, 121–5
  for the consumer, 38–40
redundancy, 136
regional shopping centre, 31
rent, 60, 66, 159
representatives, 224
responsibilities,
  Australian government, 236–7
  local government, 221
  state government, 229
responsible government, 226, 233
retailers, 28–31, 111–15
royalties, 159

S

salary, 65, 159
sales tax, 235
saving, 61
secondary industry, 91, 98–9, 131
secret ballot, 215, 225, 234
security, 63
self-employed people, 139
Senate, 233
services, 10, 12, 36, 91–2, 208
shire council, 213
sickness and accident insurance, 166
skilled workers, 145
social security benefits, 66, 69, 163
solicitor, 201
specialisation, 106–7
  in government, 210–12
  in industry, 92–5
  of labour, 130–3
  results of, 136–7, 172
specialised society, 26, 46, 60
specialty store, 30, 112

standard of living, 69
Standards Australia, 22–3
State Government, 189, 224–30
statement, 123–4
  bank, 75–6
  bank reconciliation, 76–8
status
  and money, 63
  and wants, 6
strikes, 170
subsistence society, 45
superannuation, 164–5
supermarket, 31, 112
Supreme Court, 192, 193

T

TAFE, 153
technical jargon, 21
technology and wants, 4
tertiary industry, 91, 94, 100, 133
trade unions, 168–72
trades, 146

U

unemployed people, 139
unemployment, 207
unordered goods, 36
unskilled workers, 145

V

voluntary agencies, 163
voting, 215, 225, 233, 234

W

wages, 60, 157–8
wants, 1–3, 4
welfare services, 220, 228, 235
wholesalers, 28, 110
word processors, 150
workers' compensation, 166–7
workforce, 138–9
  participation rate, 140–1
  why people work, 144–5